Publishing the Nonprofit Annual Report

Publishing the Nonprofit Annual Report

Tips, Traps,
and Tricks of the Trade

Caroline Taylor
Foreword by Kathryn S. Fuller

JOSSEY-BASS
A Wiley Company
www.josseybass.com

Published by

 **JOSSEY-BASS**
A Wiley Company
989 Market Street
San Francisco, CA 94103-1741

www.josseybass.com

Jossey-Bass books and products are available through most bookstores. To contact Jossey-Bass directly,
call (888) 378-2537, fax to (800) 605-2665, or visit our website at www.josseybass.com.

Substantial discounts on bulk quantities of Jossey-Bass books are available to corporations, professional
associations, and other organizations. For details and discount information, contact the special sales
department at Jossey-Bass.

We at Jossey-Bass strive to use the most environmentally sensitive paper stocks available to us. Our
publications are printed on acid-free recycled stock whenever possible and our paper always meets or
exceeds minimum GPO and EPA requirements.

The Council of Better Business Bureaus standards regarding the use of funds in Chapter 1 are from "CBBB
Standards for Charitable Solicitations" [http://www.give.org/standards/cbbbstds.asp] and are reprinted
with the permission of the Council of Better Business Bureaus.

The American Friends Service Committee mission statement in Chapter 3 is reprinted with the permission
of American Friends Service Committee.

The World Wildlife Fund executive message in Chapter 3 is reprinted with the permission of World
Wildlife Fund.

The Population Action International mission statement in Chapter 3 is reprinted with the permission of
Population Action International.

The Christian Children's Fund mission statement in Chapter 3 is reprinted with the permission of Christian
Children's Fund.

The Girl Scout language illustrating the theme "where girls grow strong" presented in Chapter 6 is reprinted
with permission from the *Girl Scouts of the USA 1999 Annual Report.*

Library of Congress Cataloging-in-Publication Data

Taylor, Caroline, date.
   Publishing the nonprofit annual report : tips, traps, and
tricks of the trade / Caroline Taylor ; foreword by Kathryn S.
Fuller.—1st ed.
       p. cm. — (The Jossey-Bass nonprofit and public
management series)
Includes bibliographical references and index.
     ISBN 0-7879-5410-1 (alk. paper)
   1. Corporation reports.   2. Report writing.   I. Title.
II. Series.
     HG4028.B2 T38 2001
     658.15'12—dc21

2001005160

PB Printing   10 9 8 7 6 5 4 3 2 1   FIRST EDITION

The Jossey-Bass
Nonprofit and Public Management Series

For John and B. B.—always there, loved always

Contents

Tables, Figures, and Exhibits

Foreword

A NONPROFIT that works in a remote region of the country or the world must find a way to tell its story to people who have never been to that region and have never seen what the organization is doing there. Similarly, a nonprofit whose mission focuses on showcasing the talents of local artists, or on making neighborhoods safer for children and the elderly, must also find a way to tell its story to people who can benefit from its work. Our job at World Wildlife Fund (WWF), for example, is to save the earth's endangered places and the wild species that inhabit them. Why are they threatened? What are we doing to protect them? Are we making a difference? We could tell our story in a magazine, as many nonprofits do. We could tell our story on our Web site, and we do. But sometimes the story needs to be told as a coherent whole, not parceled out in monthly or bimonthly doses or presented as a series of menu options on a Web page. We have found that the annual report makes an ideal vehicle for conveying information about our struggles and successes, in a form that will allow our story to be kept and even shared with others.

When Caroline Taylor first came to work as publications director for WWF, in 1993, we had been publishing an annual report for nearly thirty years. Over that period, our organization had grown considerably in size and complexity. Not surprisingly, the scope and size of our annual report had also increased: what had once been twenty-four pages long was now more than three times that size. Our deadline, however, had not changed. Caroline, using many of the approaches described in this book, kept our annual report on track. Her knowledge of how annual reports are produced, together with her ability to speak the language of designers and printers, made the process function more smoothly. Her background in design and editing helped our report tell a more compelling story through integrated text and visuals. For seven years, our annual reports were of sufficiently high quality to win numerous awards for communications excellence.

Just as WWF benefited from Caroline's knowledge and experience, so will the readers of this book. CEOs of newly established nonprofits, as well as nonprofits that have not previously published an annual report, will find tips for planning the report, setting the direction, writing the president's letter, and measuring the report's effectiveness. Staff of nonprofits that already put out annual reports will find helpful hints on choosing a theme; budgeting for writing, design, and printing; sticking to a schedule; managing reviews; finding photographs; and working with designers and printers.

In short, there is an abundance of information in this book for any nonprofit organization that is contemplating its first annual report—or its best one ever. There is help for those suffering from migraine-strength headaches caused by the inability to secure copy reviews in a timely manner. There is advice for those who want to make a document written by committee read as if it had been written by one person. Readers will see how the annual report fits into an organization's overall communications strategy, learn what an annual report is *not*, and benefit from a look into the crystal ball to see if, in the not too distant future, online annual reports will eventually become the norm rather than the exception. In this respect, the book draws from survey data of Fortune 500 companies and other businesses that publish annual reports, to validate one of my own personal beliefs: there will always be a need for a printed annual report.

Indeed, the many similarities between nonprofit annual reports and corporate annual reports constitute a common thread that runs through the book. Both types of report are used as image pieces, both are used to sell the organization or company and its "products," and both are used to inform investors or donors about how their money has been used. There are several books available to help investors read financial statements in corporate annual reports, and it is clear that corporate annual reports offer much to be emulated. Until now, however, there has not been a book devoted exclusively to the nonprofit annual report.

For all nonprofit organizations with an important and urgent story to tell—a story that becomes more complex but no less urgent with every passing year—this book provides the blueprint for making that story as compelling and rich as it must be to capture supporters' sympathies.

Kathryn S. Fuller
President, World Wildlife Fund

Preface

THE IDEA FOR this book occurred to me one day a couple of years ago as I handed my boss the World Wildlife Fund annual report, hot off the press. He flipped through the pages, admired the cover, and said, "How are you going to top this next year?"

It was a good question, one that kept me awake for several nights even though I had been putting out the World Wildlife Fund annual report since 1993. Every year, I had to figure out how to make the report fresher but still familiar, better but still within budget.

I am not alone. Thousands of nonprofit associations face the same challenge every year. The nature of the challenge may differ according to whether the organization is a mid- to large-sized nonprofit with adequate staff and resources or a smaller or newer nonprofit struggling to make ends meet. This book aims to make the process run more smoothly for larger, established nonprofits and, for smaller and newer nonprofits, to serve as a guide to producing a report that serves their purposes without breaking the budget. So, although it might be tempting to remain a "high priestess" of the secrets of annual report publishing in the nonprofit sector, the greater temptation is to tell all—the tips, traps, and tricks of the trade that can help nonprofit associations, both large and small, become more visible to the public and, as a consequence, raise the funds that they need to advance their vitally important missions.

The book is based on interviews with people responsible for producing annual reports for a wide spectrum of nonprofits, from relief agencies and youth organizations to cultural, environmental, and other charitable nonprofits. I also interviewed writers, designers, accountants, and printers to get their perspectives and have been guided by my own experience in managing the production of annual reports for the National Trust for Historic

Preservation, World Wildlife Fund, the National Endowment for the Humanities, and the U.S. Department of Education. Although the latter two institutions are government agencies, the process proved just as painful and protracted there as elsewhere. Whenever possible, I have used actual examples from annual reports. In some cases, however, it was necessary to invent some hypothetical nonprofits—the American Geography Education Foundation; Dames, Inc.; Friends of the Ferret; Operation Teddy Bear—to illustrate particular points. Any resemblance to nonprofits of a similar name or nature is entirely coincidental.

While researching this book, I was cautioned by corporate annual report guru Sid Cato that corporate annual reports have nothing but their name in common with nonprofit annual reports. I chose to treat this advice somewhat skeptically because I had already drawn heavily from surveys of Fortune 500 companies, corporations that had recently issued initial public offerings, and investor-relations professionals conducted by the Potlatch Corporation in 1995 and 2000 and by the National Investor Relations Institute in 1999. These surveys, combined with much useful information gleaned from *Ragan's Annual Report Review,* showed that a lot can be learned from the business world about the structure, planning, content, visuals, costs, and future of annual reports, information that applies to both the for-profit and the nonprofit sector. For that reason, I have borrowed freely from the for-profit sector those tips and processes that can be adapted to the nonprofit world:

- Keep it simple.

- Keep it accessible to general readers.

- Tell the truth.

- Make an impact visually.

After all, the average annual report has just thirty seconds to make an impression with readers and potential investors (that is, funders). This book offers the collected wisdom of many experts who know how to make every second count.

Washington, D.C.   Caroline Taylor
August 2001

Acknowledgments

I AM GREATLY indebted to the following people for the time they took out of their busy days to share their experiences with me regarding annual report publishing: Sid Cato, president of Cato Communications, Inc.; Kathleen Courrier, vice president for communication, the Urban Institute; Penny Cuff, senior program officer, Partners for Livable Communities; Benita Dale, editor, the Alliance for Cultural Enrichment; Kathryn Fuller, president of World Wildlife Fund; Shirley Geer, senior information officer, Consultative Group on International Agricultural Research; Jimeequa Harris, communications coordinator, Christian Children's Fund; Jeffrey Hon, director for public information, National Council on Alcoholism and Drug Dependence; Herschel Lee Johnson, senior communications manager, NAACP Legal Defense and Educational Fund, Inc.; Nancy Kelly, communications and outreach officer, Asia Foundation; Eric Kessler, senior communications coordinator, Ducks Unlimited; Alex Kopelman, director of communications, Girls, Inc.; Gilbert D. Kulick, director of communications, New Israel Fund; Dana Lane, chief of publications, International Finance Corporation; Carol Leben, senior writer-editor, corporate communications, American Heart Association; M'Annette Ruddell, associate director for donor communications, American Friends Service Committee; Lee Salber, director of communications, Ducks Unlimited; Natalie Waugh, senior vice president for Constituent Programs, National Wildlife Federation; Bill Warren, senior writer, Development Services, National Trust for Historic Preservation; Jim Wilson, associate publisher, Boy Scouts of America; and Jennie Ziegler, director of external relations and corporate secretary, Ethics Resource Center.

Bruce Bunting, Curtis Clifton, and William Eichbaum of World Wildlife Fund spared no small amount of time giving me their perspectives, wisdom, and experience as content experts. Louis Bayard and Ellen Schorr gave excellent advice about the writer's approach to interviewing content experts and the other principals necessary for writing the review of operations and executive messages.

I am also indebted to Marc Meadows of Meadows Design Office; Jim Pizzo and Barbara Koontz of Curran and Connors, annual report designers; and Jane D'Alelio of Ice House Graphics for their advice on what designers need and the strengths they bring to the annual report production process; to Annie Argüeso Williams, account representative for Virginia Lithograph, for her gems of wisdom regarding correct file preparation, how to understand "print-speak," and other insights on print production; to Jack Noble and Lawrence Amon for explaining the legal requirements; to Tom Nichols for guidance on meeting standards of the Council of Better Business Bureaus; and to Carla Langeveld for her invaluable research assistance.

To Peter Porosky go my heartfelt thanks for his scrupulous review of the manuscript, and to my editor, Dorothy Hearst, much appreciation for helping to make this book possible.

—C. T.

The Author

CAROLINE TAYLOR, a consultant on annual reports, earned a B.A. degree in literature and history from the University of the State of New York and an M.A. degree in liberal studies from Georgetown University. She has more than twenty years of professional experience producing annual reports for nonprofit associations and government agencies. Annual reports that Taylor has produced over the course of her career have won twenty-one awards for communications excellence.

From 1996 to 1999, Taylor taught in the Georgetown University School of Professional Development. Her course, which involved integrating all the processes involved in producing an annual report, was the capstone course for certificate candidates in the Editing and Publications Program. From 1993 to 2000, Taylor served as director of publications for World Wildlife Fund. She had previously been communications director for the assistant secretary for postsecondary education in the U.S. Department of Education; editorial policy director at the U.S. Department of Education; publications director and editor of *Humanities* magazine at the National Endowment for the Humanities; and general publications editor for the National Trust for Historic Preservation. She has written and edited a wide variety of publications on the environment, higher education, historic preservation, the humanities, and publications management.

Introduction

NONPROFIT ASSOCIATIONS have issued annual reports for more than fifty years. These products vary in quality and cost. Some nonprofit annual reports could go toe to toe with annual reports produced by Fortune 500 companies. Other reports show signs of suffering from lack of funds for quality photography, design, and printing. This book is intended to help large, sophisticated associations troubleshoot what often is a needlessly long and painful procedure, and to guide smaller, perhaps even newly founded associations in developing the structure and processes necessary to produce a high-quality annual report within the constraints of a tight budget and a small staff.

This book does not cover the financial sections of the annual report in any detail. Because audited financial statements are obtained from independent auditors and may not be altered or edited, the financial sections are essentially dropped into the report, usually near the end of the production process. If space is at a premium, or if the financial statements are particularly complex, they may be presented selectively, in shortened form, as financial highlights—usually by the person on staff with the greatest understanding of the bottom line—with readers invited to write to the organization if they wish to obtain a full set of audited financials. (The important differences between financial statements and financial highlights are covered in Chapter Three, and readers searching for more detailed information about financial statements in annual reports can find it in many accounting and finance books, some of which are listed in the Recommended Reading section at the end of the book.)

The primary reason why this book focuses on the annual report's production process is that publishing an annual report is not as straightforward as it may appear, even for associations that publish other materials. For example, many nonprofit associations issue magazines and newsletters. These periodicals, because of their frequency and content, may be very labor-intensive productions, whereas the annual report, issued only once a year, and with content that simply distills what has undoubtedly already been said in other publications, may seem simpler and less time-consuming to put out. But annual reports are deceptively complex. They are difficult to plan (everybody has a different idea about what should be covered), challenging to write (whole programs must be described in pithy, specific, bite-sized chunks of text), tricky to illustrate (especially on a small budget), complicated to design (visual elements must not overwhelm or be at odds with the central message), and most often, very late getting to the printer, with little leeway for extending the deadline. All these factors combine to make the process laborious and often frustrating, no matter how many times one has gone through it.

My students at Georgetown University, having enrolled in the capstone course of the Editing and Publications Program in the School of Professional Development, learned just how vexatious the experience of publishing an annual report can be. The course was designed to help certificate candidates understand how editing and design are interwoven in the publications process, and the students were asked to produce their own annual reports for companies or groups that they had invented.

The students initially believed that producing the reports would be boring and not nearly as much fun as producing a magazine or a newsletter. Their ennui quickly changed to panic as the deadline for completion of the class projects drew closer. Pictures that the students had selected on the basis of visual appeal turned out to be editorially inappropriate for the reports. Text had to be rewritten at the last minute because it did more to sell an organization's cause or a company's products than to report on what the institution had accomplished during the year covered by the report. Layouts that worked well for the executive message and review of operations became problematic for the financial statements and management analysis. The students discovered that there wasn't enough time to type up a list of fictitious officers, let alone fictitious donors. And why were there so many last-minute glitches at the copy store—incorrectly translated fonts, corrupted files, bleeds not quite bleeding, binding obscuring parts of the text? The students' experiences were a microcosm of the many problems that editors of annual reports face in the real world.

This book is based on the premise that multiple problems can be solved most easily if they are broken down into smaller, more manageable tasks. Chapter One begins this process by explaining why many nonprofits publish annual reports, and how an annual report fits into an organization's overall communications strategy.

Chapter Two identifies the key players, from the chief executive officer to the mail house. In addition to defining their roles and responsibilities, this chapter explains how they work together to produce an annual report that achieves its multiple objectives.

Chapter Three divides the annual report into its separate elements and explains which are mandatory (to satisfy watchdog agencies) and which are optional (although perhaps useful in presenting a compelling picture of the organization and its work). The chapter takes examples of each element from actual nonprofit annual reports.

Chapter Four explores the organizational tools that can help editors plan, schedule, and track production. Although there is no legally mandated deadline for release of the nonprofit annual report, as there is for the corporate annual report, many organizations strive to publish their annual reports by a specified date (sometime after the close of the fiscal year and before the next board meeting). Because time is a precious commodity for lean-staffed nonprofits, making a plan and sticking to it as closely as possible are keys to meeting that deadline. This chapter includes a sample plan, a production schedule, a sample synopsis, and a tracking matrix.

Chapter Five offers guidance for writing the executive message, which experts tell us is the most-read feature of the annual report. The chapter covers the key elements of the executive message, including examples of how some nonprofit CEOs have handled the bad news in their messages, as well as tips for writers, to help them make their words sound like a CEO's. The chapter also offers a sample executive message for a fictitious nonprofit.

Chapter Six is about writing the review of operations, which constitutes the bulk of the text. Readers will find tips for themes that work, as well as advice about taking turgid, arcane background material and turning it into sparkling, succinct prose that nonexperts can easily understand.

Chapter Seven explains why the editor of the annual report does more than edit the text. The chapter does offer tips for substantive editing and copyediting, but it also illustrates how the production process works, and it outlines what the editor must do to manage that process. One task is to find the most appropriate illustrations and graphics—a daunting job for a time-strapped editor on a small budget, or for an editor whose organization's mission is not easy to represent visually.

Chapter Eight discusses the role and responsibilities of the designer, the person who integrates text and visuals. As the production process wends its way through the design and production stages, the designer and the editor become a team and must work together to achieve verbal and visual coherence. Included in this chapter are tips for finding a good designer, a list of design no-no's, and information about the design process itself.

Chapter Nine provides some assistance with the arduous search for visuals. It suggests sources of photographs or illustrations, offers tips for working with a photographer, and describes different types of photo captions. Also included in this chapter is an explanation of the various forms of graphics and how to make them communicate clearly and powerfully.

Chapter Ten covers what editors need to know to work effectively with printers and mail houses. It includes tips on what to look for in reviewing printers' proofs, from bluelines to color proofs. (A glossary of special "print-speak" terms, intended to save editors money and heartache, appears at the back of the book.)

Chapter Eleven offers suggestions for evaluating success and spotting signs of trouble. This process often involves peering into a murky future in search of award-winning solutions to problems identified during the post-mortem period that often follows the report's release, when the key players get together to discuss ways to thwart Murphy's Law. (Murphy's Law, of course, states that if anything can go wrong, it will, and usually at the worst possible time. Many of the experts interviewed for this book attest that the annual report is particularly vulnerable to it.) This chapter also explores what's happening to annual reports on the World Wide Web and collects the thoughts of corporate and nonprofit annual report producers on whether the brave new world of electronic publishing will eventually make the printed annual report a relic of the twentieth century.

At the dawn of the new millennium, however, the annual report remains a staple of nonprofit publishing because it serves so many useful purposes, not the least of which is showcasing the organization. Although nonprofits may not compete for market share, they certainly do compete for funds. For many small, cash-strapped nonprofits that are just getting started and need every penny for their programs, using those funds prudently can pose a challenge. If the annual report is but a single tool in a communications strategy designed to advance the organization and its cause, wouldn't a newsletter or a brochure better serve this purpose? Why publish an annual report?

Chapter 1

Why Publish an Annual Report?

ASSOCIATIONS ARE powerful forces in our society. They have existed in this country since the first communities grew large enough for people to band together to protect hard-earned freedoms from government meddling, advance their members' common interests, and alleviate social or economic ills. Alexis de Tocqueville ([1835] 1945, p. 342) noted that association members, as enlightened members of the community, "cannot be disposed of at pleasure or oppressed without remonstrance"; by defending their rights and interests against the interference of government, he said, these associations save "the common liberties of the country."

The word *association* is used in this book to mean an organization of people who have an interest in common; it does not convey the more specialized meaning often assigned to it in the nonprofit world, where it denotes a banding together of several nonprofit organizations. And, although the word *association* can refer to trade associations of businesses that have common interests, this book focuses on nonprofit associations that have charitable or cultural missions.

Despite the important role that associations play in American society, they are neither highly visible nor well understood. When we consider that 70 percent of Americans belong to at least one association (Sheets, 1999), this invisibility is astonishing. The work of associations is often accomplished with little fanfare or notice: they are so busy doing their work, they don't have time to talk about it, and those associations that may have the time may not have the funds to publicize their work. Even with ample funding and plenty of time, however, some associations believe that precious funds should not be devoted to self-promotion. Lack of visibility may not be critically important to associations that are entirely supported by membership dues, but nonprofits that must raise funds to support their work know that a little self-promotion can go a long way toward keeping the association afloat and functioning.

Why use an annual report to promote the organization? Why not spend precious resources on a book, a magazine, a newsletter, or, better yet, a Web site? All these vehicles play key roles in a nonprofit's overall communications strategy, and many have multiple purposes that include informing, educating, and enlisting support.

Indeed, as we shall see, some nonprofits have taken the approach of publishing the annual report in an issue of the association's magazine, or as a special issue of that periodical, and many nonprofits publish their annual reports on their Web sites (see Chapter Eleven). But the annual report has some distinct advantages over other forms of communication. For example, annual reports are shorter and less comprehensive than books. That makes them more appealing to all but the minority of readers, as rare as giant pandas in the wild, who want to know absolutely everything that can be known about the organization.

Magazines or newsletters, of course, are also shorter than books. In these publications, however, the need to distinguish the publisher's "spin" from factual reporting makes them less than ideal vehicles for showcasing the organization's work. To avoid confusing readers, nonprofits that use their magazine or newsletter to make annual financial disclosures usually also create a strong visual distinction between the periodical's regular copy and the copy that belongs to the annual report. Even so, there is a slight risk of alienating subscribers who expect the association's magazine or newsletter to be—or at least appear to be—objective rather than self-promotional. And good annual reports always promote.

A Web site, at first glance, may seem to be the ideal vehicle for the succinct, highly visual content of an annual report. A current major drawback of this approach—although times are changing—is that a Web site lacks the personal touch: it is one thing to give a prospective donor an annual report that can be perused at leisure; it is quite another to invite a donor to find out about the organization by logging on to its Web site.

Given the limitations inherent in magazines, newsletters, and Web sites, it is no wonder that the nonprofit organization's annual report often plays a special role in the organization's overall communications strategy. We'll explore that strategic role in the section that follows.

Strategic Role of the Nonprofit Organization's Annual Report

In the tools they employ to communicate—Web sites, press releases, special reports, magazines and newsletters, "sales" brochures and other advertising, conferences, annual reports—nonprofits share many vehicles with corporations. Some of these vehicles—special reports, magazines, journals, newsletters, books—have an objective focus in the sense that the organizational bias is not apparent. Other communications tools—press releases, sales pieces and other advertising, conferences—have a more subjective emphasis and are clearly intended to present the organization in the best light. Two of these tools—the Web site and the annual report—successfully combine factual reporting with organizational self-promotion.

Needless to say, the larger the nonprofit, the greater the number of communications tools it can afford to employ. Some large organizations, such as the National Geographic Society, Ducks Unlimited, and the National Wildlife Federation, have their own television productions. Other nonprofits, small and newly formed, are obliged to concentrate their communications in order to conserve their resources (see Table 1.1).

Small and large organizations alike must have, at the very minimum, a brochure or a one-page handout that explains who they are, why they were founded, what they do, how they are funded, and how people can become members or offer other kinds of support. A Web presence is de rigueur in the Internet Age, and this information can be put on the organization's Web site. (The Web site of a small group, of course, need not be as sophisticated as that of a larger, more established organization.) That said, the organization still needs an informational piece to answer "snail mail" inquiries from the public and to give to job applicants, prospective donors, and business and political contacts.

The same information could be provided at greater cost in the organization's annual report, but an annual report must do more than provide general information. For example, only the annual report discloses funding sources and covers what the organization did with donors' funds during the year covered by the report. Of course, simply mailing audited financial statements to donors, or making copies of IRS forms available to them, could save money, time, and aggravation. But the annual report can play a role larger than the one required by law.

Legal Requirements

The Securities and Exchange Act of 1933, which emerged from the stock market crash of 1929, regulates publicly held, for-profit corporations (those that have shareholders) by holding them accountable to strict requirements for reporting and financial disclosure. Financial disclosures are necessary to protect public investors from poor or illegal business practices. Corporations must make annual audited financial disclosures to their shareholders by a certain date.

TABLE 1.1

Communications Tools Needed by Small to Large Nonprofits

Type of Tool	Small	Medium	Large	Comments
Web site	Yes	Yes	Yes	The size and complexity can vary greatly, depending on resources.
Annual report	Yes	Yes	Yes	Ditto. Also publish a Web version.
Information brochure	Yes	Yes	Yes	Ditto.
Press release	Yes	Yes	Yes	Also publish on the Web.
Direct-mail appeals	Maybe	Yes	Yes	Can generate new members and revenue. Also put appeals on the Web.
Newsletter (external)	Maybe	Maybe	Maybe	Consider whether this information can be more cheaply disseminated on the Web.
Newsletter (internal)	No	Maybe	Maybe	Consider whether this information can be more cheaply disseminated by meetings and memos or on an intranet.
Intranet	No	Maybe	Yes	Especially useful in organizations with far-flung field offices.
Conference program	Maybe	Maybe	Maybe	Consider only if the organization holds conferences.
Magazine	No	No	Maybe	Magazines are expensive and labor-intensive and should be considered only if they can be supported by advertising.
Journal	Maybe	Maybe	Maybe	Consider only if the organization's mission is to publish research or educational materials.
Books	Maybe	Maybe	Maybe	Ditto.
Book list/catalog	Maybe	Maybe	Maybe	Consider only if the organization publishes books and sells them. Also put on Web site.
Special reports	Maybe	Maybe	Maybe	Depends on the organization's mission.
Fund-raising case statement	Maybe	Maybe	Yes	Useful when seeking a large number of major donors; otherwise, can be expensive and time-sensitive.
Public service ads	Maybe	Maybe	Yes	Nothing ventured, nothing gained—but placement and timing are not optimum and the ads may never appear.
Paid advertising	Maybe	Maybe	Yes	If funds permit, go for it.
Merchandise catalog	No	No	Maybe	Can be a source of scarce nonrestricted revenue.
TV productions	No	No	Maybe	Ditto.
Radio productions	No	No	Maybe	Ditto.

The various stock exchanges have different requirements for when the annual reports of member corporations must be delivered to shareholders (usually 10 to 15 days before the annual meeting of shareholders, and 90 to 120 days after the close of the fiscal year). Corporations' annual financial disclosures must also meet various state requirements.

On the nonprofit side, the Internal Revenue Service requires charities that solicit funds within the United States, that have gross receipts of at least $25,000, and that are not controlled by churches or religious orders to file Form 990, "Return of Organization Exempt from Income Tax." The 990 form—much like an annual report, although in a much more standardized format—gives comprehensive information about a charity's program activities, finances, and governance.

In most states in this country, nonprofits that want to raise money are required by state solicitation bureaus to produce audited financial statements. This requirement may apply only to organizations whose annual revenues exceed a certain limit (say, $100,000); the limit depends on the state. To gain the seal of approval of watchdog groups like the BBB Wise Giving Alliance (a merger of the National Charities Information Bureau and the Council of Better Business Bureaus), a charity is also required to publish an annual report. The nonprofit annual report serves as the organization's description of its activities for the year and should offer more detail than what is provided on the IRS Form 990: the 990 cannot substitute for either a good annual report or financial statements audited by an independent certified public accountant.

Simply mailing the audited financial statements to donors or making Form 990 available to them would save money, time, and aggravation, but someone had a better idea. In 1959, Litton Industries produced the first annual report that packaged corporate financial data in a glossy, colorful booklet. Investors liked this newfangled report because it told them about more than the company's financial condition. A packaged annual report gives stockholders of corporations, and members and donors of nonprofit organizations, a more complete picture of operations, products (or results), and plans for the future, through the eyes of the person at the top (Potlatch Corporation, 1994).

The CEO's Baby

Whether it is issued by a public corporation or by a nonprofit association, the annual report, more than any other publication or communication vehicle, expresses the personality, philosophy, vision, and taste of the CEO. Herring

(1990, p. 9), discussing the corporate annual report's importance to CEOs, points out that the way in which they are presented to their stockholders and to the public is of great interest to these executives. The CEO is the one who signs the executive message. The CEO's picture is right next to that message, and the remainder of the report talks about the company's successes and failures.

Kathryn Fuller, president and chief executive officer of World Wildlife Fund, takes a similar view of the annual report's importance. "The annual report is always the most important stand-alone communications vehicle of the year. It is our signature piece," she says, because "we don't have a magazine that conveys core messages to key constituents." The core message may take a different form from one year to the next, Fuller says, but "our 'take home' message is basically the same: Conservation is an urgent cause. The challenges are enormous, yet World Wildlife Fund is making significant headway with the help of its supporters."

The nonprofit association's supporters are fundamentally its investors, and so it is logical that there will be many similarities between the annual report produced by a nonprofit organization and a corporate annual report. Whereas corporations must satisfy the reporting requirements imposed by the Securities and Exchange Commission and must produce their annual reports by a fixed deadline, nonprofit organizations face their own set of challenges.

The Challenge for Nonprofits

Annual reports are expensive. Getting the most for your money may be as important for nonprofits as it is for corporations, but nonprofit budgets can be tight.

Because the annual report is published once every twelve months, it may seem that there is a whole year available to get it out. In reality, however, no one can devote full time to one publication, even one as crucial as an annual report. Moreover, the feast-or-famine nature of publications in the nonprofit world usually means that crunch time for the annual report is also crunch time for several other urgent publications. That's why it usually takes nine to fifteen months of intensive concentration, from conception to birth, to produce an annual report. Yet a nonprofit's staff tends to be small; and imagine the effort it takes in order for this document, essentially produced by a committee, to speak with one voice, engage, inform—even entertain—and still come out on time. Especially important is what the annual report says, and how it says it. Therefore, management pays scrupulous attention to every word and image, and so do many of the report's readers.

The people responsible for writing and producing annual reports say that one of the biggest challenges they face is lack of time. "My biggest problem in putting out the annual report for the New Israel Fund was getting the report out on time," says Gilbert Kulick, who published two reports for that organization. "We would plan for mid-June, but then there would be delays getting the audited financials, and the report didn't come out until July or even early September."

Jennie Ziegler, director of external relations and corporate secretary for the Ethics Resource Center, reports a similar experience. "I would like to have more time to do the report because I believe it is key," she says. "Theoretically, it could be completed in two months, but it gets pushed off for other, more pressing deadlines."

Why, apart from the legal requirements, must the nonprofit annual report come out by a particular deadline? As long as the report comes out annually, why not just start writing and editing it when there is time, and publish it when everyone is satisfied with the copy? For one thing, many annual reports are tied to the annual meeting of the board and serve as reports to the board. Therefore, they must be published in time for that meeting. For another, nonprofit annual reports are often vehicles for generating financial contributions.

The Annual Report as a Fund-Raising Tool

Annual reports that come out in the summer, when hearts turn to vacations, or that reach donors' mailboxes in the spring, right after the taxman cometh, are not going to produce the same generous impulse as reports issued in the fall or winter. Thanks to the Internal Revenue Service, people tend to think about charitable contributions only at certain times—usually before the close of the tax year, when the spirit of giving shines most brightly. "Our report needs to come out in mid-fall," says World Wildlife Fund's Kathryn Fuller, "just in time for end-of-year fund raising."

A survey of corporate annual reports conducted by the Potlatch Corporation (1995) shows that 70 percent of investment portfolio managers used annual reports to make investment decisions. Nonprofit annual reports are likewise an excellent tool for attracting future members or donors. Between a report's covers can be found information about what the organization does, what it has accomplished during the past year, who manages and governs it, what the organization does with its donors' money, and who its current supporters are. (There's nothing like seeing the names of current donors to prompt the feeling of being only a few hundred dollars away from seeing one's own name in such august company.)

M'Annette Ruddell, associate director for donor communications at the American Friends Service Committee, says that the association's annual report brings in $400,000 to $500,000 each year. Likewise, approximately $220,000 in donations received by World Wildlife Fund in 1999 could be directly traced to the organization's 1998 annual report, according to WWF's development staff. But tracking the funds raised by the annual report can be problematic if the report is part of another publication. (As already mentioned, some nonprofits publish their annual reports as special issues of periodicals that they already produce; for example, the Environmental Law Institute featured the full text of its 1998 annual report in the May-June 1999 issue of *Environmental Forum,* and the Trust for Public Land devoted the Fall 1999 issue of its magazine, *Land and People,* to the organization's 1999 annual report.)

The Annual Report as a Financial Disclosure Document

Members and donors need to know how their support is helping the organization carry out its mission and what portion of donated funds is devoted to administrative costs. Watchdog agencies also rate charitable nonprofits according to their stewardship of funds and the portion of devoted to administrative costs. The Council of Better Business Bureaus (CBBB) has established standards to promote ethical practices by charities, which it calls "soliciting organizations." With regard to the use of funds, the CBBB's standards require that "a reasonable percentage of total income from all sources shall be applied to programs and activities directly related to the purposes for which the organization exists" (Council of Better Business Bureaus, 1999). Reasonable use of funds requires that

> *At least 50 percent of total income from all sources be spent on programs and activities directly related to the organization's purposes*
>
> *At least 50 percent of public contributions be spent on the programs and activities described in solicitations, in accordance with donor expectations*
>
> *Fund-raising costs not exceed 35 percent of related contributions*
>
> *Total fund-raising and administrative costs not exceed 50 percent of total income [Council of Better Business Bureaus, 1999]*

Financial disclosure also gives nonprofits an opportunity to show supporters and potential supporters at first hand how the organization compares to other nonprofits engaged in similar work. Unlike corporations, nonprofits tend not to compete overtly with colleagues engaged in similar work, but they certainly can use the annual report to build their image.

The Annual Report as an Image Builder

Respondents to the 2000 Potlatch survey of corporate annual reports ranked the annual report fourth among the most important communications resources available to a company (after a Web site, analyst conferences, and press coverage), and a survey conducted earlier (Potlatch Corporation, 1995) reveals that nearly 80 percent of securities analysts, portfolio managers, and individual investors thought they could learn something from reading a company's annual report. Nonprofit investors no doubt share the same views. How well the report is designed, written, and produced speaks volumes about the organization's self-image.

"The image we portray in the annual report is important," says Jim Wilson, associate publisher for the Boy Scouts of America. "We send copies to each member of Congress, the top executives of the Fortune 500, and to the top seventeen charitable organizations in the United States."

But, according to M'Annette Ruddell of the American Friends Service Committee, image building can also pose problems for the association that has a need to explain its mission, but whose core principles do not embrace self-promotion:

> *Every year, we try to shrink that distance between the bureaucracy in Philadelphia and the work in the field and bring home to the reader why we really exist. We exist for that child in a Kosovo refugee camp. We exist for that Asian American kid in San Francisco who is suffering from violence or that woman in West Virginia who has two children and no education, whose husband has abandoned them. We give her a dictionary and some paper so that she can get her G.E.D. But we also must try to interpret this story in a modest and not too prideful way.*

Even when the organization's image is portrayed as eloquently as Ruddell has done it, the careful reader may feel the need to understand the organization's track record over time. Are the organization's principals real professionals, or are they rank amateurs? Do they tell a straight story, or do they slant it? Do they actually accomplish anything, or do they seem to be making the same claims over and over again? One need only check previous annual reports to find the answers, and that's why the nonprofit annual report serves yet another useful purpose: as an archival record.

The Annual Report as an Archival Record

According to the Potlatch Corporation (1995), the shelf life of an annual report is longer than the period in which it is initially read. Reports are frequently filed for future reference and are even shared among colleagues and friends.

"People save our report," says Kathryn Fuller of World Wildlife Fund. "We spend a lot of time and money on getting good nature photography, but it's worth it because people keep the report as a daily reminder of our work."

Aside from the obvious appeal of any photos they may contain, there are other reasons to keep an organization's annual reports. Who originally served on the board? Has the board's size or role changed over time? How much has the organization grown in the years since it was founded? Has the organization stuck to its original mission, or does it seem to be suffering from "mission creep"? Have key staffers steadily advanced in their careers, or are there signs of heavy job turnover? Are administrative costs held in check from year to year, or are they also creeping up? Because the nonprofit annual report presents a year-to-year description of the organization's work, it becomes the organization's official history.

Financial progress, for example, can be detected in a comparison of the 1997 and 1998 annual reports of the Consultative Group on International Agricultural Research (CGIAR). In 1997, the executive secretary, Alexander von der Osten, reported that "in 1996, funding was $304 million and in 1997, $320 million" (Consultative Group on International Agricultural Research, 1997, p. 5). In 1998, he reported that "funding for the CGIAR's research grew from $320 million in 1997 to $340 million in 1998" (Consultative Group on International Agricultural Research, 1998, p. 7).

Because many donors target their support, a year-to-year comparison of annual reports will indicate whether progress has been made or whether the story remains basically unchanged. In the 1998 annual report of the Christian Children's Fund, for example, the story about its work in Angola reported that $1.5 million had been spent to help children affected by the civil war and that a war-trauma training program had trained 4,511 caregivers to help "children who are unaccompanied, displaced, orphaned, and those demonstrating psychosocial problems due to exposure to violence" (Christian Children's Fund, 1998, p. 2). By 1999, it was clear that some progress had been made: the same story about Angola reported that $1.7 million in assistance had been devoted to helping children in that war-torn country and that the fund had trained 5,158 caregivers (Christian Children's Fund, 1999, p. 3). Activities described (but not quantified) in the 1998 annual report as including "the rehabilitation and construction of schools, community kindergartens and child centers" (Christian Children's Fund, 1998, p. 2) took more concrete form in the 1999 report: "Additionally, the program has built or rehabilitated seven community kindergartens and 14 primary schools, three soccer fields, and one playground" (Christian Children's Fund, 1999, p. 3).

As fund raiser, financial disclosure tool, image builder, and archival record, the nonprofit annual report must please many audiences. The key word here is *please,* for the annual report is uniformly upbeat and positive, even when delivering bad news (see Chapter Five). The challenge for the editor is to fulfill these many purposes and satisfy the report's multiple audiences by assembling the various players needed to make the report into a coherent yet succinct whole.

Chapter 2

Key Players: Their Roles and Responsibilities

BECAUSE the annual report speaks for the institution as a whole, it is a stew produced by many chefs. The key players discussed in this chapter must know their roles and execute them responsibly. They must work together as a team. For this concoction to be palatable to its audience, however, it must appear to have been assembled by one master and to communicate with one voice.

Just as the master chef must orchestrate the teamwork required to produce a seven-course gourmet meal, the editor of the annual report must ensure that all the key players understand their roles and responsibilities and execute them in a timely fashion. Many key players are at the highest levels of the organization; others are more junior. When they must interact with one another and with outside consultants, for design or writing or both, achieving one voice can be a challenge.

Compounding that challenge is the tendency of staff members, who are often overburdened, to view the annual report as a necessary chore but one that is frequently overshadowed by more pressing priorities. The organization with a lean staff finds it difficult to tend to its primary business while also allowing time for staffers to grant interviews to a writer, review draft copy, and collect necessary information from people outside the organization.

Says Gilbert Kulick, who edited the annual report of the New Israel Fund, "Getting donors to approve how their names were listed was a real problem for me until we adopted the negative response: 'If we don't hear from you, this is how you will be listed.'"

That kind of firmness is but one of the qualities the editor will need in order to ensure that the key players function as a team. The editor must also be a leader and a diplomat, for the most important player in this process is the organization's highest-ranking person: the chief executive officer.

The Chief Executive Officer

No other publication expresses the nonprofit's vision, values, goals, and performance more fully than the annual report. The CEO is the one best positioned to speak for the organization as a whole—to articulate its vision and aspirations, express its values and goals, and report annually on the progress made toward achieving those goals.

"The CEO's responsibility is to review the content and emphases to ensure that they adequately reflect our positioning and priorities," says Kathryn Fuller, president and CEO of World Wildlife Fund (WWF). "My message and the chairman's message must complement one another and present key and timely aspects of WWF's work."

As in the corporate world, the CEO's audience is the people who have invested their money. They want to know that their investment was wise, and that there is a return on their investment—ferrets saved, refugees rescued, alcoholics rehabilitated, historic buildings preserved, and so forth—even though the return is more intangible.

According to Natalie Waugh, senior vice president for constituent programs at the National Wildlife Federation, the CEO's primary responsibility is to review themes and options and then delegate the report's production to a trusted member of the staff (usually known as the annual report's editor). "Set the direction," says Waugh. "Trust your staff."

The greatest trap for the CEO or executive director of a newly established nonprofit is to become overly involved in the project and try to make the annual report be too much. Waugh has these words of wisdom for those just beginning the process of creating an annual report:

> Don't put too many eggs in the annual report basket; it makes the stakes too high. The annual report is one tool, but not the only tool. It doesn't have to be the greatest document in the history of the world. Remember that readers will spend at most ten minutes thumbing through the report— looking at the pictures, reading the captions and perhaps an article. The annual report has to get the essence of the organization right and communicate in a way that donors can understand and love. And that's important. But it can't take care of every situation.

Indeed, the wisest thing any leader can do, says Waugh, is to "remember your funding constituency and tailor the report to them, just the way a corporate CEO would tailor his report to shareholders. Don't create the report for yourself or your staff. Create it for the customer."

"Too many cooks can spoil the broth," warns World Wildlife Fund's Kathryn Fuller. "The CEO must make sure that the annual report represents the institution as a whole and is not the wish list of a set of individuals." Of course, the customer is always right, and the CEO's duty is to tell all the major customers what the organization has done with their money. Nevertheless, said Fuller, "an annual report for a nonprofit can and should be much more than a statement of its financial health and management."

The visionary CEO retains the big-picture institutional perspective and the long-term vision of where the organization should be heading while leaving the details of describing how it is getting there to content experts, the next group of critical players in the annual report's production process.

Content Experts

Content experts are the staff people who execute the organization's primary mission. They know how the organization is structured and what has happened during the past year that merits coverage in the annual report. Content experts, particularly the chief financial officer, or CFO, may occupy management positions in the organization, but they may also be the organization's chief scientists, analysts, or advocates.

The role of the CFO is to ensure the accuracy of the financial information, which includes any charts or graphs, and to explain what the numbers mean. Other content experts provide essential information to the writer about what the organization has accomplished, and they review draft copy for accuracy and completeness. Some content experts, according to their roles in the organization, may also know how best to communicate with the intended audience.

"We must give the writer the basic facts, at best," says Bill Eichbaum, World Wildlife Fund's vice president for endangered spaces. "But we also need to give the spin on those facts and direct the writer to where he can find information, inside and outside the organization."

Content experts are responsible for verifying to the CEO that the material for which they are responsible is indeed accurate and complete. They are also responsible, at the beginning of the process, for making themselves available to be interviewed. By the very nature of their roles in the organization, however, content experts often cannot conduct interviews or review copy at the particular times when the annual report's production schedule calls for them to perform these vitally important functions. They may be traveling or on vacation, or they may be caught up in resolving an urgent crisis.

According to Kathleen Courrier, vice president for communication at the Urban Institute, "My biggest headache editing the annual report for World Resources Institute was finding that the people who needed to review copy were away on travel. That is not a problem here at the Urban

Institute because there are fewer people involved in the review process, but resolving differences when I get contradictory feedback is never easy."

The need to resolve contradictory feedback is quite common in complex organizations, where people with different skills and talents often work on the same issue. It is natural that they bring their own perspectives to bear on the issue, and the individual perspective is crucial; without it, the report is likely to contain errors.

"Errors in a nonprofit annual report may not be subject to lawsuit, as is sometimes the case in the corporate world," warns Bruce Bunting, vice president of World Wildlife Fund's Center for Conservation Finance. "But an organization that prides itself on accuracy should be extra careful to ensure that its annual report is not riddled with errors."

The long lead time that usually exists between the planning and the production of the report can also be a challenge. "It's awkward to have to begin thinking in the second quarter of the fiscal year about what we are going to want to say at the end," says World Wildlife Fund's Bill Eichbaum. "I have to speculate about what I am going to accomplish in the next six months."

Although it may be possible to surmount problems associated with the production schedule, dealing with content experts can pose other challenges. For example, many content experts tend not to be skilled interview subjects.

"Even the helpful experts need to be guided on what's newsworthy," said Louis Bayard, who has written the annual report of World Wildlife Fund for several years. "They tend to be too involved in the process—workshops, management plans, et cetera—so I find myself having to ask them, 'What's the story here? What's newsworthy?' It's amazing how many people don't know what their story is."

Furthermore, some content experts may be too busy to pull together all the details that the writer needs. Others may feel put on the spot by the request for an interview; they may prefer to provide written background material. Still others may conclude that being interviewed was a waste of their valuable time because the writer—the next key player—did not ask them the right questions.

The Writer

When it comes to deciding who will write the annual report, there are two choices: a writer on the organization's staff or a freelancer from outside the organization. If the organization can allocate sufficient time to a staff writer for this task, both money and time can be saved. Because staff writers are already being paid to write about the organization, they understand its mission, organizational structure, and activities. This understanding can be vitally important, says Shirley Geer, senior information officer for the Consultative Group on International Agricultural Research (CGIAR).

"Ideally," says Geer, "the annual report is written by a staff writer because CGIAR is very complex, and the language we must use is highly nuanced."

A freelancer, by contrast, will need to be briefed on the organization and its mission. Most often, the freelancer is given extensive background information—usually by someone fairly senior, who may not have the time for a thorough background briefing. Unlike a staff writer, however, the freelancer can build into the estimate a certain amount of money to cover what Ellen Schorr, a development and communications consultant for nonprofits, calls "the pain and suffering index":

> *Clients need to pay a premium if they are playing havoc with your schedule and other projects by asking for unreasonable turnaround or failing to meet their own deadlines. What is the pain-and-suffering index? Do I need to ask three times for promised background material? Are appointments kept, on time, and limited to the time allotted? Is there one contact person, or am I going to be fielding calls to and from half a dozen staffers? Are requests for further information met reluctantly or forthcomingly? Will a contact person streamline staff and board comment into one manageable document for my revision, or will four different board members be calling me at home at night to nitpick about comma placement? Do they appreciate my work? Do they pay invoices on time?*

Staff writers, of course, are just as likely to be subjected to the same difficulties. The difference is that they can't automatically raise their salaries to cover "pain and suffering."

It may seem that the possibility of this extra expense means one must always use staff writers, but that isn't necessarily true. Simply because they often know the organization too well, staff writers may not be the best communicators. For example, a staff writer may think the following sentence is perfectly clear: "Our work this past year with HBCUs helped ensure that they remain fiscally sound and academically rigorous." A freelancer, by contrast, will ask, "What are HBCUs?" For further help in making the crucial decision about whether to use a staff writer or a freelancer, see Table 2.1. Regardless of whether the writer is on staff or is a freelancer, Schorr cautions that "it's best to think like an outsider—to be on guard for jargon, obscure terminology, unclear thinking, unexplained assumptions, and anything else that may make the writing less accessible and powerful."

If an organization employs writers on its staff, they are probably fully occupied with other publications and may have little additional time to devote to researching and writing the annual report, let alone conducting interviews. Finding the time to write the annual report has been a major

TABLE 2.1

Relative Merits of Staff Writers Versus Freelancers

Issue	Staff Writer	Freelancer
Tight time frame for production	Maybe. Usually has other responsibilities but won't need lengthy briefing or research.	Maybe. Can be hired on the basis of availability but needs time for briefing and research.
Loose time frame for production	Maybe. Depends on other responsibilities.	Yes.
Cost	Covered in salary.	Can range from $1,000 to $10,000+.
Knowledge of organization	Yes. But may be too close to subject matter.	No. But adds outsider's perspective.
Freshness, novelty	Maybe. But likely to have an insider's mind-set.	Yes. But may be too fresh or too novel.
Quality of writing	Known by other work.	Unknown except for samples, reputation.
Need for rewrite	Maybe. Depends on quality of first product, other duties.	Maybe. First draft may suggest a rewrite not worth the time or cost.
Cost of rewrite	Covered in salary.	Can range from $50 to $75 per hour.
What other nonprofits do[a]	75 percent.	25 percent.

[a]Percentages based on nonprofits interviewed for this book.

challenge for Lee Salber, director of communications for Ducks Unlimited. "During the first six months of the year that our annual report is in production," he says, "we are also working on television shows, a radio show, the Web site, press relations, an annual convention and leadership conference, and two outdoor festivals." Using a staff writer exclusively to write a publication that comes out only once a year is a waste of precious contributions from supporters.

A recent survey of corporate annual reports showed that 64 percent of corporate annual reports were written by in-house staff as compared to 13 percent that were written by consultants from outside firms (National Investor Relations Institute, 1999). If the annual report producers who were interviewed for this book can be considered guides to the nonprofit world as a whole, then 75 percent of nonprofits use staff writers and 25 percent hire freelancers to write their annual reports (the annual report of the American Friends Service Committee was written by a staff person in 1997 and by a freelancer in 1998 and 1999). The choice very much depends on budget, staff resources, the complexity of the message, and the kind of writing that the organization thinks will work best in its annual report.

The writer's role is to pull together disparate pieces of information from different sources, which include the information supplied by content experts and various kinds of background material, and transform these pieces into a coherent narrative of what the organization accomplished during the year under review.

"You're basically working with a variety of different sources, from published material to technical documents not written in 'English,'" says Louis Bayard. "The challenge is to weave them into a concise, comprehensible picture that gives readers a sense of what the organization has been doing."

Sometimes the writer is expected to develop an outline, but often the writer is given an outline or synopsis with which to work. The writer's responsibilities are as follows:

- Conform to the outline

- Collect source material

- Listen to and carefully record the words of any content experts who are interviewed for the report

- Understand the tone and approach that are appropriate to the writing

- Submit a polished draft by the requested deadline

- Rewrite the draft if requested to do so

Unless a staff writer is new to the organization, he or she will probably have little trouble understanding the approach to take and the tone to use.

"I recall a draft submitted by a staff writer that really missed the mark," says M'Annette Ruddell, associate director for donor communications at the American Friends Service Committee. "This person was new to the organization and, although well intentioned, didn't quite achieve the right tone, even though he had read previous reports."

Writer Ellen Schorr's advice to staff writers is to build in extra time to collect input from the many different staff members who must be interviewed. "Ask a few trusted colleagues what's been wrong or right with past reports," she says. "Use their suggestions to shape the next one."

Outside consultants—and, most likely, new staff as well—will benefit from specific guidance in the form of a writer's assignment (see Exhibit 2.1). The assignment spells out length, deadlines, tone, and approach and usually includes an outline or synopsis of what is to be covered. Our next key player—the editor—is the person who prepares the writer's assignment and works most closely with the writer.

EXHIBIT 2.1
Sample Writer's Assignment for Friends of the Ferret Annual Report

Start Date: March 2

Final Draft: May 4

Purpose: To disclose the financial condition of Friends of the Ferret and to encourage donors and members to give additional support by describing our mission and accomplishments for the fiscal year covered by the report, as well as any new threats to ferrets and our plans to address these threats.

Audience: Major donors, corporations, foundations, members giving $50 and up, similar animal-rescue organizations, and conservation-related local, state, and federal agencies.

Approach: Writing must be accessible to a high school graduate with no background in natural science; no jargon or abstractions; all specialized terms defined.

Theme: "With a little help from our friends."

Tone: Factual, lively, somewhat colorful but never purple; businesslike but not overly formal; positive but never "gee whiz."

Coverage: *Review of Operations:* In the three major sections (Antipoaching, Homeless Ferrets, Education and Outreach), focus on the *ends* (ferret protection, either in shelters or in the wild) while discussing the *means* (antipoaching measures, adoption programs, rescue operations, care of injured ferrets, public education). Single out for emphasis specific volunteers and other friends who are helping us achieve these ends (700 words for each section).

Executive Messages: Chairman will focus on major support received (major gift); on legislative successes in Georgia and Nebraska; and on appreciation to retiring board member John Heller (100 words). President will focus on internal restructuring (reasons why, what it portends for future effectiveness) and thank management consultant J. D. Shumate for donating his time; on *Ferret Fancier* magazine award; on growth of adopt-a-ferret program; on gift-of-time donation by veterinarians in Sussex County, Delaware; and on how these friends are helping us help ferrets (250 words).

Editor will supply mission statement, management analysis, "ways to give," and lists.

Note: Because this is an institutional publication, you will not be given a byline. You will be expected to do at least one rewrite of any section or subsection that needs it. Deadlines will be negotiated at the time the rewrite is requested.

Should the overall work product be deemed unsatisfactory to Friends of the Ferret, you will be paid a kill fee of one-half your estimated total fee.

Enclosures: Annual report synopsis and production schedule
Background information for Review of Operations sections
Contact information for staff to be interviewed

The Editor

Whether the editor is a member of the communications staff, with responsibility for the organization's publications, or a member of the development staff, with responsibility for donor outreach, he or she is in a key position to understand how the organization wishes to present itself to the public and what it is trying to communicate to its various audiences. For this reason, the editor most often plays two roles: in addition to editing the text for content, tone, approach, grammar, and style, the editor directs the production process from beginning to end.

The editor's role in editing is to ensure that the writer's tone and approach are appropriate to the audience and, if not, to correct these problems. And, of course, the editor must ensure that the text is grammatically and stylistically accurate. Cutting copy to make it fit the highly restricted space of the annual report is another major concern.

The biggest editorial challenge for M'Annette Ruddell of the American Friends Service Committee has been to condense a large amount of material so that it would fit into a limited space. Her experience is echoed by Jimeequa Harris, former communications coordinator for the Christian Children's Fund, who said future reports would be better if she could cut even more text while still capturing the essence of the fund's daily work.

The editor's role as process manager is more fully explained in Chapters Four and Seven. For now, suffice it to say that it is the editor who must bring all the ingredients together at the appropriate time and transform them, by the necessary deadline, into a finished, coherent, accurate, stylistically consistent annual report, with help from the next key player in the annual report's production process: the development office, the editor's major partner in integrating all the elements of the text and ensuring that the message is on target.

The Development Office

A nonprofit that does not use its annual report for fund raising may not need to involve the development staff, but all other nonprofits should take heed. The organization's fund raisers know more than anyone else, other than the CEO, about the type of donor prospect they are trying to cultivate. As front-line recipients of communications from donors, development staff people also know what pleases and displeases current donors. For example, if last year's complete audited financial statements seemed incomprehensible and needlessly complex to some donors, then the development office will probably be the one to suggest that this year's annual report offer financial highlights instead of detailed statements. Or, again, if donors believe that not enough was said last year about where the organization is headed, or about how the organization overcame a decline in membership or some other adversity, then the development office will undoubtedly inform the CEO about this reaction so that the executive message can address the issue. Finally, the development office generates the donor lists for the report and decides what is to be included in the mailing package when the report is sent to current and prospective donors.

The text and the lists of donors may not be ready for typesetting at the same time. One nonprofit may collect donors' names right up to press time, making last-minute changes as necessary to ensure that the names appear the way donors want them to; another nonprofit may establish a cutoff date for donor acknowledgments and receipt of donors' names (usually sometime after the close of the fiscal year). The donor list of a small or newly formed nonprofit is usually short enough not to pose problems for the design and layout of the report. The larger nonprofit, with a lengthier donor list, must get its list into the hands of the next key player—the designer—before the report's actual length and layout can be determined.

The Designer

A National Investor Relations Institute survey (1999) of corporate annual reports showed that 64 percent of annual reports were designed by outside firms, 19 percent were designed by both in-house staff and outside firms, and 14 percent were designed solely in house. Moreover, 82 percent of Fortune 500 companies that responded to another survey (Potlatch Corporation, 2000) said they had used outside design consultants for their annual reports, and 75 percent of the associations interviewed for this book used outside design firms. Some large organizations do employ full-time graphic designers, but outside consultants are most often chosen to design annual reports, a decision in direct contrast with decisions about who writes the report.

The designer's role is to render the text's message in visual terms through shape, size, color, and illustrations. According to Marc Meadows of Meadows Design Office, "We must develop a good balance between visuals and narrative so that the publication functions as a cohesive document and reflects the image of the organization."

Jim Pizzo, account representative for Curran and Connors, Inc., a firm that specializes in designing annual reports, is acutely aware of the need to take account of clients' likes and dislikes. "We do not slavishly adhere to the latest design trends," says Pizzo, "unless, of course, that's what the client wants. Basically, we design until the clients are happy."

Design trends sometimes do not dovetail with effective communication. For example, a typeface that is too small or otherwise too difficult to read may be the height of design chic, but if it is likely to strain the sometimes age-challenged eyes of potential donors, the designer must choose something more readable. The need to balance design with editorial concerns makes it especially important for the designer and the editor to speak the same language.

The designer, as already noted, is usually not a full-time employee, and so the editor retains ultimate responsibility for ensuring that the report's visual presentation is consonant with the organization's image and values. Suppose, for example, that the designer has chosen brown as the dominant color in the annual report for the fictitious organization Friends of the Ferret, and that the president of the organization dislikes all shades of brown. The editor must persuade the designer to find another color, even though the designer probably chose brown because it seemed the best color to represent the earth tones associated with ferrets and nature.

"The designer's overall responsibility," says Marc Meadows, "is to represent the client's intent accurately." Clearly, the designer must have a solid understanding of what the client organization wants to convey before he or she can attend to the nuts and bolts of design, which will encompass the following tasks:

- Ensuring that text and visual elements are integrated to enhance the report's overall impact

- Choosing a readable type style for the text

- Making sure that the report's format and other features of the design are appropriate, economical, and physically possible to print

The final item in the preceding list accounts for why the designer is often the one who works most closely with our next key player: the printer.

The Printer

The printer's role encompasses several tasks:

- Putting ink to paper

- Keeping the editor and the designer informed of any production problems or delays

- Correcting printing problems on press

- Folding, trimming, and binding the report

- Delivering the report by the requested deadline, even if meeting it means working overtime

The quality of printing varies, from what printers call "basic" (sometimes referred to in the trade as "quick and dirty") to a medium level called "good" to premium and showcase levels (sometimes called "museum quality" because the color reproduction must match the original as closely as technically possible). Naturally, the higher the quality, the greater the cost, and the nonprofit constrained by a tight budget may find basic- to good-quality printing adequate to its needs. At the other end of the scale, funds permitting, the nonprofit that uses the annual report to highlight the organization and its mission may opt for premium- or even showcase-quality printing.

Many printers specialize in annual reports; a printer knows that a good job on the first report is likely to mean many more years of printing that report. But doing a good job on an annual report means more than printing a high-quality product. The printer who specializes in annual reports also recognizes that timing is everything.

The printer comes on the scene toward the end of the production process and is expected to make up for time lost earlier while not sacrificing a bit of quality. To print the report within an abbreviated time span, the printer must have several different presses that can print the text and the cover simultaneously. In addition, the printer needs a bindery that can handle different types of binding, and the printer's schedule needs to be flexible enough to allow last-minute changes before the report goes to press, or even after it is on the press. (Fortunately, the Internet has made it possible for the printer to download large text and graphics files, produce digital proofs quickly and efficiently, send the proofs to the client by express mail, receive the client's changes via the Internet, and keep the whole process moving.)

According to Annie Williams, account representative for Virginia Lithograph, "Designers tend to expect that printers will pore over every detail of the file. . . . [But] the printer can't read the designer's mind." The printer knows that a good designer—that is, a designer who understands the complexities of printing—is a priceless partner. The designer's written specifications can be misinterpreted, and so the best way for the printer to ensure the customer's satisfaction is to work closely with the designer and eliminate misunderstandings, especially when it comes to electronic file preparation.

In some cases, the printer may handle distribution. Very often, however, the printer delivers the bulk of the printed reports to our final key player: the mail house.

The Mail House

Sometimes the annual report is mailed out by the organization's staff. (And some organizations distribute their annual reports via the World Wide Web; see Chapter Eleven.) When a report is to be mailed, and when there are more than about five hundred entries on the list of addresses, it is usually more economical to have the report mailed by a professional mail house.

The role of the mail house is to assemble the package—the annual report, a letter from the CEO, a preprinted reply envelope for contributions, perhaps a gift table, and the outer envelope—and mail it, by the requested deadline, to the parties whose addresses are on the list supplied by the organization. Someone on the organization's staff, either the annual report's editor or someone from the CEO's office or the development staff, takes charge of collecting the CEO's letter, the envelopes, and the address labels and ensures that everything is delivered to the mail house in time for this labor-intensive operation.

Once the elements of the package and the number of addresses are known, the mail house can estimate how much time the mailing will take. (This estimate, of course, depends in part on whether the report is to be sent at the first-class rate or at another rate.) The nonprofit organization must gauge the advantages of getting the report out quickly but at greater expense, by sending it at the first-class postal rate, or taking more time but saving money on postage, by mailing the report at either the third-class rate or the book rate. A recent survey (National Investor Relations Institute, 1999) showed that 60 percent of annual reports were mailed at the first-class rate, 23 percent at the third-class rate, and 5 percent at the book rate.

The patrons of a restaurant judge a meal according to how well its various ingredients are blended together by the restaurant's many chefs. Likewise, readers of an annual report judge its quality by how well the key players discussed in this chapter have worked together to produce a coherent whole with many different elements.

Chapter 3

Elements of the Annual Report

ALTHOUGH there may be exceptions (for example, in the scholarly world), most readers do not open the cover of a book and read every word in the table of contents, foreword, preface, and acknowledgments before beginning the first chapter, nor are they likely to reach the end of the text and then proceed to read every word of the back matter (glossary, notes, references, and index). Likewise, readers usually don't read a magazine from cover to cover, which is why a magazine tends to be subdivided into feature stories and such departments as the advice column, travel tips, fashion, money management, and nutrition. Readers can locate these items by thumbing through the pages rather than searching the table of contents. Like the departments in a magazine, each of the annual report's sections has a clear purpose. This chapter describes the essential elements of the nonprofit annual report and the purposes that each element serves.

Even when there is a table of contents, the readers of an annual report are going to do some fairly predictable things. First they will thumb through the report, looking at the photos and reading the photo captions. In a corporate annual report, readers will then turn to the executive message, to get the gist of what happened to their investments and what is likely to happen next. In a nonprofit annual report, particularly if its readers have donated funds to the organization, they will probably search for their names in the donor list before turning to the executive message. In both the corporate and the nonprofit report, readers will then scrutinize the financial statements. According to the extent of their interest in the company or organization, some will read further sections of the report.

To take advantage of these well-established reading patterns, annual reports are subdivided into some fairly constant elements, some optional and others absolutely necessary. One necessary element is the cover. It may be advisable not to judge a book by its cover, but because no one is obliged to read an annual report, it is judged first and foremost by its cover.

The Cover

Every publication has a cover, even if the cover is printed on the same paper stock as the text. Because the cover is the first thing people see, it literally sells the publication. If the cover catches the reader's eye, half the battle is won.

The critical test of an annual report's cover is whether it clearly designates that the publication is a particular organization's annual report for a specific year. Coca-Cola, for example, issued its 1995 annual report with a solid-red cover in the unmistakable shade associated with the corporation and the words "Our Company" superimposed in Coca-Cola-style script. Home Depot's 1998 annual report, with a cover that showed the apron worn by its employees, made very effective use of the orange and white that have become the company's signature (according to a Home Depot manager of public relations, orange prompts people to act because it is a color that cannot be ignored; Sweet, 2000b). One annual report by the American Institute of Architects had a cover featuring black type on a beige background, with the look of a page that had come out of an old-fashioned manual typewriter, for an overall impression that was clean, simple, spare—in a word, architectural.

At work in each of these examples is a principle that applies to annual reports of all types, corporate or nonprofit: put your product on the cover. The Boy Scouts of America does this with engaging photographs of scouts of all ages. Girls, Inc., uses appealing photographs of girls in action. World Wildlife Fund uses photographs of wildlife that it is working to protect. The National Trust for Historic Preservation uses old buildings. Ducks Unlimited uses ducks. At any rate, the particular way in which the organization's name and logo are rendered is a matter of design. Indeed, good design plays a major role in making sure that the cover of the annual report conveys a sense of the organization, the importance of its work, and the type of supporters on its membership rolls.

It goes without saying that the typical nonprofit organization, unlike Coca-Cola, is not so well known that it can dispense with putting its name on the cover of its annual report. The challenge arises when the organization's "product" is not one that is easily illustrated with a photo. The more abstract the organization's mission, the more likely it is that some kind of art-oriented photograph or graphic treatment will be a good choice. For example, the World Bank Institute commissioned colorful art by children, depicting their visions of the future, for the cover and major sections of its

1999 annual report (see Exhibit 3.1). The children, from refugee camps in Macedonia and elsewhere in southeastern Europe, had participated in the institute's "Competitiveness and a Vision of the Future" program.

The Urban Institute's mission—providing information about domestic policy issues to government and nonprofit agencies—is another abstract concept that is difficult to communicate through photographs. To convey that much of the institute's work involves sociological studies and measurements, the cover of the Urban Institute's 1999 annual report integrated a color photograph of three children's faces overlaid by a gridlike structure suggesting graphs and charts (see Exhibit 3.2).

To surmount the challenge of visually portraying the mission of the International Finance Corporation on the cover of the organization's 1999 annual report, illustrator James Steinberg created a sophisticated color montage depicting a person of indeterminate gender against a combined backdrop of a city building and a globe. On these images he superimposed a spigot dripping water onto a corn crop, a satellite dish, and a chart. Having read the tagline, "Improving Lives Through Building the Private Sector," readers could easily understand what this drawing was all about (see Exhibit 3.3). Likewise, the photograph of ripples on water on the cover of the 1998 annual report of the Consultative Group on International Agricultural Research suggested, subtly but clearly, the idea of impact, which conformed to the tagline "The Impact of Knowledge" (see Exhibit 3.4).

It is true that these organizations are large and well financed; no doubt they have the funds to cover the commissioning of photographs or illustrations and the creation of photomontages, if not simply the purchase of stock photos. The nonprofit that has both an abstract mission and limited funds can still put an effective cover on its annual report by making creative use of typography. For example, the blue-and-green cover of the Ethics Resource Center's 1998 annual report used the organization's logo and its mission statement—"Our vision is an ethical world"—along with a clip-art globe to convey the organization's central purpose (see Exhibit 3.5).

If the cover has done its job, the reader will open the book and probably search for the next important element: the executive message.

The Executive Message

Readers of corporate and nonprofit annual reports want to hear from the person at the top. The executive message—a short, straightforward, upbeat letter from the leader—is where the CEO "tells it like it was" when the organization was founded, to set the context for telling readers what happened during the year being reported and how the organization has grown or

EXHIBIT 3.1

Cover, World Bank Institute 1999 Annual Report

Source: *World Bank Institute 1999 Annual Report.* Illustration by Igor Ivanovski, Skopje, FYR of Macedonia. Reprinted by permission.

EXHIBIT 3.2

Cover, Urban Institute 1999 Annual Report

Source: *Urban Institute, 1999 Annual Report.* Design by Levine & Associates, Washington, D.C. Reprinted by permission.

EXHIBIT 3.3

Cover, International Finance Corporation 1999 Annual Report

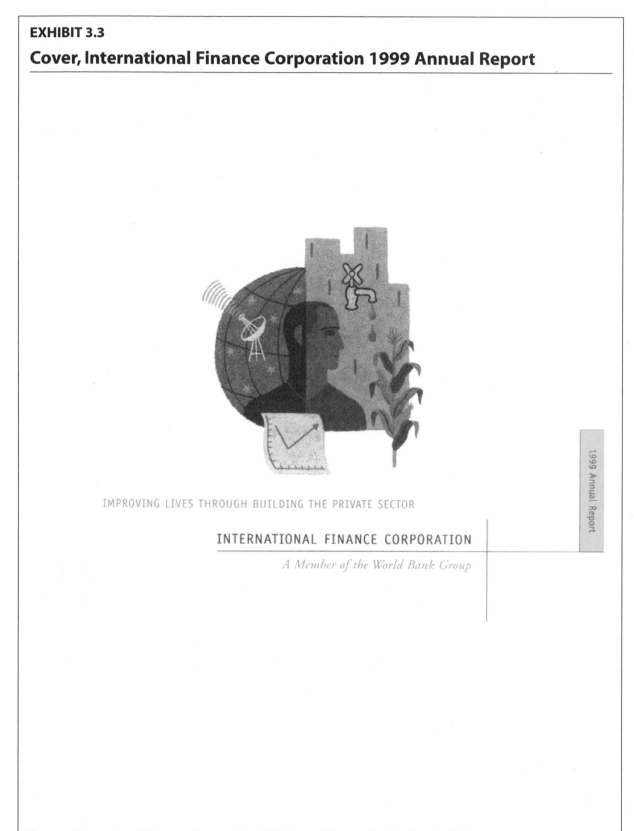

IMPROVING LIVES THROUGH BUILDING THE PRIVATE SECTOR

INTERNATIONAL FINANCE CORPORATION

A Member of the World Bank Group

1999 Annual Report

Source: *International Finance Corporation 1999 Annual Report.* Design by Grafik Communications, Ltd., Alexandria, Va. Illustration by James Steinberg. Reprinted by permission.

EXHIBIT 3.4

Cover, Consultative Group on International Agricultural Research 1998 Annual Report

Source: *Consultative Group on International Agricultural Research 1998 Annual Report.* Reprinted by permission. Design by Daddona Graphic Design LLC.

EXHIBIT 3.5

Cover, Ethics Resource Center 1998 Annual Report

Source: *Ethics Resource Center 1998 Annual Report.* Reprinted by permission.

changed. The bulk of the message summarizes the year's accomplishments. It concludes with a forward-looking statement about where the organization will be focusing its attention in the year to come.

"It is important to give a vision of where the organization is headed," says Kathryn Fuller of World Wildlife Fund. "My message, in one form or another, is intended to motivate or inspire our constituents. My statement is not so much about the institution as it is about the imperative of conservation."

The executive message may be written by the president or chief executive officer or by the board chairman. There may be two separate executive messages—one by the CEO and one by the board chairman—or a joint message from both (see Chapter Five).

Readers unfamiliar with the organization can glean a lot from the executive message, but they are also aided by some explanation of the organization's purpose and its values. That explanatory element, which is not mandatory, is the mission statement.

The Mission Statement

This short organizational profile gives readers a succinct, often eloquent description of what the organization is, how long it has existed, its mission and values, and how it carries out its mission. It is here that powerful, persuasive prose can be a potent weapon for engaging readers' sympathies and encouraging them to reach for their checkbooks. It would be difficult, for example, not to respond to this mission statement: "Christian Children's Fund is an international child care agency which demonstrates God's universal love of children by serving the health and educational needs of impoverished children regardless of gender, race, national origin or creed" (Christian Children's Fund, 1999, p. 2). Or to this one: "The American Friends Service Committee believes in the infinite possibilities of the human spirit. Our programs toward social and economic justice, peacemaking and guiding youth are imbued with hope that springs from the Quaker principle that the Light of God is within each of us. Our determination to forge a better world is renewed with each hand that joins ours—to lend and to receive help" (American Friends Service Committee, 1998, p. 1).

The mission statement may be long or short. Here is one example of a long mission statement:

> We seek to save a planet, a world of life. Reconciling the needs of human beings and the needs of others that share the Earth, we seek to practice conservation that is humane in the broadest sense. We seek to instill in people everywhere a discriminating, yet unabashed, reverence for nature and to balance that reverence with a profound belief in human possibilities.

From the smallest community to the largest multinational organization, we seek to inspire others who can advance the cause of conservation.

We seek to be the voice for those creatures who have no voice. We speak for their future. We seek to apply the wealth of our talents, knowledge, and passion to making the world wealthier in life, in spirit, and in living wonder of nature [World Wildlife Fund, 1997, inside cover].

And here is an example of a short mission statement: "Population Action International works to make clear the linkages among population, reproductive health, the environment, and development" (Population Action International, 1998, inside cover).

There is no preordained place for the mission statement, although its logical placement would be somewhere near the front of the report. Sometimes it may be on the inside front cover, sometimes next to the executive message, and sometimes on the inside back cover for those readers who tend to open books from the back. In its 1997 annual report, the Consultative Group on International Agricultural Research (CGIAR) devoted the first full page of its report to explaining its mission (see Exhibit 3.6).

The section that actually describes the organization's accomplishments for the year usually also carries with it some sense of the group's mission and values. That descriptive section, the essence of the report, is the review of operations.

The Review of Operations

In both a corporate and a nonprofit annual report, the bulk of the narrative consists of a review of what the company or organization did during the year being reported. This section is called the "review of operations" in the business world, and we will apply the same term in discussing the nonprofit annual report. To meet the watchdog agencies' standards, the text for this section must be arranged according to the way the separate expenditure streams are accounted for in the financial statements. For example, if one function of Friends of the Ferret is to provide adoptive homes to orphaned or abandoned ferrets, then the text describing what was accomplished will be matched in the statement of functional expenses by a category titled "Ferret Farms Program" or the like.

The review of operations may be written in a narrative style or in a short descriptive "box and bullets" style. Chapter Six covers the review of operations in greater detail and gives some illustrations of these different styles. Usually, however, the review of operations does not concern itself with actual dollars and cents. These monetary issues are covered in another element: the management analysis.

EXHIBIT 3.6

Mission Statement, Consultative Group on International Agricultural Research 1997 Annual Report

Our mission is to contribute, through our research, to promoting sustainable agriculture for food security in developing countries. Throughout the pages of this report runs the theme nourishing the future through scientific excellence, which exemplifies the CGIAR in action.

Source: *Consultative Group on International Agricultural Research 1997 Annual Report.* Reprinted by permission. Design by Daddona Graphic Design LLC.

The Management Analysis

The management analysis—sometimes called the "funding and financial overview" in nonprofit annual reports—precedes the financial section of the report. Many nonprofits include the management analysis in their annual reports because it offers a chance for the organization to tell readers who dislike tables and charts the story behind the numbers in the financial statements. Says Lawrence Amon, vice president for finance and administration of the National Wildlife Federation, "I think any donor making a sizable contribution wants reassurance that the organization is stable and healthy."

The tone of this message is businesslike, and the messages are targeted. "If you have a diverse funding base," says Amon, "you include the major revenue categories and percentages of the total. If revenue categories are growing, you highlight it. If supporting services are a reasonable percentage of total spending, you make that point."

The analysis also offers an opportunity to single out the most significant donations for recognition. "If you want to give credit to—and earn points from—a major foundation, corporate, or individual gift, highlight it," says Amon. "You want to tell a financial story that makes the best case to the donor."

There is always at least one story behind the numbers in the financials. Suppose, for example, that Friends of the Ferret's review of operations contains a section titled "Education Programs," which speaks of a greatly expanded program for veterinary students through distance learning. The expenditures that made this expansion possible will show up in the financials and must be acknowledged in the management analysis; otherwise, a reader may infer that Friends of the Ferret arbitrarily decided to allocate more money to education programs than to its other charitable endeavors. If the same reader supports Friends of the Ferret only because of its ferret-rescue program, the organization risks losing that reader's support and also some money.

Sometimes the management analysis explains how expenses were allocated, even though there may also be a pie chart showing those allocations. For example, in the 1998 annual report of the International Fund for Animal Welfare, the following textual explanation was right next to a pie chart illustrating the allocation of expenses (see Exhibit 3.7): "38.9% of program funds were spent on Animals in Crisis and Distress, 40.7% on Commercial Exploitation and Trade, and just over 10% each on Habitat and Public Affairs" (International Fund for Animal Welfare, 1998, p. 51).

EXHIBIT 3.7

Funding and Financial Overview, International Fund for Animal Welfare 1998 Annual Report

Thanks to the continuing generosity of our long-term supporters and growth in our donor base, IFAW raised a record $62.3 million in fiscal year 1998, up from $54.9 million the previous year. Annualized growth from 1994 to 1998 has been just over 20%. This robust growth continues a pattern of increasing interest in and support for IFAW's critical animal welfare work around the globe. Over 90% of this support comes from direct mail and annual giving. In the coming years IFAW will be working to continue building and diversifying this funding base.

1998 represented the second year into the current strategic plan and organization of our work into four key areas (our Animals in Crisis and Distress, Habitat, Commercial Exploitation and Trade, and Public Affairs efforts). 38.9% of program funds were spent on Animals in Crisis and Distress, 40.7% on Commercial Exploitation and Trade, and just over 10% each on Habitat and Public Affairs.

Even though IFAW attracted growing support for its work and became better known around the world in 1998, it becomes ever more apparent that the need to support animal welfare, whether it is for pets in China, seals in Canada or whales throughout the oceans, continues to vastly outstrip the resources we have available.

For its part IFAW is committed to continuing growth and improving the efficiency and effectiveness with which funds are allocated so that more of these critical needs can be addressed.

IFAW's complete audited financial statements may be obtained by writing to IFAW, Membership Correspondence, 411 Main Street, Yarmouth Port, Massachusetts 02675, or to the regional office listed on the back cover.

Program Expenses FY98

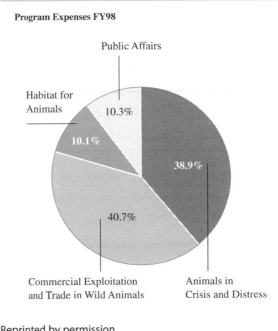

Source: *International Fund for Animal Welfare 1998 Annual Report.* Reprinted by permission.

Sometimes the financial overview explains the purpose of each of the organization's discrete programs. Suppose, for example, a reader looking at the 1999 annual report of the National Wildlife Federation had noted that the sum of $44 million was expended for the category called "Other Nature Education Programs" and wondered what these programs did. The financial overview offered this convenient explanation: "Other nature education programs represent expenses to create and market nature education merchandise to raise public awareness and concern for wildlife and natural resources" (National Wildlife Federation, 1999, p. 31).

In the 1998 annual report of the Boy Scouts of America, the management analysis, titled "Report of the Treasurer," defended a surplus of $17 million dollars in simple terms: "Surpluses are important for two reasons. First, they demonstrate fiscal responsibility. Adequate resources are available to satisfy all obligations. Second, they allow special initiatives which might not otherwise be possible" (Boy Scouts of America, 1998, p. 31). In equally simple language, the treasurer went on to explain a decline in net results of supply operations: "Net results of [supply] operations were $1,583,000 below 1997 primarily because of incremental jamboree activity during 1997. While wholesale sales fell because of the absence of jamboree activity in 1998, retail sales continued to grow with the addition of new Scout shop outlets and as a by-product of growth in traditional Scouting membership" (p. 31).

Total revenue from corporations and foundations can add up to a significant sum. When a large part of that money comes from two or three entities, the financial overview often mentions them by name. Once gains and losses have been explained to readers, the stage is set for the next absolutely mandatory element: the financial statements, which are the annual report's raison d'être.

Financial Statements

The nonprofit annual report may present either a full set of audited financial statements, accompanied by notes and the auditor's report, or financial highlights that summarize the information in the full set of audited financials, with an invitation to readers to request the full set. The organization's "numbers cruncher"—the chief financial officer or whoever is in charge of accounting—chooses the information to be presented in the financial highlights, with a view to presenting the best possible picture of the organization's performance (Loth, 1993). The full set of financial statements, by contrast, is a more comprehensive view of the organization's performance and is certified by independent auditors. The question then becomes whether to publish highlights and offer to provide readers with a complete set of audited financials or to publish the audited financials themselves, complete with auditor's opinion and notes explaining the numbers in the financial tables.

In Lawrence Amon's view, "Not only can audited financial statements be a little too complicated for the average reader, it is also possible that audited financials may raise more questions than they answer because of the possibility of misinterpretation of accounting treatment." Financial highlights, because they present a condensed version of the organization's performance, are designed to give readers only a quick overview. These highlights do not tell readers which accounting methods were used, for example, or whether those methods changed from one year to the next, nor can readers see whether the auditor's opinion is unqualified. Moreover, because financial highlights offer comparisons of only two years, their usefulness in helping readers judge long-term trends in the nonprofit's performance is highly limited (Loth, 1993).

The problem for many nonprofits, however, is that audited financial statements take up expensive space, even when the financials are printed in one color, on cheaper paper stock, for insertion into the report at the binding stage. The full set of audited financials in the 1999 Ducks Unlimited annual report covered nine pages. Compare that to two pages for financial highlights in the 1999 annual report of the National Trust for Historic Preservation (see Exhibit 3.8).

For most nonprofits, the solution is simple: offer readers a set of financial highlights that meet watchdog agency standards, and invite them to request the full set of audited financials if they want more detailed information. To meet watchdog agency standards, soliciting organizations must present, according to the Council of Better Business Bureaus (1999), "adequate information to serve as a basis for informed decisions." This information includes but is not limited to the following items and circumstances:

- *Significant categories of contributions and other income*
- *Expenses reported in categories corresponding to the descriptions of major programs and activities contained in the annual report . . .*
- *A detailed schedule of expenses by natural classification, presenting the natural expenses (e.g., salaries, employee benefits, occupancy, postage, etc.) incurred for each major program and supporting activity*
- *Accurate presentation of all fund-raising and administrative costs*
- *When a significant activity combines fund raising and one or more other purposes (e.g., door-to-door canvassing combining fund raising and religious ministry, or a direct mail campaign combining fund raising and public education), the financial statements shall specify the total cost of the multi-purpose activity and the basis for allocating its costs [Council of Better Business Bureaus, 1999]*

EXHIBIT 3.8

Highlights, National Trust for Historic Preservation, 1999 Annual Report

Financial Report Fiscal Year 1999
(First Year Operating Without a Federal Appropriation Since 1968)

STATEMENT OF ACTIVITIES
September 30, 1999 and 1998

	Unrestricted Operating	Temporarily Restricted	Permanently Restricted	1999 Total	1998 Total
Operating Revenues					
Federal appropriation	0	0	0	0	3,500,000
Other grant income	$2,124,627	0	0	2,124,627	2,958,643
Contributors	11,258,830	6,311,872	0	17,570,702	11,711,051
Membership dues	3,886,639	0	0	3,886,639	3,851,098
Historic site admissions & special events	3,778,808	0	0	3,778,808	3,432,908
Investment income	5,198,940	354,554	0	5,553,494	4,495,424
Contract services, article sales & advertising	4,600,182	0	0	4,600,182	4,385,115
Rental income	1,126,577	0	0	1,126,577	1,204,248
Miscellaneous income	1,306,264	0	0	1,306,264	1,334,603
Net assets released from restrictions	7,055,437	(7,055,437)	0		
Total Operating Revenues	40,336,304	(389,011)	0	39,947,293	36,883,090
Operating Expenses					
Historic sites	11,568,952	0	0	11,568,952	11,347,711
Preservation services	12,850,825	0	0	12,850,825	11,220,178
Publications	3,061,392	0	0	3,061,392	3,132,503
Education	3,650,597	0	0	3,650,597	3,263,751
Membership outreach	3,811,004	0	0	3,811,004	5,085,648
General and administration	2,620,279	0	0	2,620,279	2,874,781
Fundraising	3,807,252	0	0	3,807,252	3,400,045
Total Operating Expenses	41,370,301	0	0	41,370,301	40,297,617
Revenues over (under) expenses[1]	(1,033,997)	(389,011)	0	(1,423,008)	(3,414,527)
Realized & unrealized capital gains	3,705,676	4,801,729	0	8,507,496	(3,834,031)
Unexpected restricted contributions	0	8,748,590	2,359,119	11,107,709	6,070,508
Change in net assets	2,671,770	13,161,308	2,359,119	18,192,197	(1,178,050)
Net Assets—beginning of the year	48,047,315	37,364,223	16,489,183	101,900,721	103,078,771
Net Assets—end of the year	$50,719,085	50,525,531	18,848,302	120,092,918	101,900,721

[1]*Operating expenses in excess of operating revenues funded by the National Trust Independence Fund, designated in net assets by the Board of Trustees to assist in funding FY '02 operations as part of a long-range financial plan responding to the loss of the federal appropriation.*

EXHIBIT 3.8

Highlights, National Trust for Historic Preservation, 1999 Annual Report, Cont'd.

BALANCE SHEETS
  September 30, 1999 and 1998

Assets	1999	1998
Current Assets:		
Cash & cash equivalents[1]	$2,648,367	2,074,439
Accounts receivable, net	2,716,524	2,200,022
Contributions receivable	7,977,129	2,211,661
Merchandise inventory	693,802	749,386
Prepaid expenses	476,494	742,519
Properties held for resale	1,395,500	200,000
Total current assets	15,907,816	8,178,027
Investments at market:		
Revolving loan funds	7,188,847	8,250,026
Endowment and similar funds	93,506,382	77,578,006
Other investments[1]	12,032,276	10,429,191
Total investments	112,727,505	96,257,223
Contributions receivable, net of current	9,363,441	5,748,166
Other assets	6,197	64,033
Property and equipment, net[2]	3,748,493	3,399,300
Total Assets	141,753,452	113,646,749
Liabilities and Net Assets		
Current Liabilities:		
Accounts payable	2,435,514	1,486,413
Accrued expenses	1,381,726	1,475,354
Deferred income	3,360,914	2,988,615
Current portion of notes payable	500,000	505,454
Current portion of amounts held for others	2,000,000	0
Total current liabilities	9,678,154	6,455,836
Notes payable	3,750,000	4,336,032
Amounts held for others	7,191,901	0
Other liabilities	1,040,479	954,160
Total liabilities	21,660,534	11,746,028
Net Assets:		
Unrestricted:		
Available for operations	2,589,094	3,804,795
Net investment in property and equipment	3,748,493	3,399,300
Board designated	44,381,498	40,843,220
Total unrestricted	50,719,085	48,047,315
Temporarily restricted	50,525,531	37,364,223
Permanently restricted	18,848,302	16,489,183
Total net assets	120,092,918	101,900,721
Total Net Assets and Liabilities	$141,753,452	113,646,749

[1]*Additional cash reported as other investments.*

[2]*National Trust follows the accounting practice of not including in its assets the cost or appraised value of any of its historic sites.*

Source: *National Trust for Historic Preservation 1999 Annual Report.* Reprinted by permission.

The financials tend not to take up much of the editor's time simply because the editor is not expected to edit them. But they can cause headaches. For example, the auditors and accounting experts who are responsible for the accuracy and completeness of the financials often do not meet their review deadlines, and their tardiness may affect the final production deadline. Moreover, just to be safe, because even a certified public accountant may make mistakes, the careful editor, mathematically inclined or otherwise, adds up the numbers in tables and any graphs or charts that accompany the financial data.

Financial statements or highlights give readers important information about the organization's business performance and financial position at the close of the year. For that reason, they are the most carefully scrutinized section of any annual report, at least in the hands of readers who understand how to read and interpret them. For the numbers-challenged reader, or for the reader with a short attention span, there are other ways to judge the organization's performance and staying power. One way is to see what other people think of the organization by examining the next important element: lists.

Lists

Who governs the organization? The list of the board members gives their names and affiliations so that the board's expertise can be inferred at a glance. Most organizations choose board members for their prestige, expertise, and deep pockets. From the board's perspective, this latter qualification is helpful because watchdog agency standards prohibit board members from receiving any remuneration. CBBB standards stipulate that "soliciting organizations shall have an independent governing body," and if more than 20 percent of the board's members are compensated, either directly or indirectly, for their services, they will not meet CBBB standards (Council of Better Business Bureaus, 1999).

It also helps readers to know who is actually running the organization day to day, from the CEO on down. (How far down depends on the size of the organization and on how important it is to the organization to list everyone on the staff rather than only those staffers whom the public may want to contact.) The list of staff members is not mandatory, however. When it does appear, its placement varies widely from one report to another. In the Urban Institute's 1999 annual report, for example, the staffs of each of the institute's major centers are listed in the review of operations, which describes each center's work (Urban Institute, 1999).

The small organization that lists every employee, from mail clerk to president, conveys two messages: "Look how much we accomplish for how small we are" and "Everyone who works here is important to us." In its 1998 annual report, the Pinchot Institute for Conservation listed all fifteen staff members and included a group photograph featuring some of them. But once an organization has become so large that listing every staff member would take more than two pages, some readers may form the negative impression that the organization has become an unwieldy, unresponsive bureaucracy. Worse, a lengthy staff list can convey the impression that donors' support is paying salaries and overhead rather than helping the organization serve its charitable purposes.

An annual report that is used to raise funds usually publishes a list of donors. This feature of the nonprofit annual report, second in popularity only to the photo captions, shows readers who supports the organization and, generally speaking, how much they have given; the implication is that potential donors will be in good company should they decide to give. Although the donor list may go on for pages, it is space well spent. Because many of the report's readers are donors to the cause, it is only natural for them to want to see their own names in the donor list and to find the names of other people who have given just as generously.

Here the little details really matter. Checking and rechecking the donor list can consume precious time, but woe to the editor who misspells a donor's name or places it in the wrong category! According to Bill Warren, now a senior writer for the National Trust for Historic Preservation, "My biggest headache at institutions I've previously worked for is the condition of the donor lists. There has to be a better way to make sure the lists are accurate throughout the year." The donor list in the National Trust's 1998 annual report was followed by this statement: "The compilers have carefully reviewed the names that are listed. If you find an error, please accept our apologies and contact the Development Office . . . so that we may correct our records" (National Trust for Historic Preservation, 1998, p. 21).

Donors come and donors go, but the report should mention only those people whose gifts arrived during the fiscal year covered by the report. A donor may give a small gift at the beginning of the year and then decide to give another, larger gift. Take, for example, a list that includes the name of Catherine E. Coxwriter under the $10,000–$25,000 category and the name of Katherine E. Coxwriter under the $50,000–$99,999 category. Both entries should be checked: Could there be a Catherine Coxwriter and a Katherine Coxwriter, both with the same middle initial? Perhaps, but it's unlikely. Or could it be that she needs to be listed only once, in the $100,000+ category and with her first name spelled correctly?

Donors often have oddly spelled names. The editor who encounters the name of John Priston Gaines and arbitrarily changes his middle name to "Preston" without consulting the development staff person who provided the list will probably not survive to edit the list another year. Likewise, the organization itself is unlikely to survive if its annual report does not offer readers information about how they can support the organization's cause, and that thought brings us to the next element: information about making a donation.

How to Help

The annual report that is used as a fund-raising tool anticipates readers' questions about how they can support the organization's work. The "how to help" section informs potential members or donors about the many forms their contributions can take and tells them where they can get further information. Forms of contributions may include straightforward unrestricted gifts, contributions restricted to one aspect of the nonprofit's mission, or bequests, annuities, and other forms of planned giving.

The New Israel Fund, for example, devoted a full page in its 1997 annual report to how the fund could be supported, listing three categories of gifts: general support, designated gifts, and gifts to the endowment fund. The report then listed the many forms that these gifts could take: cash or checks, securities, Israel bonds, matching gifts, life insurance, real estate and tangible property, bequests, or trusts (New Israel Fund, 1997, p. 24).

In the same vein, the National Wildlife Federation devoted one page of its 1999 report to short descriptions of the many ways in which interested readers could help the organization fulfill its mission. For specified sums of money, readers could become Heralds of Nature, Guardians of the Wild, or members of the Leaders Club, and they could participate in matching gifts or workplace giving in addition to making a gift to the organization as part of an estate plan (National Wildlife Federation, 1999, p. 32). A much smaller, pamphlet-style annual report put out in 1998 by the American Friends Service Committee simply reminded readers that their contributions were tax-deductible and suggested some language that could be inserted into a will for readers who might choose to make bequests (American Friends Service Committee, 1998, p. 5). The 1999 annual report of the Volunteers of America had a slip-in card attached to an envelope, which made it easy for readers to check off a level of contribution, ask for a brochure on planned giving, or get information about including the organization in their wills (Volunteers of America, 1999). The Trust for Public Land had a similar device bound into its 1999 annual report: under the photograph of a man on horseback were the words "A gift of stock makes great horse sense," and on the back of the card-envelope, readers were invited to "increase the horsepower" of their gifts by donating stock or by giving through an annuity (Trust for Public Land, 1999). Some nonprofits also include a gift table, which tells readers generally what a gift of a certain amount will help the organization accomplish. A gift table for Friends of the Ferret might look something like the one shown in Table 3.1.

The person most likely to respond to gift tables and other information about how to support Friends of the Ferret is someone who has seen what ferrets look like and finds them appealing. Likewise, supporters of the Christian Children's Fund want to see photos of the children whom the fund is working to protect, and supporters of Ducks Unlimited want to see pictures of ducks. That is why the typical annual report uses some form of visual element to attract readers and enhance the report's visual impact.

Visual Elements

More than 88 percent of Fortune 500 companies responding to a survey on corporate annual reports expressed the belief that annual reports need photography if they are to retain readers' interest (Potlatch Corporation, 2000). Limiting the photos in an annual report—or, worse, eliminating them entirely—may dilute the impact of the report's message. For many nonprofits, however, the challenge of illustrating the annual report may be nearly insurmountable: pictures of refugees, or scenes of poverty or war, may be powerfully poignant in a newspaper or a magazine, but in an annual report they may suggest to readers that the organization is failing to care for refugees or deal with the effects of poverty or war.

"Positive pictures can be effective," said Jeffrey Hon, former director for public information of the National Council on Alcoholism and Drug

---

TABLE 3.1

How to Help Ferrets

Your Gift of ...	Can Help Us ...
$25	Feed one homeless ferret for a week
$50	Transport volunteers to a community outreach event
$100	Teach one family how to care for a ferret
$500	Heat the homeless shelter during the coldest months

Dependence. "But how do you show a person in recovery?" Hon's most effective visual solution—and his personal favorite—was to use cartoon-style drawings in the council's 1992 annual report. The theme of the drawings was "hearing what kids have to say" (see Exhibit 3.9). The drawings would have seemed out of context without the accompanying captions.

The Ducks Unlimited 1999 annual report offered gorgeous full-color photographs of various duck species. One such species, the wood duck, was vividly pictured on the front cover, but the photo could have been used to

---

EXHIBIT 3.9

Illustrating a Difficult Subject with Cartoons and Captions

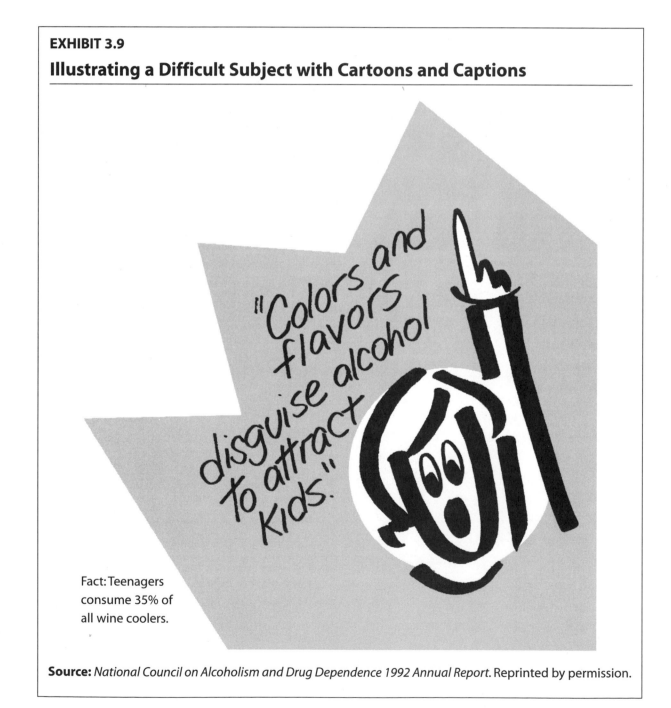

"Colors and flavors disguise alcohol to attract kids."

Fact: Teenagers consume 35% of all wine coolers.

Source: *National Council on Alcoholism and Drug Dependence 1992 Annual Report.* Reprinted by permission.

better advantage if the caption had not simply identified the species but also given readers some information about wood ducks—for example, their habitat, habits, and the threats they face.

Finally, even though it is usually obvious that the photograph appearing on the same page as the CEO's or chairman's message, or on the opposite page, is probably a photo of the CEO or chairman, it helps to identify the person in the photograph, especially if the message is a joint one by the chairman and the CEO. Readers want to know who's who. In cases where

EXHIBIT 3.9

Illustrating a Difficult Subject with Cartoons and Captions, Cont'd.

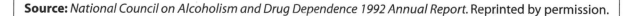

"Stuff happens to you you don't remember the next day. You can do things that get you into real deep trouble."

Fact: Many college students who commit violent crimes or who are the victims of violent crimes— including date rape, assault and robbery—have been drinking prior to the crime.

Source: *National Council on Alcoholism and Drug Dependence 1992 Annual Report.* Reprinted by permission.

the CEO's picture has been taken "in the field," readers will want to know where the place is and what prompted the visit by this busy leader. (For more about photo captions, see Chapter Seven; tips for finding visuals that work and integrating them into the text are covered more completely in Chapter Nine.)

As the preceding discussion has shown, each of the annual report's various elements is different in style and function. The editor's challenge is to pull them together and make them into a coherent whole in time to meet the final production deadline. The report's length and complexity, the number of players involved in providing content and reviewing copy, and the amount of time the editor can devote to the annual report's production (when that is probably not the editor's sole responsibility) can make the challenge seem daunting. That is why planning and organization are so vitally important.

Chapter 4

Planning, Scheduling, and Tracking Production

WE LIVE IN an age of instant gratification. Modern technology has made it possible to get nearly everything we want in less time than ever. But some things still take time. Culinary experts tell us, for example, that it is not advisable to roast a Thanksgiving turkey in a microwave oven because it will taste as if it had been steamed rather than roasted (Cunningham, 1994); a twelve-pound turkey, to come out right, must be cooked slowly for several hours. If the host waits until the guests arrive to put the turkey in the oven, they will either be deep in their cups or asleep by the time dinner can be served. So the thoughtful host starts roasting the turkey far enough ahead of time to allow even late arrivals a chance to enjoy at least one cocktail before dinner. This is called *planning*.

Editors of annual reports are acutely aware of the need to plan—and are sometimes acutely frustrated by the expectations of the organization's managers. Because the annual report is essentially the CEO's baby, it is the CEO who sets the tone and the theme, defines the parameters, and often directs the design. There are CEOs who micromanage the process and CEOs who let the report get well under way before coming in with critical decisions; it is for the latter group that tips for CEOs are offered in Exhibit 4.1.

The CEO's values and vision are difficult enough to execute without having to do so in a rush. "You've got desktop publishing, haven't you?" says the impatient boss. "You should be able to publish this in a day!" Sure: one copy, perhaps, and then only if the writing, editing, copy reviews, basic design, and photo research have all been completed.

Aside from the need to allow time for planning the contents and producing the report, the preparation of the financial statements that form the core of every annual report cannot begin until the annual independent audit is complete. And yet reports that are used for fund raising must still

---

EXHIBIT 4.1

Tips for CEOs

- Be sure that the report answers the questions that donors are most likely to ask. Your message should especially explain why donors should open their checkbooks.
- Choose a competent, trusted person to manage the project and then support that person throughout the process.
- If you have strong opinions about the theme and the design, make sure that you express these preferences early in the planning stages. (You can always ask to review the rough layouts to be sure they coincide with your preferences, but changes at that stage should be minimal.)
- Make yourself the first, not the last, person to review the draft. You will not be scrutinizing content so much as making sure that all the relevant stories have been included and that the tone and approach are right for the audience. (You can always be the last to review, but it helps to give your blessing to the initial draft's style and approach so as to fend off extraneous comments by other reviewers.)
- The annual report is usually reviewed by many content experts, their supervisors, the chief financial officer, and, often, the legal counsel. These individuals can literally unravel a coherent story by nitpicking the text to death to suit their own ideas of how the organization's work should be described. Tell these people that their input is essential but that their role is to focus *solely on factual errors*, not on tone, approach, or editorial style.
- Fend off last-minute requests to replace stories with others that are more current and more reflective of success. The report covers the fiscal year, and those late-breaking stories are best held until next year's annual report.
- Let the production professionals review color separations and blueline proofs. Because corrections at this stage are very costly, they should be restricted to technical problems with color separations or errors made by the printer when outputting to film. (If, however, a major textual error has been brought to your attention, of course it should be corrected.)

---

be published at the ideal time: that magical period, usually right before the end of the year, when the spirit of giving prompts donors to make final decisions about their charitable contributions for the taxable year.

It is much more complicated to plan and schedule an annual report than to serve the traditional Thanksgiving turkey dinner, but the annual report and the turkey have something in common: the best and most effective annual report, like a well-roasted turkey, has benefited from planning and scheduling that took place far enough in advance to allow for both the completion of key players' assigned tasks and a "contingency cushion" that can accommodate the publishing equivalent of a late dinner guest: Murphy's Law.

Murphy's Law, which we met earlier, states that if anything can go wrong, it will, and usually at the worst possible time. In the case of the annual report, the tighter the production schedule, the more likely it is that something will go wrong and that the report will be delayed. Therefore, the wise planner draws up a production schedule that contains enough extra time to allow for illnesses, accidents, acts of God and nature, and equipment failures at the printing plant or bindery. Before a production schedule can be drawn up, however, the editor needs to plan the report's contents.

Planning

Thanksgiving guests may be enjoying the most delicious turkey they have ever tasted, but they are not likely to consider the feast a success if that is all they are served. The host must plan the entire meal, and planning the meal means deciding such things as what dishes go best with turkey, what wines to serve, how to dress the table, and whether the occasion merits formal or informal attire. These decisions are based, not on the host's personal preferences, but on what is most likely to please the guests. The host may be wild about macaroni and cheese as a side dish but will probably serve the more traditional dishes that family and guests are expecting. The host may prefer to wear jeans and a T-shirt, but the occasion may call for a coat and tie. Similarly, the annual report's editor may prefer long narratives, but cost constraints may dictate a shorter "news bite" style. The annual report's designer may prefer a small type size that allows for more white space on the page, but a larger, more readable type size may better serve the report's readers.

If the carefully planned Thanksgiving dinner turns out to be a smashing success, the clever host will serve the same meal in the future, and that's true for an annual report, too. If a report fulfills its many purposes, there may be no need to change its format, contents, or theme. Indeed, one trap entailed in producing an annual report is succumbing to the temptation to freshen it up.

Suppose that, year after year, the report has had the same general approach, tone, and style and has received positive internal and external feedback. To the editor and others producing the report, however, it's getting to be a bore. Nevertheless, repetition may be comforting to the report's readers: it has been a year since the last report showed up in their mailboxes, and here it is again.

Change merely for the sake of change can backfire; it is best to hold off changing the look of the annual report until a time when the organization has changed or expanded its mission. This is not to suggest, however, that all change is risky. Change to improve the report's impact or effectiveness, or even to reduce costs, may very well be warranted. In such a case, a postmortem (see Chapter Eleven) is effective because it takes feedback on the report that has just been published and turns it into questions to be answered during the planning of the next report.

In fact, in its most basic form, the planning of the annual report consists of finding answers to several key questions. They may be questions that have already been answered numerous times in numerous ways, but it is nevertheless helpful to ask them again, just to be sure the report gets off on the right track. The simple plan for an annual report shown in Exhibit 4.2 is intended as a basic guide, both for those who are planning a first annual report and for those who are contemplating a change.

EXHIBIT 4.2

Annual Report Plan

Publisher: Who are you? What is your mission? The answers to these questions will help determine how the copy is written and how the report is designed.

Purpose of the report: Is the report to satisfy financial reporting requirements? Sell the organization and its mission? Encourage donations? Satisfy a legislative mandate? All of the above?

Audience: Given the purpose or purposes you have identified, who should get this report? Members? Current and prospective donors? Other nonprofits similar to yours? Key decision makers? The press? The answers to these questions will help determine how many reports to publish. But, more important, if you give some thought to constructing a demographic profile of typical readers—age, income level, years of education, tastes—you will be able to decide which approach and tone work best for them.

Approach: To what reading level should the writing be pitched? How many specialized terms will the typical reader need defined or stated in more general terms? Is the typical reader fairly knowledgeable and sophisticated? Does the reader need to be swayed emotionally or persuaded intellectually that your cause is worth supporting?

Tone: All annual reports should be positive in tone, even when reporting disappointing news or financial performance. But the report can also be lyrical or no-nonsense, casual or formal, humorous or straight—again, the tone depends on the likely reactions of typical readers.

Content: In addition to the executive message, review of operations, management analysis, financials, and board and staff lists, which of the elements described in Chapter Three should be included, and why?

Design: Given the demographics of typical readers, what design treatment represents your organization and its mission visually while also appealing to these readers? Clean and spare? Cluttered and busy? Bold and daring? Trendy? Traditional? Elegant? Funky? Simple? Complex? What type styles and sizes, colors, and formats will best represent your organization visually while also appealing to typical readers?

Illustrations: What images best help sell the organization and its mission? Photos are the most-read feature of any annual report, but sometimes it is difficult to find appropriately positive images of the organization and its work. Will you need to commission photography or line drawings to illustrate the report, or are appropriate images readily available? Will the report also have maps, or figures and graphs?

Printing: How many pages should the report have, and in what format? To be effective, does the report need to be in full color on glossy paper stock, or could it be equally effective—and perhaps more palatable to the typical reader—if it is printed in one or two colors on an uncoated paper stock?

Distribution: Will the report be mailed first class? Distributed at a meeting or meetings? Will the mailing package also include a transmittal letter? A gift table? A reply envelope for donations?

Those who are producing an annual report for the first time should take heed of the advice offered by Jim Wilson of the Boy Scouts of America: "Determine who approves the final report, and get them involved from the start of the project. Very early on, get an outline and story treatment approved. Likewise, pursue very early approval of the layout and photos. Getting this early approval and buy-in to the concept will generally avoid last-minute changes."

What better way to get this buy-in than at a planning meeting? At this crucial meeting, management conveys the directions, focus, theme, and general content of the annual report. If these things are already known, there is probably no need for a planning meeting. Still, the planning meeting represents an ideal opportunity, if no formal mechanism exists at the end of the process, to conduct a postmortem of the previous year's report, as a basis for improving the new report. The scope of those improvements will depend to some extent on the budget.

Budgeting

The host who has entertained the same number of people on a previous Thanksgiving knows approximately how much the dinner will cost, from the turkey and other food items to the flowers, aperitifs, and wine. Likewise, if an annual report has been published before, if everyone was pleased with it, and if there are to be no major changes in length, type of paper, or colors used, then the report's cost can be determined fairly easily by simply updating what was done last year. Suppose, however, that recipients of the previous year's report have complained that it looked too glossy and too expensive. Donors, after all, want their money to be spent on the cause, not on reports about it. Or suppose that the board members think the previous year's report was so self-effacing that it did not get noticed at all.

The budget for a corporate annual report tends to be large because the competition for future stockholders is keen; two-thirds of corporations that responded to an annual report survey said they didn't mind the company's spending more for a better-looking annual report as long as the company's financial performance was strong (Potlatch Corporation, 1995). The budget for a nonprofit annual report tends to be leaner: funds earmarked solely for efforts to reach the nonprofit's goals far exceed the organization's unrestricted funds, which cover administrative costs. Nevertheless, nonprofits would do well to heed the voices of nearly half the corporate respondents in the survey just cited, who agreed that "annual reports made from cheap materials signal that business is not very good" (p. 23).

The challenge of budgeting for the nonprofit annual report is to find that happy balance between controlling administrative costs and ensuring that the report is sufficiently impressive to garner the confidence that brings in additional funds. The organization publishing its first annual report may find it difficult to gauge costs without the benefit of previous experience. Estimating the overall cost of a new publication can be tricky if the number of pages and halftones, the format, and the type of paper and ink are unknown, yet the question most likely to be asked by management in the planning meeting for a first-ever annual report is "How much is this going to cost us?"

The well-prepared editor will have an answer ready, one that slightly overestimates the cost, to ensure that the report will be under budget when the last bill comes in. The most precise way to get an estimate of the total cost is to draw up a set of specifications that reflect, as closely as possible, the specifications of the actual report. Here is what communications consultant Ellen Schorr needs to know about an annual report before she can estimate the cost of writing it:

> *How well do I know the organization? How complex are the issues and activities to be covered? What is the target length? (Word count is infinitely more useful than number of pages.) Is the provided background material well written and succinct or voluminous and unmanageable? How many interviews will be needed, and will I be given any guidance or asked to develop my own questions? How many revisions does the client intend to do and with how many eyes on each draft? Will I be asked to participate in photo selection, caption writing, proofing, or any other production tasks?*

As is evident from these requirements, it is really not possible to get an accurate writing estimate without first having a plan for the report. To get design and print estimates, it is necessary to know the details shown in Exhibit 4.3, even if many of them are guesses at this stage.

An estimate is not an actual bid. A designer or a printer who provides an estimate may not actually get the job when exact specifications are known and actual bids are solicited, so giving estimates tends not to be a high priority for designers and printers. But suppose management wants the numbers now. In that event, two shortcuts suggest themselves. The first is to estimate the budget on the basis of what it cost to produce a previous publication that is similar enough in format, length, and so on, to be in the same cost neighborhood. The second is to draw up a set of invented specifications that are as close as possible to what the eventual report will reflect

EXHIBIT 4.3

Specification Sheet for Cost Estimates

Design

Number of typescript pages, double-spaced

Format of report (8.5 by 11 inches is standard for annual reports, but 11 by 8.5 inches is also an option, along with a range of other shapes)

Number of images to be included, and whether they are full color, duotones, or black and white

Number of tables, graphs, charts, maps, and so on

Level of complexity or number of columns (one, two, or multiple and complex columns)

Printing

Format of report

Approximate number of typeset pages

Self-cover or plus cover (see the glossary of graphic arts and mailing terms, p. 193)

Approximate number of halftones (whether color, duotone, or black and white)

Approximate number of bleeds and reverses

Paper stock: coated or uncoated (specify a weight and brand—for example, 70-pound Lustro Offset Enamel, dull or gloss-coated text and/or cover, if known)

Whether photos are FPO (for position only, to be scanned in by the printer) or already scanned in

Types of proofs needed—blueline, color keys, match prints, and so on

Whether there will be a press inspection (highly recommended for reports of more than two colors)

Whether printer will be asked to handle mailing

Approximate number of destinations for delivery of the report

and then ask vendors for ballpark estimates based on their past experience with similar publications. (In this case, it helps to give a short deadline—no more than a day—so vendors understand they are not expected to work up actual specific estimates.)

Another question that management might ask is "What *should* the annual report cost?" The organization probably doesn't want to have the most—or the least—expensive annual report on the block; it probably wants to be right in the middle unless the target audience expects the report to be either really slick and glossy or as inexpensive as possible. There may not be time for the editor to survey similar nonprofits to see what their reports have cost, and they in turn may not be willing to share that information. Even organizations that are willing to provide the information may not consider the request a high priority.

Another approach is to find out what businesses usually spend for their annual reports. Data from a recent survey show slightly more corporations with annual report budgets in the $20,000–$149,999 range than in the $150,000–$399,000 range and a median total budget amount of $138,800 (National Investor Relations Institute, 1999). To remain in line with what most corporations are budgeting for their annual reports, the editor could decide on a budget as low as $20,000 or as high as $150,000, but for a small nonprofit even $20,000 is too much; that is why organizations with twenty or fewer staff members tend not to publish annual reports at all.

Partners for Livable Communities, with a staff of twelve, does not publish an annual report primarily because of the expense, although Penny Cuff, senior program officer, also says that an annual report is a not a useful tool for her because it does not serve the organization's mission. The Alliance for Cultural Enrichment, which showcases the talents of African American writers and artists in the Washington, D.C., metropolitan area, would like to publish an annual report but cannot do so because of the expense. Only three years old, the organization has twelve unpaid staff members. Benita Dale, editor of the alliance's *East Dialogue* magazine, says that the organization will have to grow before it can afford an annual report.

Even when funds are scarce, however, costs can be contained. In the early 1990s, for $10,000, the National Council on Alcoholism and Drug Dependence published, on coated stock, five thousand copies of a black-and-white, sixteen-page annual report. In 1998, the council was able to halve the expense by publishing, on uncoated stock, two thousand copies of a two-color, twelve-page newsletter-style report. For major donors, the American Friends Service Committee printed, on uncoated stock, twelve thousand copies of its eight-page, two-color 1999 annual report for $2,160, or eighteen cents a copy. For seventy-three thousand other recipients, the organization printed a four-page version, still in two colors and on uncoated stock, for $4,015, or about five and one-half cents per copy.

General ballpark figures may be sufficient unless management wants to know the cost per copy. In that event, it will be necessary to break out the discrete costs of production. Using the fictitious organization Friends of the Ferret as an example, let's assume that the report needs to be in full color so that readers can get a true sense of how appealing ferrets are. Some images are available from staff members, but others, and probably the cover image, will have to be obtained from stock houses. It is estimated that $3,000 should cover the photo fees.

The writer estimates that it will cost $3,700 to write the text. The designer quotes a ballpark figure of $7,700 to design and typeset the report.

The freelance proofreader, who will be a savior at the end by catching typos and other inconsistencies that other key players can no longer see because they have read the report too many times, estimates her fee at $1,600. The mail house quotes a ballpark figure of $1,800 to assemble the mailing and apply labels. So far, the budget looks like this:

Writer: $3,700

Editor: (in house—included in overhead)

Proofreader: $1,600

Designer (estimate includes press inspection): $7,700

Photography: $3,000

Printing (8,000 copies): ?

Distribution (excluding postage): $1,800

At this point, there are too many unknowns to get an accurate estimate of printing costs. The editor doesn't know how many typeset pages there will be or the total number of photos. The editor doesn't know whether the designer is going to recommend a fifth color as an accent or a varnish to keep the cover ink from smearing onto readers' hands. To render the ferrets' fur in all its glossy, rich detail, however, it will probably be a good idea to print the report on coated paper.

So far, the estimated expenses total $17,800. Because it won't be possible to print eight thousand copies for $2,200, the budget for the Friends of the Ferret annual report is not going to be at the low end of the corporate range. (It may be possible to save money by printing a two- or three-color report on uncoated stock, but would it have as much impact as a four-color report?)

Suppose it's likely that management will find a cost per copy of $2–$3 reasonable and a cost of $4 or over too steep. (The cost per copy is determined when the printing cost is divided by the number of copies printed.) To keep the cost per copy in the range of $2–$3, the printing budget will be between $16,000 and $24,000, and the total budget (rounded off) will be between $34,000 and $42,000. Just to be on the safe side, should this figure be padded—$37,000 at the low end, and $45,000 at the high—to allow for contingencies like higher paper costs or more expensive photography? That is a judgment call. If the purse strings are tight, the editor may be asked to trim the budget. If management is heavily committed to issuing a high-quality annual report and willing to pay, within reason, whatever it takes, then adding a few thousand dollars to the budget will certainly mean fewer sleepless nights in the months ahead.

After the issue of funds has been settled, it is time to map out how much time it will take to get from planning the annual report to assembling the mailing package.

Scheduling

When do the sweet potatoes need to be put into the oven so they'll be done when the turkey is ready? How long will it take for the green beans to steam? The host's production schedule may be entirely mental, or it may be scribbled in a note somewhere, but it's not very different from any other kind of schedule that requires bringing separate elements together at the optimum time to ensure that the end product is coherent and complete. Just as the host knows that potatoes take longer to cook than beans, but far less time than a twelve-pound turkey, the annual report's editor knows the sequence of events in producing a publication. For those who have never produced a publication from writing through distribution, the production process, in simple form, looks something like what is shown in Figure 4.1, although there are many occasions on which there is more back-and-forth than the figure indicates.

The production schedule (see Exhibit 4.4) is based on the editor's assessment of how long it will take for each of the steps in the publication process to be completed. (Of course, some steps can take place simultaneously.) Working backward from the delivery date, the editor records the date by which each step must be completed. The schedule is then literally reversed when it is finally distributed.

There are a few things to be noted about schedules. The dates are the dates by which certain tasks should be completed. If these things can be done earlier than indicated on the schedule, then there will be more time to accommodate the vagaries of Murphy's Law later on in the process. Also, the various tasks do not have to be accomplished one step at a time. For example, the clever editor sends text to the designer before the CEO has approved it. This gives the designer and the editor time to see where the copy needs to be cut, and to work on refinements to the design. Unless the CEO demands a complete rewrite of the text (and the editor should know whether the text is likely to be acceptable before asking for the CEO's valuable time), it will take less time to make text corrections than to hold up the entire production process while awaiting the CEO's approval of the text.

Reading the draft in its entirety presents the first opportunity for management to gauge the coherence and balance of the story told by the annual report. "I look for overall cohesion," says Kathryn Fuller of World Wildlife

FIGURE 4.1

Annual Report Production Process

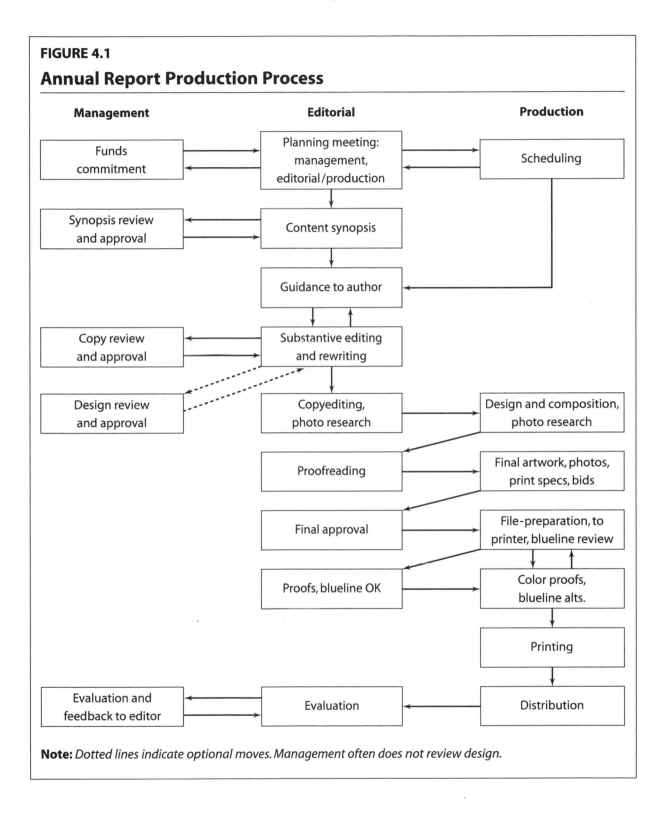

Note: *Dotted lines indicate optional moves. Management often does not review design.*

EXHIBIT 4.4

Annual Report Production Schedule

Draft Schedule (working backward)

11/22	Mailing completed
11/15	Report delivered
11/3	Blueline, color proofs approved
11/2	Blueline, color proofs due from printer
10/6	Files, images to printer
10/2	Final design corrections, photo substitutions; CFO completes review of financials
9/29	CEO approval of text
9/22	Final text to CEO for review; financials to CFO to review
8/28	Donor lists and proof corrections to designer
8/10	Development approval of donor lists
7/28	Management team approval of revised text; proofs due from designer
7/14	Revised text to management team; layout review
6/30	CEO comments due on initial draft
6/16	Draft to CEO for initial review; layouts started
6/5	Photo research started
5/15	Draft due from writer
3/30	Management team approval of synopsis; assignment to writer
3/15	Synopsis to management team for review
3/1	Planning meeting

Fund, and she reads it to see "whether it captures our breadth and priorities, and whether it is generally well written and appealing."

At this initial stage, it is highly probable that the CEO or the management team will tinker with the coverage and want to change or even omit what they have already approved. The wise editor expects changes but can deal with them more effectively at the early stages than later on, after the report has been designed and laid out.

It is also advisable to begin photo research at the moment the initial draft is in hand and while it is being reviewed, even if there are likely to be substitutions down the line. Obtaining photographs can be time-consuming and frustrating, and so the earlier this process begins, the more likely it is that the most appropriate photos can be found. Beginning early also allows enough time to commission photography if it is needed, and if the budget permits it.

Once the schedule has been developed, the next step is to develop an outline of what the report will cover.

The Annual Report Outline

Building on what has worked, discarding or modifying what didn't work, and hearing from the people at the top about what they want the new report to be will set the stage for writing an outline or synopsis of the contents.

"It's critical to work from an outline," says Kathryn Fuller, adding that World Wildlife Fund "is a complicated organization. We need to get the right balance of stories, themes, people, and places. Without the outline, there are likely to be omissions discovered late in the process, or perhaps an overemphasis on some topics."

Many organizations establish a theme for the annual report. The editor weaves this theme into the synopsis while listing what particular items will be covered. Again, the annual report is not a yearbook-style report of everything that occurred during the year being reviewed. It is a selective picture of the organization's accomplishments in the key areas of its operations.

Suppose that the three major objectives of Friends of the Ferret are to prevent illegal hunting and trapping, provide shelter to injured or orphaned ferrets, and educate the public about the responsibilities of owning a ferret as a pet. Suppose further that management wants the theme of the annual report to be "With a Little Help from Our Friends." The synopsis of the annual report might look something like what is shown in Exhibit 4.5.

Tracking Production

Once the synopsis is approved and the writer has begun to work, the editor will need to track production to be sure the project remains on schedule. The simple matrix shown in Table 4.1 helps the editor keep track of the status of many discrete tasks by showing what has been done to date and what remains to be done by the scheduled completion date. Listing any roadblocks to meeting these incremental deadlines can also help the editor suggest improvements to the process for the next year's annual report.

In the case illustrated in Table 4.1, the CEO's travel-related absence delayed the incorporation of the final text changes, and the files were sent to the printer later than had been called for in the schedule. Therefore, to ensure that the final delivery date would be met, the editor authorized overtime charges with the printer, and all's well that ends when it was supposed to. Note, however, that tracking documents are confidential, closely held internal records of what actually happened so that improvements can be made the next time; the wise editor knows that it is counterproductive, not to mention risky, to point out faults and lay blame.

EXHIBIT 4.5

Friends of the Ferret 2001 Annual Report: Synopsis

Chairman's message: To be decided in March
President's message: To be decided in March
Board of Directors list
Mission Statement

Review of Operations

Antipoaching Efforts (L. Robinson, vice president for antipoaching operations)
- West Virginia: Braxton and Webster Counties wildlife officers enlist local hunters in reporting any sightings of illegal traps or poachers
- Georgia: Progress in lobbying the state legislature to outlaw steel-jaw traps
- Nebraska: Pilot program launched in Burt County to compensate farmers for damage to crops caused by ferrets

Homeless Ferrets (V. Campbell, vice president for shelter operations)
- Massachusetts: Opening of new community-sponsored shelters in Fitchburg and Lowell
- South Carolina: Recruitment and training program for volunteer shelter staff in Greenville
- Delaware: Volunteer veterinarians of Sussex County donate one day a month to operating on injured ferrets

Education and Outreach (E. Hooper, vice president for education operations)
- International: Major donor helps launch Friends of the Ferret Web site
- National: Adopt-a-Ferret program now active in at least one city in each of the fifty states
- National: *Ferret Fancier* magazine wins a community involvement award from a major farm organization

Management Analysis
Financial Highlights
Donor list
Staff list
Ways to Give

At this point, it may be tempting to ask whether all these tools are necessary. After all, the annual report is a single publication that comes out at the same time every year. Why not just start with the writing and plod on until the report is printed? The answer is that an annual report is not like a book that has a single author. The writer does not assemble the board, staff, and donor lists or monitor the progress of the financial statements through the audit process. The management analysis is usually written by the chief financial officer. The "How to Help" section is written by the development staff. With so many parts of the report provided by so many different people, the editor must manage the process so that all the elements come together at the optimum time. Chapters Five through Ten describe how the editor manages this process, beginning with the writing of the executive message.

TABLE 4.1

Annual Report Tracking Document: Status as of November 30, 2000

Task	Scheduled date	Actual date	Reasons for delay
Planning meeting	3/17	3/22	CEO rescheduled
Synopsis to management team	4/7	4/7	
Management approves synopsis	4/14	4/30	VP for development traveling
Assign writer	4/17	4/17	
Draft due from writer	6/2	6/2	
Begin photo research	6/5	7/30	Stock images mostly inappropriate
Initial draft to CEO	6/16	6/16	
CEO comments due	6/30	7/5	
Revised draft to management team	7/14	7/14	
Layout review	7/28	8/4	VP from education on vacation
Galleys due from designer	7/28	8/7	
Development approves donor lists	8/10	8/18	Database errors
Donor lists to designer	8/28	8/28	
Galley corrections to designer	8/28	8/28	
Final text, captions to CEO	9/22	9/22	
CEO approves text, captions	9/29	10/6	CEO on travel
Final design corrections, photo substitution	10/2	10/9	CEO changes delayed
File, images to printer	10/6	10/17	See above
Blueline, color proofs due	11/2	11/6	Files late to printer
Blueline, color proofs OK'd	11/3	11/7	See above
Report delivered	11/15	11/15	(authorized overtime with printer)
Mailing completed	11/22	11/22	

Chapter 5

Writing the Executive Message

Dear Friends of the Ferret:

I gave you some money last year, but before I write another check, I want to hear from you. How many ferrets have you saved lately? Did you spend my money on ferret protection? Or did you spend most of it on redecorating your office? What happened with your plans to have a farm for homeless and injured ferrets? What are you going to do to fight proposed laws that would prohibit ownership of ferrets as pets? Is there any reason why I should give you more money than I have in the past?

A Ferret Fancier

THE EFFECTIVE EXECUTIVE MESSAGE answers each of the "ferret fancier's" questions. In this executive message, which sets the tone for the remainder of the nonprofit organization's annual report, the CEO or executive director speaks directly to readers. The CEO, as the person running the organization, knows what readers need and want to know about the organization. The executive message is where the CEO reminds readers why the organization was founded, to set the context for telling readers what happened during the year covered by the report and how the organization has grown or changed. The bulk of the message summarizes the year's accomplishments. The message concludes with a forward-looking statement about where the organization will be focusing its attention in the year to come and with a note of thanks to the organization's supporters.

CEOs who do not write their own executive messages—and many do not—must still convey exactly what they want to say and how they want it expressed. Some CEOs can do this well, and some have difficulty, but almost all are very pressed for time. It is understandable, then, that they will turn for assistance to a trusted staff member, perhaps a speechwriter or the writer of the annual report.

The writer must try to penetrate the mind of the CEO and intuit what needs to be said as well as how the CEO would say it. "Some executives tend not to be prepared to talk about this topic," says writer Lou Bayard. "There is a lot of dead air and floundering around, so I sometimes don't get anything useful out of the interview and have to create the message solely from the synopsis." Bayard finds the interview most helpful in getting a sense of what the CEO thinks is the important take-home message: "Talking to them in person gives personal details that make the message come alive. And, of course, I expect the message will be rewritten—or at least heavily edited—by the principal."

The executive message is second among the most frequently read features in the annual report (just behind photo captions), and it must address questions that readers, especially potential donors, are likely to have. Donors who want information about the organization's fiscal health can find it in the financial statements, but they are also likely to peruse the executive message to reassure themselves that the organization has been a good steward. Richard Morrill, chairman of the Christian Children's Fund, bolstered donor confidence by citing independent authorities: "Very few organizations can claim to be among the 'nation's most charitable charities,'. . . as recognized by *Consumer's Digest.* . . . A number of other publications such as *Parenting Magazine, The Chronicle of Philanthropy, The NonProfit Times,* and *Money Magazine* have recognized us for our high degree of fiscal responsibility" (Christian Children's Fund, 1999, p. 2).

Essential Elements

Most executive messages contain the following key elements:

- A brief summary of the organization's mission
- A description of what the organization does to fulfill its mission, and a statement (modest, of course) about why it can do this better than other, similar organizations
- A description of any changes in focus
- A listing of significant accomplishments
- Any bad news that is reflected in the financial statements
- A description of what the organization did or plans to do to deal with any setbacks

- An explanation of any significant increase or decrease in support
- An outline of plans for the coming year
- An expression of thanks to supporters
- A call for renewed commitment
- A photograph of the executive issuing the message

The actual executive message shown in Exhibit 5.1 illustrates some of these key elements. Note that the bulk of the message is about the organization's accomplishments during the preceding year.

The executive message always comes from the top. Sometimes the president or executive director of the organization issues this message; sometimes it comes from the chair of the organization's governing board. Sometimes it is a joint message from the president and the chair. Sometimes the president gives one message, focusing on the organization's accomplishments, and the chair gives another, focusing on the organization's external affairs.

Just as investors in a business want to know how the company has performed, investors in a nonprofit want to know what the organization has done with their funds during the previous year. A survey of corporate annual reports (Potlatch Corporation, 1994) asking what market analysts looked for in a CEO's letter, reports that they expect a brief summary of the company's operations, an explanation of which divisions performed well and which did not, and a look forward combined with an indication of any changes that were in the works to improve future performance.

In contrast to what is true for a corporation, the bottom line for a non-profit organization is not earnings but accomplishments. A nonprofit—whose work, by definition, is almost never accomplished—may find it difficult to discuss what it actually did during the preceding year. In most cases, it is nearly impossible to discuss outcomes: the number of species saved, refugees repatriated, out-of-wedlock births prevented. It also can be difficult to give as specific an outlook for the future as some readers would like. In one annual report (Girl Scouts of the USA, 1999, p. 1), a case in point is the joint executive message of the president, Connie L. Matsui, and the executive director, Marsha Johnson Evans: "Our vision of serving all girls shines bright as we continuously develop ways to reach underserved populations. We are developing new partnerships and collaborations through government and corporate funding opportunities to expand current and new programs as we pursue our eventual goal to reach every girl." Readers who wonder exactly what these new partnerships and funding opportunities are will have to read the following year's report. Nevertheless,

EXHIBIT 5.1

Example of an Executive Message

A YEAR OF ACHIEVEMENT, AND GROWING THREATS

brief summary of mission {

Throughout 1998, IFAW expanded its animal welfare and conservation activities around the globe. From our support for Caribbean projects teaching children to better understand and preserve whales, to a new partnership to conserve Asian elephant habitat in China, we have continued to broaden our programs to protect the earth's most majestic inhabitants. Through our Emergency Relief and Pet Rescue efforts, IFAW reached out hands of compassion to oiled seabirds in Germany, rare deer in Asia, threatened wildlife on the African plains and homeless pets around the world in need of shelter and caring.

highlights of significant accomplishments {

Our pragmatic, hard-hitting advocacy campaigns won important victories in the halls of government last year. As this report goes to press, news comes that an unethical spring bear hunt in Ontario has finally been brought to an end following an intense, year-long campaign. IFAW's unique partnership with The Schad Foundation, highlighted in this report, made this victory possible. Other creative partnerships with private industry and government led to new maritime regulations, signed off by President Clinton, to avoid ship strikes of the northern right whale. This was an important step in safeguarding this critically endangered species in its Atlantic Ocean habitat.

The accomplishments of the past year have been grati-

fying, but the threats to animals have increased as well. In Canada, the commercial seal hunt has reached levels that scientists warn are simply not sustainable. A resurgent trade in ivory bodes ill for the African elephant. Plans for industrial development threaten pristine gray whale habitat in Baja, Mexico. And on the world's oceans, whaling by Japan and Norway took its highest toll in over a decade.

setbacks that set the stage to renewed efforts }

We are waging important campaigns on many fronts, and there is much to do. But I have hope that as the new millennium dawns, IFAW's blend of scientific research, policy development, media advocacy, education and hands-on protection efforts will help usher in an era of more enlightened coexistence between humans and the wild creatures with whom we share the earth.

how IFAW will address threats in the coming year }

The steadfast support of donors and contributors around the world is what makes the work outlined here possible. We are privileged to be able to pursue this vital effort on your behalf.

thanks to supporters }

Gratefully,

Fred O'Regan

Fred O'Regan
President and Chief Executive Officer

6

Source: *International Fund for Animal Welfare 1998 Annual Report.* Reprinted by permission.

patience is a virtue in the nonprofit world, and being too specific about prospective partnerships and funding opportunities would be too much like counting chickens before they hatch.

Some nonprofits step right up and tell readers some fairly specific goals for the future. In another joint executive message, for example (Volunteers of America, 1999, p. 2), Walter C. Patterson, chairman, and Charles W. Gould, president, made the following statement: "Our goal is to significantly increase our annual service dollars and our public support, to expand our geographic reach into an increasing number of communities across the nation, and to initiate an international outreach program." For readers in search of specifics, they went on to say, "We want to triple our annual service dollars by 2010. . . . We can measure the impact of our expanded efforts by increasing the number of people we serve from today's 1.5 million per year to a goal of 4 million people in 2010; and by increasing our volunteers from 31,000 in 1999 to about 150,000 by 2010" (p. 2).

In the executive message, only the major accomplishments are summarized. They are usually presented as the tiny steps necessary to reach what, for most cause-related organizations, is a distant, often unattainable goal. If the group was founded to discover an AIDS vaccine, for example, then the CEO will discuss such things as research breakthroughs, successful tests, and any significant increases in federal or other funding. If the group was founded to feed the homeless, the message will quantify the number of meals served, discuss what was done to acquire food at little or no cost, and describe any new kitchens or shelters that were opened. Conservation CEOs talk about setting aside new parkland or protected areas, securing legislation that protects endangered species or regulates pollution, and encouraging businesses to be more responsible environmental stewards.

For example, a message from one organizational president, Mark Van Putten (National Wildlife Federation, 1999, p. 2), told readers, "This report records the amazing strides made this year toward recovering once-threatened wildlife like America's national symbol, the bald eagle. It describes how the National Wildlife Federation's award-winning classroom and outdoor education programs are building a foundation of knowledge and planting a seed of stewardship in tomorrow's leaders." Readers can find details of these accomplishments in the review of operations. In a somewhat more abstract vein, another president, James D. Wolfensohn (World Bank Institute, 1999, p. 1), discussed the accomplishments of his organization: "The World Bank Institute has taken a leading role in developing official and private-sector partnerships, creating think-tank initiatives, and joining nongovernmental organizations on issues truly important to the world's people. The institute is leading the Bank's work in promoting distance learning. It is at the forefront of the Bank's efforts to fight corruption by involving civil society and using diagnostic tools to strengthen civil liberties." These two examples demonstrate how the executive message "teases" readers to look further for details. By offering only broad-brush highlights, the executive message reflects the big-picture viewpoint of the CEO and leaves specific details to the review of operations. As a big-picture expression of the CEO, then, the annual report's executive message is short, positive, visionary, and honest (see Exhibit 5.2).

Handling Setbacks

An annual report that contains surprises—especially unpleasant ones—suggests that the organization either is not well managed or has some big communication problems. If there is bad news about the organization's performance, especially if it shows up in the financial statements, the executive message must deliver this unfortunate news: it is best that readers learn about it from the person at the top. Because this is the CEO's letter, however, the events can be put in context, and readers can be given a look ahead if they are told what actions are under way to prevent similar problems in the future.

Only after the nonprofit's accomplishments are trumpeted does the executive message tackle the bad news. Some messages are clearer than others. Here's how Peter Woicke, executive vice president of the International Finance Corporation, put a positive spin on a financial loss: "Despite substantially increasing our loan provisioning as a hedge against possible losses and absorbing a first-quarter loss—our first ever—we ended the year by posting positive net income of $249 million" (International Finance Corporation, 1999, p. 5). Note that Woicke delivered the bad news in a straightforward

---

EXHIBIT 5.2

Checklist for Writing the Executive Message

Ideal Length: 500 or fewer words

Tone: Positive, visionary, honest

Approach: Direct and simple (no jargon, technical terms, or obfuscation; unfamiliar terms defined)

Style: Colorful but not overemotional; never self-congratulatory

Content: All necessary ingredients covered, with anticipation of questions that supporters are likely to ask

fashion but cushioned the blow by ending the sentence with a report on the financial turnaround.

In similar fashion, Richard Moe, president of the National Trust for Historic Preservation, described what the organization did to weather its first year of surviving without a congressional appropriation:

> *The end of our dependence on a federal appropriation confronted us with a wide range of opportunities and challenges, chief among them the loss of $3.5 million in funding—roughly 30 percent of our core unrestricted budget. . . . We have launched efforts to increase our endowment and raise funds for annual operating support and special projects, to develop a range of new earned-income initiatives, and to create an Independence Fund to ease the transition to reliance on private-sector funding. . . . Thanks to the generous support of the board of trustees and the efforts of our staff, we've achieved a sizable increase in our endowment [National Trust for Historic Preservation, 1998, p. 3].*

Paul Wood, president of the National Council on Alcoholism and Drug Dependence, took a very straightforward approach to explaining why the council could not accept the Ad Council's offer of free air time to broadcast public service announcements offering a new toll-free number for people in need of help: "I knew we couldn't afford to accept the generous gift. . . . We simply didn't have enough money to pay for all the calls we would receive if the spots were aired on network television during prime time. . . . I had to tell the Ad Council no" (National Council on Alcoholism and Drug Dependence, 1990, p. 2). Wood then explained the steps the council took to address the problem: "Since then, however, I'm happy to report that we may never have to say no again. We recently purchased equipment that will enable us to answer the HOPE-LINE at our national headquarters instead of contracting with an outside service provider. Now it will cost us only a third of what we paid previously . . . if the usage remains the same" (p. 2).

Even when the bad news is truly horrific, it must be delivered with candor. An excellent example of this principle is the executive message from the president and secretary general of the International Federation of Red Cross and Red Crescent Societies, citing setbacks that included the deaths of Red Cross and Red Crescent workers and volunteers brought about by turmoil in the countries where they worked (International Federation of Red Cross and Red Crescent Societies, 1996). Seldom do setbacks of this magnitude go unnoticed, even if they appear only once on the evening news, or in the international section of the local newspaper. That is why the CEO must meet the bad news head on, as the federation did. Having acknowledged the bad news, the federation's leaders went on to say that both the safety of its workers and respect for their humanitarian work were critically important. The federation did not specifically outline a strategy for reducing the likelihood of future deaths in the line of duty, but it did promise to assess trends and continue to improve working standards.

The urgency of a cause may be undeniably clear, but failing to be specific about the actions taken to address it can make leaders of even the most prestigious organizations seem either blasé or burned out. After all, how many years can one spend trying to find a cure for Parkinson's disease before the mission tends to become business as usual? How hard can one work to achieve the impossible in an indifferent world before one succumbs to enervating but less risky endeavors like assessing trends or improving standards? In all likelihood, those who can no longer fight off the blahs and the blues are destined to find their leadership challenged and their successors already warming up in the bullpen.

For-profit corporations can explain financial losses in a number of ways. What do nonprofits do to explain membership declines? By and large, they don't. The popularity of causes waxes and wanes: once upon a time it was infantile paralysis; today it's AIDS. Economic recessions cause some people to have to cut back on charitable giving; when the economy rebounds, so will membership rolls. Much more stark than the actual numbers themselves are the outcomes of significant declines in membership: projects that cannot be carried out for lack of funding, reorganizations that involve staff reductions, or changes in organizational missions that restrict the organization's focus.

Outcomes of this magnitude should be covered in the executive message, but with a positive, forward-looking spin along the lines of "Yes, there have been setbacks. Things might be bad now, but we've taken steps to turn the bad news into good, and here's what we're going to do." Or, to borrow an example from the fictional organization Friends of the Ferret:

> *Although Friends of the Ferret hoped to open a farm for injured and homeless ferrets this past year, a feasibility study of land acquisition and construction costs indicated these plans would have to be deferred until we can be sure we have sufficient resources to sustain the farm's operation over the long term. A survey of current and former members [conducted by worried executives to find out why the organization had lost three thousand members during the previous year] indicates some promising new directions for the organization. [Note that the executive is not obliged to tell annual report readers why the survey was conducted.] In the months ahead, we will be shifting our focus away from urban population centers to suburban and rural areas where ferret ownership is on the increase and where education about ferret ownership is most needed.*

Expressing Gratitude

Because so much cause-related work is unfinished by nature and depends on the continuing support of members and donors, the concluding pitch of most executive messages is sometimes an expression of thanks to supporters and almost always a call for renewed commitment. Here is an example from Max A. Schneider, chairman of the National Council on Alcoholism and Drug Addiction: "In one critical respect, we remain unique: the unwavering support of our dedicated volunteers and donors throughout the country . . . means that alcoholics, other addicted persons, and their families will continue to have an organization exclusively addressing their needs well into the next century" (National Council on Alcoholism and Drug Addiction, 1998, p. 4).

Very often these words of appreciation take on a note of eloquence and passion, as in the farewell message from Matthew B. Connolly Jr., retiring executive vice president of Ducks Unlimited: "I'm very proud of the work we have done together—all the money we raised, all the acres we conserved, all the fun we had. But most of all I'm proud of the legacy we have left our children—a legacy of wild places full of wild creatures" (Ducks Unlimited, 1999, p. 3).

A survey of corporate annual reports indicates that those responsible for publishing them concentrate on the executive's letter to shareholders more than on any other single element of the report (Potlatch Corporation, 1995), and the same can be said for the executive message in the nonprofit annual report. Never negative or defensive, the tone of the message appeals to the generous impulse in all of us. The message can be tailored to a sophisticated audience without alienating less informed readers; it is simple but artfully constructed. The opening, for example, must immediately capture readers' attention and give them something they will remember six months later. Terms are defined; every nuance of meaning is scrutinized to ensure that the leader says what needs to be said.

Writing for the CEO

As already mentioned, time is such a precious commodity for the person at the top that often the executive message is written by a staff member or by the writer hired to write the rest of the annual report. When that is the case, the voice of the message must sound like the CEO's (see Exhibit 5.3).

"Obviously," says Kathryn Fuller of World Wildlife Fund, "I play a part in outlining what I want to say in the president's message, and what is the appropriate context for the chairman's message. It's helpful to have the per-

---

EXHIBIT 5.3

How to Make Your Words Sound Like the Boss's

- Study the CEO's speeches and other written communiqués to get a sense of his or her voice.

- Seek guidance from the CEO on what needs to be covered.

- Interview the CEO, if possible, to get as much of the message as possible in his or her own words.

- Ask open-ended questions designed to elicit colorful, pertinent answers that also reveal the leader's character and personality. Examples: What made you get into this line of work in the first place? What, in your opinion, is the heart and soul of this organization? What was the most difficult decision you had to make this past year? If there were one thing you could change overnight, what would it be?

- Use only those answers that help you cover the essential elements of the message.

- Be prepared to have your draft message altered, sent back for a rewrite, or disregarded entirely.

---

son who wrote the annual report text write these messages, to ensure that there are no redundancies or false notes."

Of course, the CEO is likely to edit and even rewrite the message, to position it exactly as it should be. "I typically spend some time on the final edit," says Fuller, "but I prefer to have the writer do the initial draft."

Louis Bayard has written speeches and executive messages for Fuller for several years, and so he is quite familiar with her voice and style. "If I were dealing with a new writer," says Fuller, "I would tell him that I am very particular about prose. It should draw people in with language that is alive, crisp, and clear at the same time. I have very little tolerance for pieces that are wordy or overblown."

The first step in writing the executive message is to interview the person at the top to see what he or she would like to say. Usually CEOs have a very clear idea of the central messages they want to convey, and they expect writers to flesh out the details. The executive message (shown in Exhibit 5.4) for a fictitious charity called Dames, Inc., can be used in conjunction with the step-by-step guide in Exhibit 5.5 to draft the elements of a typical executive message for a nonprofit annual report.

The CEO's Photo

The final element is visual. A photograph of the CEO should appear with the message to reinforce the idea that the CEO is communicating directly with the report's readers. A "mug shot" is standard when the budget is tight, but there are other options. Which one is chosen will depend on the image that the CEO wants to convey. According to Jane d'Alelio, president

EXHIBIT 5.4

Executive Message for Dames, Inc.

From the President

At the annual convention of the National Organization for Women (NOW) this past year, something I overheard made my spirits soar. A well-dressed, confident-looking African American woman was telling her young friend, perhaps her daughter, "Dames, Inc., helped me get started back when I thought nobody cared about my dream of owning the shop. Now look at me: five years later, and I'm opening branch number three!"

The NOW conference was in Detroit, a city that has seen a 20 percent growth in Dames, Inc.–supported business startups in just one year. When you add up all the women-owned businesses that Dames, Inc., has helped get off the ground—more than 3,600 on the date this report went to press—you soon realize that the woman in Detroit and women like her in Dallas, Omaha, Chicago, and Albany have come a long way in the very short five years since Dames, Inc., was founded.

Business startups supported by Dames, Inc., showed even more phenomenal growth in Chicago, with 83 more new businesses started in 2000. Albany and Dallas are doing well, while Omaha has shown little growth. Dames, Inc.'s new director of the Omaha program has redoubled efforts to get state and local welfare officials to refer promising candidates whose dreams of owning their own businesses can be realized with partial or full payment of tuition for a few months' training in bookkeeping, computer skills, or other skills. Because business training is such an important part of our approach, Dames, Inc., continues to expand the number of business courses for which we pay partial to full tuition.

We still have a long way to go. This past year, I received hundreds of letters from women, begging us to open chapters in cities like Denver and Cleveland and Boston. With a heavy heart, I had to ask these women to be patient awhile longer. Although the support that we have received this past year makes it possible to continue operations in the five cities we chose for our initial focus when we were founded, we are going to need to raise much more before we can begin to think of expansion.

To address the urgent need for growth, we have strengthened our development efforts and are testing the concept of recruiting members from among the ranks of business school and law school alumnae around the country. I am pleased to report that initial focus-group surveys in the West and Midwest show that this approach has promise of yielding significant results. In 2001, we will launch a direct-mail campaign to reach this vitally important potential base of support.

Fortunately, our board and major corporate and foundation supporters continue to be steadfast in their commitment to helping women take the first step toward breaking the cycle of poverty and surmounting the challenges of owning their own businesses. Like the woman in Detroit, they deserve our best efforts to help them test their wings and fly.

EXHIBIT 5.5

Guide to Drafting the Executive Message

1. Take the CEO's central message idea and make it the lead-in.

2. Tie that to the organization's mission and objectives.

3. Segue into a summary of the year's most significant accomplishments.

4. Bury the bad news, if any (positively stated, of course), amid the good news, and don't forget to be as specific as possible about what the organization is going to do to ensure that the problem is corrected in the future.

5. Sum up with a thank-you to supporters, followed by a look forward to the coming year.

6. For the conclusion, tie the forward-looking statement back to the lead-in central message.

---

of Ice House Graphics, "The setting—whether at a desk or out in a field, with the CEO wearing a suit or with shirtsleeves rolled up, alone or in a group, with natural lighting or artificial, active or posed—sends very specific vibrations to readers." Therefore, if money is available, there should be a photograph of the CEO. If the organization works in exotic or dangerous or interesting locales, the CEO should be photographed in those places. Even if the budget won't allow the hiring of a professional photographer, a candid snapshot of the CEO holding a refugee's baby, or comforting a disaster victim, or even surrounded by ferrets, tells readers that the person at the top cares about the cause, actively participates in the organization's work, and deserves readers' help.

In broad brush strokes, the executive message paints a vibrant verbal picture of the cause and its vitally important work. The ferret fancier's letter that opens this chapter is worth keeping. Answering those questions can provide the key to getting what all nonprofits so desperately seek: an open checkbook.

Chapter 6

Writing the Review of Operations

ONE LOOK at modern newspapers like *USA Today* or at contemporary Web sites would suggest to time travelers, no doubt, that one effect of the march of civilization has been the need to break up information into bite-sized chunks. We seem no longer to be capable of absorbing and digesting larger portions. Who has time to take in all that a carefully structured narrative can deliver? With television, radio, newspapers, the Internet, and the telephone all demanding our attention, where are those long periods of uninterrupted time in which to concentrate and focus our scattered attention? Civilization itself seems to be suffering from attention deficit disorder. Far from attempting to treat this disorder—and how does one try to reverse the march of civilization?—the editor of the annual report delivers what readers want.

The review of operations sums up key activities of the organization during the year covered by the report. Sometimes called the "operational overview" or the "editorial section," this part of the annual report tells what the organization does and how it accomplished its work during the year covered by the report. It is here that the annual report's theme, first expressed in the executive message, comes to full expression. Some themes are better than others.

Picking the Perfect Theme

In the corporate world, businesses use the annual report's theme to focus attention on their strengths or to highlight major changes. The themes most often used in recent years by Fortune 500 companies were business growth and company changes (Potlatch Corporation, 2000). According to Sweet (1999f), "the best themes for corporate annual reports accomplish three goals: (l) They reflect the corporate message, (2) they grab readers' attention, and (3) they continue throughout the book." The nonprofit world is no different.

The theme of the American Heart Association's 2000 annual report was "Everything we do today can make a difference tomorrow." The association carried out the theme on the opening page of each major section: "Our research can save a life tomorrow"; "Operation Heartbeat gives us an advantage tomorrow"; "Operation Stroke prepares us for tomorrow"; "Our Advocacy Program ensures support tomorrow"; "Our Education Programs will transform tomorrow."

For Friends of the Ferret, mentioned previously, the theme was "With a Little Help from Our Friends." Certainly that theme reflects the mission of this fictitious nonprofit, but it is the writer's challenge to make it grab readers' attention and to carry it out throughout the book. The National Trust for Historic Preservation (1998) suggested a theme for its annual report—reinvention and renewal—in the president's message, but the remainder of the report failed to follow through either textually or graphically. By 1999, the organization had corrected the problem: the cover stated the theme ("saving America's treasures for 50 years") and both the chairman's and the president's message began with a reference to the organization's golden anniversary. The following pages traced "a half-century of leadership" (see Exhibit 6.1).

Although management may have very clear ideas for the direction and focus of the annual report, the well-prepared editor brainstorms with colleagues, and often the writer and designer as well, to pick a theme that can be presented to management at the planning meeting. The synthesis of ideas from the top and ideas from the working level often produces the most successful themes. According to some annual report experts (Sweet, 1999f, p. 1), success is measured by whether readers remember last year's annual report. The tips shown in Exhibit 6.2 provide guidance for the editor in search of a theme.

Lurking somewhere in the background material supplied to the writer are words and deeds that can be tied directly to the report's theme. And although it may seem an extra challenge to write to a theme, the organizing principle of most themes actually makes the writing easier. Some editors—especially when tackling their first annual report—may find it difficult to imagine how to express the theme in the text, let alone manage the theme's visual expression. If truth be told, many editors consider themselves left-brain analytical types, not right-brain creative gurus. But leaving the expression of the theme solely in the hands of the writer and the designer can be

EXHIBIT 6.1

Chairman's and President's Anniversary Message, National Trust for Historic Preservation 1999 Annual Report

A Half-Century of Leadership

On the occasion of the National Trust's 50th anniversary, a look back over the past half-century shows how far the organization has come. Equally important, a review of the societal changes that have taken place since 1949 shows how profoundly historic preservation has influenced the look and livability of American communities.

When the National Trust was founded, preservationists spent most of their time and energy fighting to save landmarks threatened with demolition. Today, while sound old buildings still get razed, they aren't torn down as a matter of course. Renovation and adaptive reuse are widely regarded as viable—even preferable—alternatives to demolition.

Fifty years ago, preservationists' concerns ended at the boundaries of the "old part of town." Today we take a much broader approach to preservation, recognizing that what happens in the countryside and the suburbs has a direct bearing on the fate of older areas. And we recognize the need to save artifacts of the recent past, roadside architecture, engineering landmarks, heritage corridors—all the things that help define us as a culture and a nation.

Back then, preservation was not widely recognized as a tool for revitalization, and its economic benefits were poorly documented. Now, with decades of data on the success of the Main Street program, the impact of the historic rehabilitation tax credit, and the widespread community benefits generated by the Intermodal Surface Transportation Efficiency Act and other programs, we have firsthand knowledge of preservation's effectiveness in bringing new life to residential and commercial neighborhoods. We have a large and growing body of information on the impact of heritage tourism, the positive effect of design regulations on property values in historic districts, job creation in historic rehab projects, and the like. We've always known that preservation is good for the soul; now we know it's good for the pocketbook as well.

In 1949, the effect of preservation was confined to a relative handful of communities. Fifty years later, it is difficult to find a community, large or small, where houses and storefronts haven't been fixed up with pride, where obsolete buildings haven't been put to new uses, where historic resources haven't been identified and protected, where historic sites aren't marketed as tourist attractions. In short, the impact of preservation can be seen everywhere, and it has made a clearly discernible difference in the way American communities look and in the way Americans value their heritage.

The creation of the National Trust a half-century ago was a response to the need for a national organization to provide support and encouragement for grassroots preservation efforts. As the nature of those

1970 Study Tour program launched.

Trust files first *amicus* brief on behalf of a neighborhood association in Lexington, Ky.

1971 First Trust field office opens in San Francisco.

First Trust loans awarded to help fund rehabilitation projects.

National Preservation Honor Awards established.

1973 First National Historic Preservation Week celebrated.

1978 Trust participates in *Penn Central Transportation Co.* v. *City of New York,* in which Supreme Court upholds legality of preservation ordinances.

1979 Rural Heritage program launched.

1980 National Main Street Center established.

1982 In *National Trust* v. *U.S. Army Corps of Engineers,* Trust files first lawsuit as plaintiff.

1983 Trust wages successful campaign to save historic West Front of U.S. Capitol.

EXHIBIT 6.1

Chairman's and President's Anniversary Message, National Trust for Historic Preservation 1999 Annual Report, Cont'd.

An Anniversary Is a Celebration.
It Is Also an Opportunity for Reflection.

efforts has changed over the years, the National Trust has changed as well—in ways that have both mirrored and shaped the growing sophistication and effectiveness of the national preservation movement.

Our founders envisioned an organization whose primary purpose would be the acquisition and administration of historic sites. True to this vision, the Trust has assembled and opened to the public a unique, diverse, and expanding collection of properties spanning two centuries of American history and architecture.

Over the years, outreach programs became increasingly important as the preservation movement and the Trust itself grew and matured. The Preservation Services Fund, created in 1969, was the first of many programs to provide financial support for local efforts. Timely hands-on assistance to grassroots preservationists is provided by a network of regional offices, the first of which opened in 1971. Demonstration projects soon followed, including the National Main Street Center, which emphasizes preservation as a tool for revitalizing traditional business districts, and Community Partners, which employs a similar approach in historic residential neighborhoods. Other special programs focus on rural preservation, heritage tourism, and support for statewide preservation organizations.

Recognizing the value of public policies that support preservation, the Trust worked to secure passage of the National Historic Preservation Act, the historic rehabilitation tax credit, the Transportation Efficiency Act for the 21st Century, and numerous other federal laws, state statutes, and local ordinances. Similarly, the Trust has ensured compliance with existing laws by initiating or joining lawsuits on issues ranging from the threatened destruction of New York's Grand Central Terminal to the proposed construction of a freeway through historic neighborhoods in South Pasadena, California.

Education has always been at the core of our work. An ever-expanding array of educational vehicles—including ***Preservation*** magazine, the yearly list of America's 11 Most Endangered Historic Places, the nationwide celebration of Preservation Week, and a wide range of conferences and workshops—has been highly effective in spotlighting issues, rallying public support for preservation, and providing training for emerging leaders. This is today's National Trust.

Celebrating a half-century of leadership, we are doing the job we were created to do: building and sustaining communities that are truly livable, saving our irreplaceable legacy from the past as our gift to the future.

1988 First list of America's 11 Most Endangered Historic Places issued.

Trust helps save Manassas Battlefield from intrusive commerical development.

1989 Heritage Tourism program created.

Historic Hotels of America launched.

1994 Community Partners program established

Statewide Partnerships launched to help strengthen statewide preservation organizations.

Trust takes leadership role in successful campaign to halt development by Walt Disney Co. in Virginia's historic northern Piedmont.

1997 Trust works with Montana Historical Society to save boomtowns Virginia City and Nevada City, Mont.

1998 Save America's Treasures program launched by White House, with Trust as main private-sector partner.

Preservation **wins National Magazine Award for General Excellence.**

Federal funding for Trust ends.

Source: *National Trust for Historic Preservation 1999 Annual Report.* Reprinted by permission.

EXHIBIT 6.2

Annual Report Themes That Stick

- *Brainstorm* with colleagues—the creative types like the writer and the designer—and the content experts who are most knowledgeable about the organization's work and the challenges it faces.

- *Test* the theme on people who aren't involved in producing the annual report, including people outside the organization who do not know much about it. (Usually there is no time or money for focus-group research, but a quick poll of friends and family can give sufficient feedback to know whether the idea is on target or a real bomb.)

- *Write it up* for management. The exercise of having to flesh out the theme and defend the choice will show how workable it may be for the writer and designer. If you can't make it work, neither can they.

- *Manage* the theme's textual and visual expression. Don't let the writer overemphasize the theme or forget it midway through the draft. Don't let the design carry the theme on its back with no textual support from the writing. And don't pick a theme that simply can't be conveyed in a design treatment.

---

risky. The editor remains the person who knows most about the organization. And dealing with themes can actually be fun.

Ducks Unlimited (1999) used the theme "taking stock in waterfowl" in its annual report. Playing on the double meaning of "stock" (because Ducks Unlimited stock is traded on the National Stock Exchange), the message from the president, Julius F. Wall, began, "Last year was a record year for U.S. stock markets; it was also another record year for Ducks Unlimited" (p. 3). A tissue-thin flyleaf at the front of the book reproduced, in faint blue ink, a newspaper's daily stock quotations, with the "D" section at the reader's eye level.

The Consultative Group on International Agricultural Research (CGIAR) used the theme "nourishing the future through scientific excellence" for its 1997 annual report. The cover visually introduced the theme with a photograph of a farmer's hands holding a mound of grain. The review of operations was then divided into the categories of encouraging biodiversity conservation as essential for sustaining agriculture, conducting research to improve food crops and cropping systems, and promoting policies to reduce poverty and improve food security and nutrition (Consultative Group on International Agricultural Research, 1997).

The following year, using the theme "the impact of knowledge," the organization chose to emphasize how "knowledge, developed by CGIAR scientists and their partners, ripples outward in every direction, improving the way poor farmers grow their food and achieve better livelihoods" (Consultative Group on International Agricultural Research, 1998, p. 1). The challenge of visually representing this abstraction was solved on the cover with a photograph of ripples on a pond (see Exhibit 3.4 in Chapter Three). The three major sections in the review of operations then followed suit: the section discussing the organization's thirty-year record of generating knowledge "that has endured" opened with a photograph of tree rings; the section discussing the organization's interdisciplinary, international network opened with a photograph of a spider's web; and the final section, which discussed the organization's role as a knowledge catalyst helping to nurture the creativity of scientists, opened with a photograph of a nebula in outer space (Consultative Group on International Agricultural Research, 1998).

A much more down-to-earth theme in the 1999 annual report of the Girl Scouts of the USA emphasized the association's newly adopted slogan, "Girl Scouts: Where Girls Grow Strong." The cover, showing a diverse group of smiling scouts, asked, "What does strong mean?" The joint letter from the national president and the executive director reiterated, "Girl Scouts *is* where girls grow strong . . . in mind, in spirit, and in sense of self" (Girl Scouts of the USA, 1999, p. 1). The review of operations began with a dictionary-style definition of the word *strong,* and each succeeding subsection continued to explain the word, in a call-and-response format accompanied by an appropriately illustrative photograph:

What does strong mean? Being strong means building skills for success in the real world.

What does strong sound like? Strength is heard in conviction, in an unwavering voice that speaks passionately.

What does strong feel like? Strong is the feeling that comes from the fun, friendship, and power of girls together [Girl Scouts of the USA, 1999].

To take another example, this time from Dames, Inc., a fictitious organization that helps low-income women start their own businesses, the theme for an annual report could be "You've Come a Long Way, Boss," to emphasize the nonprofit's astounding success in providing seed money to several small-business ventures. Suppose that many of these ventures started as one-woman, home-based enterprises and are now full-fledged businesses. The theme could be visually represented a number of ways in the annual report: as before-and-after photos of the businesses when they first started and at the peak of their success or as a graphic representation of a briefcase with legs (in high heels) "walking" through the report's major sections.

Textually, the theme could be represented by callout testimonials or profiles of customers and others who have benefited from the business startups. For example, a customer could write about having to drive sixty miles to the nearest shopping mall to find fabric and sewing notions, which she can now purchase from Sew Nice, a store that got its start with seed money from the Dames, Inc. A banker's testimonial could relate how his initial reluctance to extend credit to an unemployed entrepreneur was overcome when Dames, Inc., agreed to match the bank's loan. A successful business-woman could explain how the charity's grant made it possible for her to support her two young children while working at home. (For more on how Dames, Inc., might represent the theme in layouts for its annual report, see Exhibit 8.3 in Chapter Eight.)

Choosing What to Cover

Although it may be convenient, for archival purposes, to have a complete record of everything the organization accomplished during the year, that record does not have to be in the form of an annual report. Indeed, because archives are largely for internal consumption, the complete record of what the organization has done does not even have to be a publication. But, as we have seen, annual reports have many purposes, only one of which is archival. It is the editor's responsibility to see that the report fulfills all its stated purposes. Therefore, even though the review of operations is the report's biggest section, it still must be succinct. To hold readers' attention, this section must be short, positive, and as colorful as possible, which means that not every story will be told, and some feelings will be hurt. It is here that the editor must play diplomat with great tact, saying to the anguished content expert, "We couldn't cover your program in all the detail it so richly deserves because the report is meant only to be a snapshot of the organization's accomplishments this past year," or to the vice president for regional outreach, "We can only describe three of your most outstanding accomplishments, if we want to do them justice; otherwise, we would only have room for a list."

With guidance from the management-approved synopsis, the editor must select the most representative stories of what the organization has accomplished (see Exhibit 6.3). The key stories may not be the easiest ones to obtain, and the specificity that may seem necessary to make a story credible simply may not exist, but the writer must persist—even when the pesky problem of structure rears its illogical head.

EXHIBIT 6.3

What to Keep? What to Cut?

Keep

Stories about the organization's major programs and new initiatives

Stories that reinforce the annual report's theme

Stories emphasizing the importance or urgency of the cause

Stories with concrete, exemplary results

Stories that give the organization a human face—stories about risks, heroism, responses to crises or emergencies, generosity, actions above and beyond

Stories illustrating how the organization has changed

Stories highlighting noteworthy, cause-related accomplishments of staff or volunteers (books published, awards and recognitions from independent, objective bodies)

Cut

Stories about the organization's administrative, communications, or operations functions

Stories that contradict the annual report's theme

Stories suggesting that the organization is fighting a losing battle or that the cause is hopeless

Stories that were covered in last year's report (unless progress since last year has been phenomenal)

Stories that are weak, bureaucratic, vague, or so abstract that readers will not understand them

Stories about programs that are being phased out or redirected

Stories highlighting staff or volunteers' noteworthy accomplishments that do not pertain to the organization's work (awards and recognition that are internal or unrelated to the organization's work)

Organizing the Review for Readers

The review of operations is structured the same way as the organization is structured: if there are three major activities or purposes of the organization, then the review of operations will have three sections, each reflecting one of the key activities. The institution's work may change over time, but the reporting structure—to match narratives to financials—remains the same. Usually, each division's work is covered in a separate subsection. But the editor should beware: that kind of structure may turn out to be meaningless to readers. For example, most annual reports do not cover what the human resources or administrative divisions did during the year because these are support functions rather than program functions. But even some program functions don't fit logically into a division-by-division structure.

When World Wildlife Fund was organized around the programs it oper-
ated in Africa, Asia, Latin America, and the United States, it was a challenge
to figure out where in the annual report to cover other activities, such as the
fund's research on toxic chemicals or its global efforts to combat illegal trade
in wildlife. Because the research on toxics often led to policy recommenda-
tions that were made to international bodies, the question was whether that
particular division's work should be covered in the section titled "Research
and Development" or in the section titled "Conservation Policy." The same
problem occurred with decisions about where to cover the work of the division responsible for monitoring illegal wildlife trade. The scientific staff
members in this division often published studies of the effects of trade on
bears, tigers, and even ginseng, but they also developed policy positions for
delegates to the World Trade Organization and the Convention on International Trade in Endangered Species.

Sometimes the solution to a structural problem is to place an anomaly
in a sidebar box, or to make it a lengthy caption rather than part of the regular narrative. Once issues of placement are resolved, however, the writer
still faces the challenge of describing the organization's work in colorful,
meaningful language.

Writing It Right

Writing the review of operations poses a challenge to the writer because the
information for this section often comes from background material and
interviews. By its very nature, the background material is not aimed at the
same audience as the one the writer is trying to reach. Background material tends to employ terminology, jargon, and acronyms that are quite familiar to specialized audiences but meaningless to the audience for the annual
report.

There is no room in the report for specialized language or jargon, even
though they may function as a form of shorthand. The organization's work
may involve biodiversity assessments, but the annual report will call them
studies of plant and animal diversity. The mission may be to build infra-
structure in LDCs, but the annual report will say that the mission is to build
roads, bridges, and sewage-treatment systems in less developed (or developing) countries. Jargon may be shorter, but clarity is paramount. (For more
about jargon, see the section titled "Speaking for the Institution," later in
this chapter.)

Interviews present a somewhat different set of challenges. Very seldom
does a busy content expert have time to prepare for an interview, and sel-

dom will the expert have all the necessary details at hand. Most often the expert will offer to provide the missing details later, but it will still be necessary to issue a reminder and even prod and nag to get the information.

"My biggest challenge," says writer Lou Bayard, "is getting my calls returned. I surmount this by being a nuisance. I call them so many times that they finally call me back just to stop being pestered." The key to writing the review of operations, says Bayard, is organization. He maps out the time it will take to write each section of the review, makes a calendar, lists the people who need to be called, and keeps track of their responses so that he can follow up if they have not returned his calls. "I work best with background material, and I use the interviews to point myself in the right direction."

"I try never to write reports unless the client has pulled together at least a significant body of background," says communications consultant Ellen Schorr. "At the very least, the client should provide a specific list of interviewees and what I am expected to learn from each of them."

Two things the writer can do to make sure the interview yields the necessary nuggets of information is to prepare for it well in advance (see Exhibit 6.4) and ask questions that yield the information needed for the write-up (see Exhibit 6.5).

Using Background Material

The longer the piece, the easier it is to write, yet nothing equals the annual report's story for brevity.

"One overriding challenge," says Herschel Lee Johnson, senior communications manager for the NAACP Legal Defense and Educational Fund, "is . . . to make this copy interesting for the reader, which means in part greatly reducing its potential length and trying to translate legal matters into layman's terms."

Background material may be helpful, but it needs to be mined for essential nuggets of information. Says Ellen Schorr, "If the published materials are comprehensive enough to include all the background the client wants in the report, are well written, and are not too voluminous, I prefer to work from them. If they are voluminous, the client should cull . . . and index the important points."

Those points in turn have to be reshaped into the annual report's story. Exhibit 6.6 provides an example of background material supplied to the writer of the annual report for a fictitious nonprofit association called American Geography Education Foundation. The writer's assignment was to write two short, colorful paragraphs about the foundation's high school–level

---

EXHIBIT 6.4

Interviewing Tips

- Don't ask for an interview. Many people get nervous and believe that they have to prepare for it as though it were their oral dissertation. Instead, tell the person you'd like to get their thoughts on a particular subject. You can always follow up to get specific details.

- Do your research in advance. Read the background information and decide what is missing that the content expert can provide during the interview.

- If experts are not available during the time frame you have for writing the report, ask if they would be willing to answer questions by e-mail. Most of the people interviewed for this book were interviewed by e-mail.

- Come with a list of key questions to be sure you cover everything.

- Begin by thanking the person for taking the time to talk to you, and engage in some small talk before starting the actual questions.

- Take notes and be sure to tell the people you interview that you will give them an opportunity to review the copy for accuracy.

- Probe for details through follow-up questions. If people do not have the details at hand, ask them to provide that information, and then *follow up* to get it.

- If the person answers with jargon, technical language, or inside talk, play dumb about what it means, and ask for illustrative examples. Then use those plain words in place of the jargon.

- Allow more time than you think you will need.

- End the interview by thanking the person again for taking the time to talk to you. Remind the person that there will be an opportunity to see what you have written and to correct inaccuracies.

---

geography education program. In addition to using the background information, the writer interviewed the content experts to get missing details. Note how the writer reduced the amount of inside talk and jargon so that the story could be more accessible to general readers. In addition to making the words more accessible to generalists, the writer must also be self-effacing in the sense that the strong narrative "voice" so important to powerful nonfiction writing is not at all appropriate for an annual report.

Speaking for the Institution

The organization may be doing the most noble work on Earth, but most of the people doing it are caught up in the day-to-day minutiae of institutional processes. Because of the demands on their time, they usually ask the writer to work from background material that was probably written for technical or professional audiences. The material may contain jargon and undefined terms, both of which may be difficult for general readers to grasp.

EXHIBIT 6.5

Key Interview Questions and Why They Work

What is your biggest satisfaction in your work? This is an especially good question to ask the CEO during the interview for the executive message, but it works equally well for content experts giving you information for the review of operations. This question not only helps warm up the subjects and get their minds focused on their work but also, even more important, usually yields those golden "sound bites" of eloquence that are so necessary in communicating the organization's mission. Another question that serves the same purpose would be to ask who are the person's greatest role models or teachers.

Looking back on your work this past year, is there anything you wish you could have done differently? This question helps elicit information about the challenges and obstacles that the content experts faced and what they did to overcome them. A similar type of question would be to ask what was the most difficult decision someone had to make.

What is the biggest misconception in the public's mind regarding the work you do? This question helps the subjects talk about the importance of their work and provide information that you can weave into the story. The question also helps them talk to the reader, not to someone they assume is an "insider." A similar type of question is to ask, "How do you answer those critics who say _____ about your work?"

What is the heart and soul of this organization? What makes it tick? As with the first question, you are likely to get eloquent answers that put heart into what otherwise would be a dry recitation.

What would you say to major donors about your work that would persuade them to open their checkbooks? If your report has a fund-raising purpose, this question must be asked. Often content experts get tied up in the day-to-day process and forget the overarching purpose of their work, not to mention the need for that work to be supported by donations.

What would the world/nation/city look like if you hadn't been doing what you have been doing for the past _____ years? This question elicits the all-important "track record" answer that is necessary to establish the organization's credibility with readers. Obviously, it works only if the organization has a track record of longer than five years.

What is the biggest threat to these children/wild animals/people? The answer to this question often helps put the charitable organization's mission in sharp focus for readers by conveying the important difference that the organization is making through its work.

In last year's report, we told readers you had accomplished _____ in _____ places. Are you still doing _____ in those places? This question gets to the specifics of accomplishments. Follow-up questions are often necessary: If you're still doing _____ , are there plans to expand it or expand the number of places where you do it? Are you now doing something else? If so, what is it, where are you trying it, why did you decide to do this particular thing, and what did you accomplish this past year?

Who benefits most from the work that you do? This question also gets beyond process considerations to the actual reason why the work is being done. Too often, for example, conservation involves setting aside protected areas, managing those areas, and helping provide roads, housing, and equipment to park staff. Although readers may be interested to know how many park guards were given new boots or vehicles, what they *really* want to know is how many tigers were saved as a result.

EXHIBIT 6.6

Annual Report on High School Geography Education

Background Material

MEMORANDUM

TO: J. C. Robinson, Vice President, High School Education

FROM: D. West, Senior Program Officer

RE: Field Trip, October 8–20, 2000

My trip to Cincinnati, Omaha, and Denver yielded mixed results, as follows.

Cincinnati: The curriculum guides on local geography were widely used by those teachers I interviewed. (Of the eight teachers using these materials, only five were available to meet with me.) Criticisms tended to be that the activity suggestions presumed a level of household income more likely to exist in the suburbs than in the inner city. Most of the teachers said they had benefited from our in-service seminar. Several of them said they were going to suggest improving the assessment of student outcomes because the school district's standards-based assessment rubric provided a limited view of students' knowledge and skills, especially as pertains to geography.

Omaha: Preservice teacher education programs ranked highest on the "must change" lists of the teachers I interviewed. Most of these overworked professionals thought too much emphasis was given to meeting state teacher-certification guidelines and not enough to the particular subject areas they were expected to teach. Four of the nine teachers I interviewed came from out of state and were not as well informed about the geography of Nebraska and the Plains states as they felt they should be. On the upside, our challenge grant was matched by a large insurance company. This may make development of a geography preservice program possible as early as next spring.

Denver: Teachers at two high schools in the city are promoting geography as a integrative field. They have had modest success and are now pushing to have geography education made a requirement in the state recertification process. Activity guides that we provided last fall have had moderate success. In one school I visited, the students had created relief maps based on their studies. One map of abandoned gold mines in the area around Cripple Creek was written up in the *Denver Post* (see attached clipping, and note that we got no credit, of course).

Actual Story in Annual Report

Mining the Gold in Geography

There's gold in the hills surrounding the little mining town of Cripple Creek, Colorado, and the students in Mr. Adams's geography class at Denver's Carnegie High School have found it. Student activity guides provided by the Foundation this past year helped Mr. Adams's students understand the geological history of the Rocky Mountains. They also took a field trip to Cripple Creek to see first hand the rugged mountain topography that made mining so dangerous in the 19th century. "That's why we decided to do a relief map instead of a flat one," said Mr. Adams. "We wanted folks to see just how steep those hillsides are and how hidden away some of the old mine sites are."

Adams's students are among 54,000 high school students in Denver, Omaha, and Cincinnati who are benefiting from assistance provided by the Foundation during 2000. In Omaha, a Foundation challenge grant, matched by an insurance company, is making it possible for teachers to increase their understanding of the region's geography *before* they enter the classroom. And in Cincinnati, high school geography teachers are using Foundation-supplied curriculum guides to help inner-city students understand the city's geographical history.

Content experts themselves tend to speak in jargon. Acronyms, abbreviations, and jargon all help get the message across more quickly in a fast-paced world, provided that everyone understands those terms. For example, "biome" may be the exact term to use in referring to a particular type of ecological community, such as a rain forest, grasslands, or desert, but it is probably meaningful only to conservation insiders. Likewise, "building capacity" covers in two words what can be conveyed to outsiders only in several words, and in a publication where brevity is paramount, it may be tempting to settle for those two words, but what exactly do they mean? "Building capacity" may mean helping park managers construct housing for staff or visitors, but helping a local group mount a fundraising campaign is also building capacity. Only the content experts know which definition is correct—or do they?

When people answer his questions with jargon, "I pretend I'm stupid," says Lou Bayard. "Even if I know what 'transboundary solutions' means, I tell the person, 'You have to help me here. What does this mean?' I try to rephrase and get their agreement that the rephrasing will work. Some will say, 'That's clearer,' but others—especially lawyers—cling to the exact wording, even if readers won't understand it or care to try to figure it out."

The writer must weed out jargon and write as clearly as possible. When the meaning is unclear, Ellen Schorr asks for clarification: "When you say 'the shifting health care landscape,' are you talking about the increase in managed care enrollees or the rising numbers of uninsured or something else?" she will ask. "Then I try to get them to think like an outside reader of the report: 'I'm not sure someone unfamiliar with your organization would understand that. Could you describe it another way or in a bit more detail?'"

The one person most likely to expect clarity is the one who most often speaks to the public: the CEO. Kathryn Fuller of World Wildlife Fund is quite adamant that the use of constructions like "building capacity" and "ecoregion-based conservation," as well as other undefined terms and acronyms, be kept to an absolute minimum in all of World Wildlife Fund's communications to general audiences, particularly in the organization's annual report.

Having achieved the greatest degree of clarity and brevity in the draft, the writer must let it go. There is no ownership of any writing done for an annual report; no byline is given. The draft is edited and reworked by so many people that the ultimate product often bears scant resemblance to the initial draft. Nevertheless, a writer who clearly understands why the executive message must be in the CEO's voice, and why it must reflect the CEO's thoughts, may resist changes that the CEO wants to make in the wording of the review of operations. The writer should let it go, lest the writer be let go.

Speaking for the institution presents other challenges as well. Nancy Kelly, communications and outreach officer for the Asia Foundation, cites the need to turn so many different submissions into one voice. "That is the reason we often employ a freelance consultant-writer," she says. "We want someone who is not caught up in the foundation's jargon, someone with a fresh view."

Speaking for the institution does not mean that the prose should be dry or abstract. Some organizations fight what may seem to be losing battles—against alcoholism, drug dependence, and poverty, or for measures and programs to save children's lives—but the hardships they face give a human dimension to their work. The trick is to describe the hardships, uphill battles, dangers, and risks in a style that brings home to the audience the challenges faced each year on behalf of the people or animals the organization is trying to help. As Jeffrey Hon of the National Council on Alcoholism and Drug Dependence advised, "Describe those activities that will most interest your audience, and keep the text brief and breezy."

Brief and breezy are not easy to come by in writing about programs designed to encourage ethical behavior in businesses or loans to developing countries. In fact, Dana Lane, chief of publications for the International Finance Corporation, says her biggest writing challenge is "saying something fresh and interesting year after year." Freshness has more to do with writing style, however, than with subject matter. Writing that is fresh sparkles with clarity, brevity, color, and life. Life comes from the living, and that's why the most colorful, fresh writing tends to be about people's predicaments and actions.

Searching for Freshness

One formula for freshness, employed by the Boy Scouts of America, is to single out one specific story for each section of the report. Each year, one of these sections is about the Honor Medal for bravery. In 1997, one of forty-two scouts who received the Honor Medal was ten-year-old Steven Beeson, who rescued a neighbor's two children from their burning house:

> Steven overcame his fear and quickly picked up the youngest boy, carrying him out of the house. . . . He then ran back into the house and carried the other boy to safety. With both boys outside, Steven ran back into the house a third time and rescued the dog.
>
> That might be the end of the story, but after rescuing the boys and the dog, Steven ran 200 yards down the block—still barefooted—to the nearby fire station for help. . . . Lt. Jim Collins of the San Antonio Fire Department . . . says had it not been for Steven's quick thinking, the situation could have been much worse [Boy Scouts of America, 1997, p. 25].

Not only was this part of the review written like a story, it was full of drama and action. There could have been no more powerful testimonial than a story like this one to the Boy Scout belief that character counts. Its freshness and simplicity could engage readers of all ages, from adults, whose ongoing support is critical, to children longing for that once-in-a-lifetime chance to be brave. Along the way, the image of scouting as a noble and worthwhile pursuit was burnished.

Of course, it is easy to write about people in an annual report focused on the Boy Scouts, but how do other organizations, with fewer people-centered missions, achieve freshness? The National Wildlife Federation could have written some deadly dull prose describing one aspect of its Finance and Environment Program, which involved building public awareness of the need to eliminate mercury and polychlorinated biphenyls from Lake Superior. Instead, the federation told an action story: "For nearly 18 hours straight last summer, five men paddled sea kayaks across Lake Superior, the world's largest freshwater lake. Don Dimond, Kevin Geshel . . . , Brock Hunter, Rob Tull, and Rick Wright braved the frigid storm-prone lake to help . . . build national awareness of the need for additional environmental safeguards for the lake and the people and wildlife that depend on it" (National Wildlife Federation, 1999, p. 18).

What about really abstract ideas? How can they be rendered freshly? One function of the Ethics Resource Center is to conduct surveys of employees' perceptions of their company's organizational ethic. The center chose to describe its work in this area in human terms:

> *For many companies, measuring and understanding the attitudes, perceptions, and behaviors of their employees seems a daunting task. At Lockheed Martin corporation, with 175,000 employees representing 149 business units in far reaches of our world, the task may appear impossible. But the company marched forward, working with the Ethics Resource Center to learn more about its ethical foundation. From Kannapolis, North Carolina, to Kuala Lumpur, Malaysia, the Ethics Resource Center surveyed employees on issues affecting ethical business conduct. And, for the first time, the Ethics Resource Center was able to draw key correlations between employee job satisfaction and the company's ethical practices [Ethics Resource Center, 1998, p. 9].*

Because of their immediacy and power, stories are the most compelling narrative style for nonprofit organizations' annual reports. But straight reportage also has its place. For many associations, the review of operations combines long blocks of reportage about a particular endeavor with highlights, in sidebar boxes, of particular aspects. The Consultative Group on

International Agricultural Research, in one section ("Assessing System Capabilities for the 21st Century") of its annual report, described the principal findings of the third system review of the organization (Consultative Group on International Agricultural Research, 1998). For readers who might have found this material rather dry, the report offered sidebar boxes that told ministories related to the main text. One of these, "A Tradition of Accountability and Learning," provided information about the two preceding system reviews. A second, "Biotechnology in the CGIAR," warned of the urgent need to increase agricultural production to meet the needs of a burgeoning population and then informed readers that, after convening two expert panels to study biotechnology issues, the organization would "develop needs-based, in-house biotechnology capability that will address the present and future needs of small-scale farmers" (p. 23).

When space is at a premium, as it is for the American Friends Service Committee, the box-and-bullet style of writing works best. Describing a program to achieve economic justice, an American Friends Service Committee brochure-formatted annual report first explained why the program exists and then offered a bulleted list of accomplishments:

> *The American Friends Service Committee [AFSC] believes in the power of individuals to change oppressive conditions brought on by natural disasters, wartime dislocation, or poverty. However, local initiatives often need additional resources with which to begin. Through emergency aid, followed by technical assistance and supplies, we assist communities toward long-term sufficiency. In 1998, AFSC served as your liaison in Asia, Africa, Central America, the Middle East, and the United States by:*
>
> - *Delivering 8,000 pairs of mittens and $40,000 worth of powdered milk to children in . . . North Korea. . . .*
>
> - *Distributing $90,000 worth of food and medicine to Somalis recovering from torrential rains that caused loss of human life and livestock. . . .*
>
> - *Providing a significant grant to a Chilean village to repair an earthquake-damaged water wheel needed for irrigation for a citrus tree-planting program. . . .*
>
> - *Writing and distributing more than 40,000 copies of a handbook advising welfare recipients and their advocates in West Virginia and across the country of their rights as welfare regulations change [American Friends Service Committee, 1998, p. 2].*

Note that these short, bulleted items have their own impact through specificity and color. They might have been more elaborate if there had been more room to tell them, but they still made a powerfully succinct statement about the group's accomplishments in 1998 with its program for economic justice.

Whatever style is used, the writer of the review of operations should make the writing as specific, colorful, and complete as possible. Failure to do so is an abrogation of the writer's responsibility and may result in a request for a rewrite (if time permits), rejection of the draft, or, at the very least, no future assignments. The writer who manages to combine brevity with beauty has a much better chance of being asked to write the report the next time around. And of course, a high-quality draft makes the editing phase of the process go much more smoothly.

Chapter 7

Editing and Managing Production

WHEN THE MANUSCRIPT for the annual report finally lands on the editor's desk, it is time for the editor to edit. Up to this point in the process, as discussed in Chapter Four, the editor has been functioning primarily as project leader by planning the report, scheduling production, and assigning the writing. How can this busy project leader find the time to concentrate on the actual editing of the text? It isn't easy.

Of course, in many larger associations, the project leader may actually have someone on staff who edits the text and writes the photo captions. But in smaller organizations, the editor is expected to manage the process from start to finish *and* to edit, write, and even rewrite to achieve the "one voice" so essential to an annual report.

The first step in this process of *e pluribus unum* is to read the writer's draft and evaluate whether, in addition to completeness, it has the appropriate approach and tone. Of course, the editor has already set the stage by giving the writer a word count, a deadline, and a specific set of guidelines (recall Exhibit 2.1 in Chapter Two).

Substantive Editing and Copyediting

Some editors, pencils (or pens) tucked safely behind their ears, start by reading the complete draft from beginning to end to check for coherence and completeness and to make sure that the writer has followed the guidance given in the writing assignment. Other editors plunge right in and begin marking copy. Both approaches work, but if the editor starts right off marking copy, he or she can sometimes lose sight of the forest in the search for bark on the trees. It is possible, for example, to wander four or five pages into the draft before noticing that the writer did not follow the assignment or that no theme has been established, let alone carried out.

If the writer has failed to follow the assignment, the editor must decide quickly whether to ask for a rewrite or simply rewrite the draft. Time and money are the most important factors in making this decision. Assuming, however, that the writer has produced a good draft, the ten-step editing approach shown in Exhibit 7.1 can help ensure that all the editing bases are covered.

Of course, reading the draft all the way through may not be possible when the deadline is too tight, and the text has to be edited literally section by section, as it comes in. In either case, the editor will usually edit first for substance (substantive editing is sometimes called "line editing") and next for spelling, grammar, punctuation, and consistency (this second kind of editing is usually called "copyediting"). Substantive editing tackles problems with organization, completeness, tone, approach, and even accuracy, if the editor happens also to be a content expert. In many nonprofit associations, however, the editor is not a content expert, and so the editor edits for organization, completeness, grammar, and consistency and then sends the edited text back to the content experts and asks them to review it for accuracy.

EXHIBIT 7.1

Ten Steps to a Thorough Edit

1. Read the draft for content.

2. Decide where the various pieces will go and how they might be illustrated.

3. Make sure that the draft is put together logically and that the flow is natural from one part to another and from one paragraph to the next.

4. Edit for style.

5. Edit for desired length. At this stage, the draft can be edited to approximate the desired length, with more drastic cuts postponed until the copy has been typeset and cuts are needed to fit the allotted space.

6. Edit for accuracy of statements.

7. Edit for objectivity, fairness, good taste, tone, and completeness.

8. Edit for simplicity, clarity, spelling, and grammar.

9. Edit for impact through word choice and presentation of ideas.

10. Read through the edited draft to be sure that it has properly jelled.

Source: Adapted from Edmund C. Arnold, *Editing the Organizational Publication*, p. 84. Reprinted by permission.

It may seem like a waste of time to copyedit at this stage, especially when text changes made by content experts mean that the draft will have to be copyedited again. But the content expert who spots a misspelled word or poor grammatical construction could infer that the editor has done a sloppy job, and the less confidence the content expert has in the editor, the more likely it is that the review process will be painful and slow.

Copyediting itself is a multifaceted process. Most editors find it helpful to follow a formal style guide, such as *The Chicago Manual of Style,* and many editors also edit according to a house style established by the nonprofit organization to suit the particular characteristics of the subject matter to be covered. For example, the style guide for the National Trust for Historic Preservation would contain entries explaining the difference between *Federal* and *federal* (the former being a style of architecture, the latter referring to national government), prescribing the correct use of the article *a* (rather than *an*) with the word *historic* (because only unaspirated *h* takes the article *an*), and reminding even the most tenured editor that buildings are listed *in,* not *on,* the National Register of Historic Places.

As with any other kind of publication longer than a brochure, it is helpful to create a style sheet that pertains solely to terms frequently used in the annual report. The style sheet can be clipped to the proofs of the annual report throughout the proofreading process so that the proofreader can quickly ascertain whether, for example, *child care* or *childcare* is the established style and whether *adviser* or *advisor* is the established spelling (see the sample style sheet in Exhibit 7.2).

In addition to copyediting of the text, the donor lists must be reviewed to see that they are properly alphabetized and that the spelling of names has been scrupulously checked. Nothing is more insulting than misspelling a donor's name—and some people do have strangely spelled names. The editor must double-check any oddities with the development people to be sure that all the names are correctly spelled. Some automated lists are generated in such a way that *Jr.* and *III* are buried in the middle of a name, and so the copyeditor is likely to encounter constructions like these hiding among the columns and columns of names:

John Jr. Olson

Jane and Marion Oppenheimer

Samuel P. III Page

J. P. Potsdam

Lists of officers, staff members, and board members likewise demand the editor's careful attention. The chairman of the board probably would not be

EXHIBIT 7.2

Style Sheet for Friends of the Ferret 2000 Annual Report

A-F

Adopt-a-Ferret Program

antipoaching, one word, no hyphen

adviser

Burk County (NE), not Burke

comma, use serial comma

Earth/earth, capitalize when referring to planet; lowercase when referring to soil

e-mail, not email

Ferret Fancier, title of FOF magazine on first and second reference; not *The Ferret Fancier,* not *Ferret Fancier Magazine*

Friends of the Ferret, FOF on second reference; do not use with "the"

Future Farmers of America, use with "the"

G-L

Greenville, not Greeneville, SC

Homeless Ferret Program, use with "the" (actual FOF division is called Shelter Operations)

home page, two words, lowercased

impact, use as noun only

Internet

Land and Water Conservation Fund, use LWCF in second reference only if used frequently

M-R

National Park Service, Park Service on second reference; do not use NPS

Nature Conservancy, use with The

National Wildlife Federation, not Foundation; NWF on second reference if used frequently

nonprofit, do not hyphenate

numbers, spell out one through ten; use figures thereafter

on-line, hyphenate adjective and adverb forms

program, uppercase when included with the full name of the program but lowercase when used alone

revenue, do not add "s" to this collective noun

S-Z

Shelter Operations, use only for title of FOF division; otherwise, use Homeless Ferret Program

species names, use common English names only and lowercase except for proper nouns that are a part of the name

states, spell out in text; use USPS abbreviations in lists

titles of people, uppercase when preceding name, lowercase when following

toward, not towards

use/utilize, use simpler form

Web site, not website or web site

woodlot, one word

www.ferretfriend.org, FOF Web site

ZIP code, use only in lists, with one space between two-letter state abbr. and ZIP

pleased if he were listed as "Johnson P. Smithereen III, Chairman of the Board" in the board list but as "Mr. and Mrs. John Smithereen" in the donor list.

Just to be sure all the *i*'s have been dotted and the *t*'s crossed, it is also helpful to have a checklist that can be reviewed when copyediting is finished (see Exhibit 7.3).

Readers still unsure of the differences between substantive editing and copyediting can study a passage that has been edited for substance (see Exhibit 7.4). Note how the editor has ignored small typos and inconsistencies of style and has focused instead on structure and content. Once these problems have been addressed, the editor will copyedit the revised passage (see Exhibit 7.5) before sending it out for review.

EXHIBIT 7.3

Copyediting Checklist

Audience

- No biased, slanted, or stereotyped language
- Assumes correct level of reader knowledge (no undefined terms for lay audiences, no jargon or inside talk)
- Examples used to illustrate difficult concepts
- Assertions supported by facts or footnotes

Organization

- Information presented in logical order
- Ideas clearly expressed
- No missing information or unanswered questions
- Transitions made from one idea to the next

Appeal

- Intriguing title
- Lead that invites readers to continue
- Sentences varied in length
- Active, not passive, voice
- Conclusion leaves no loose ends

Clarity

- No ambiguous concepts
- Specific, not vague, words
- No redundancies or verbosity
- No overly complex sentences
- No "Wow!" statements[a]

EXHIBIT 7.3

Copyediting Checklist, Cont'd.

Style

- Author's voice consistent throughout
- Tone appropriate to audience and topic
- No clichés or mixed metaphors
- Few if any lifeless ("to be") verbs
- Consistent use of punctuation, capitalization, and numerals

Grammar

- Pronouns with the correct antecedent
- No double negatives
- Correct subject-verb agreement
- No dangling modifiers
- Prepositions used correctly
- Pronouns in the correct case
- Split infinitives only when absolutely necessary
- *That* and *which* used correctly
- No spelling errors

Punctuation

- No surplus punctuation
- Use of exclamation marks only when absolutely necessary, not merely for emphasis
- No unintentional sentence fragments
- No run-on sentences
- Words correctly divided
- Compound constructions correctly hyphenated
- Consistent treatment of numbers and fractions

Mechanics

- Pages numbered in the upper right-hand corner
- Tables and figures, each on a separate page, numbered correctly, and keyed to text
- Chapters or main headings in text match listing in table of contents and appear in the same order

[a]*Wow statements are unsubstantiated assertions that usually provoke in readers the question "Why?" or the reaction "Who cares?": "The meeting was a resounding success." (In what respect?) "Everyone had a great time at the company picnic." (Who cares?) "The book was well received." (Why wouldn't it be?)*

EXHIBIT 7.4

Operation Teddy Bear 2000 Annual Report
Review of Operations, with Substantive Editing

Public Outreach

Twenty thousand more children received Bear
Power magazine this year, thanks to a generous
donation from the Smith (Wanaker) Foundation. The *[H]*
magazine *[also]* won an award from the Educational (Press)   *— Ck name changed to Publisher?*
Association of America for best in design of a mag-
azine for elementary school kids. But the magazine
is only a part of a concerted outreach effort that
culminated in a successful year for Operation Teddy
Bear. Although teddy bear tea parties continue to be
the mainstay of support, our direct-mail solicitation
effort also brought in much-needed revenues and
plans are underway to add two more solicitations
to our direct mail campaign next year.

[Ck Spelling]

[In addition to subsidizing]
~~The Smith~~ (Wankaler) ~~Foundation grant helped~~
~~subsidize~~ the printing of additional copies of Bear
Power Magazine, *[the grant made]* ~~making~~ it ~~also~~ possible to increase
the number of full color pages from eight to 16.

[Move up]

[According to our mailbag]
~~T~~Games and puzzles ~~have proven to be~~ *[are]* highly popolar
[children who read Bear Power ⊙]
with ~~the target audience, but they are more effective~~

EXHIBIT 7.4

Operation Teddy Bear 2000 Annual Report
Review of Operations, with Substantive Editing, Cont'd.

> children have less difficulty.

~~when rendered in full color.~~ ~~Kids can~~ following the

"path" the teddy bears take in search of honey.

~~When the puzzle is rendered in full color,~~ "I like the

teddy bear picnic puzzle," writes six-year-old Shanita

Harris. "I like helping them find the honey before

the bees do."

Teddy bear tea parties were held to benefit

name them

two area hospitals this past year, and everyone

Wow - explain why successful

agreed they were a big success. By now, most of the   *how many?*

in-patient chilren have received a bear donated by

Operation Teddy Bear. Honey "pots"—[miniature jars

of honey and jam donated by area restaraunts—

utilized at the two tea parties were later donated to

the hostipals.]— *significance not clear, ck w/staff*

Finally, the volume of mail we are getting

about Bear Power magazine or seeking to donate

teddy bears to hospitals and other institutions has

increased, making the hiring of additional staff

an imperative for 2001.

too internal

EXHIBIT 7.5

Operation Teddy Bear 2000 Annual Report
Review of Operations, After Copyediting

Public Outreach

Twenty thousand more children received <u>Bear Power</u> magazine this year than last, thanks to a generous donation from the Smith Wankaler Foundation. In addition to subsidizing the printing of additional copies of <u>Bear Power</u>, the grant made it possible to increase the number of full color pages from ~~eight~~ 8 to 16. According to our mailbag, games and puzzles are highly popular with the children who read <u>Bear Power</u>. When the puzzle is rendered in full color, the children have less difficulty following the path the teddy bears take in search of honey. "I like the teddy bear picnic puzzle," writes six-year-old Shanita Harris. "I like helping them find the honey before the bees do."

<u>Bear Power</u> magazine also won an award from the Educational Publishers Association of America for best design of a magazine for elementary school children. But the magazine is only a part of a concerted outreach effort that culminated in a successful year for Operation Teddy Bear.

EXHIBIT 7.5

**Operation Teddy Bear 2000 Annual Report
Review of Operations, After Copyediting, Cont'd.**

Teddy bear tea parties—a mainstay of our support—were held to benefit two area hospitals this year. Proceeds from the tea parties ensured that all inpatient children at St. Agnes of Mercy and Maryville Community Hospital now have a teddy bear of their own. Honey "pots"—miniature jars of honey and jam donated by area restaurants—that, in the past, have been discarded following the tea parties were given to the younger brothers and sisters of the ~~hostipalized~~ *hospitalized* children.

Managing Reviews

Copy reviews are perhaps the biggest headache in the production of an annual report. One reason is that the ball is no longer in the editor's court, and editors tend to sleep better when they are in control. Another reason is that content experts and managers are busy people, and reviewing a draft may be nowhere near the top of the list of their urgent priorities.

The resourceful editor employs a range of tricks—and traps, if necessary—to get comments back from reviewers on time, or at least not too long past the deadline. Some of the tricks and traps offered in Exhibit 7.6 are devious; many are downright juvenile. But they work.

There are several ways to collect reviews, and each has its advantages. If the editor circulates hard-copy drafts to reviewers and asks them to make their comments on these copies, the editor can then exercise a great deal of judgment about incorporating the reviewers' comments. Very often, comments by content experts tend to restore the jargon and shoptalk that editing has so carefully removed, and so the trick here is to reword reviewers'

EXHIBIT 7.6

How to Get What You Need When You Need It

Give reviewers a deadline well ahead of the date when you actually need their comments. This is not dishonest. It's smart planning. You can't be expected to know what is on the calendar of everyone who must review the copy. Even if people have received a copy of the annual report production schedule and noted on their calendars that they will be asked to review copy and turn it around by a certain date, they may be unable to meet this obligation because of unexpected travel, illness, or other emergencies. It may also be the case that you were late getting the copy to them. A corollary rule, however, is to be sure to give reviewers enough time to review copy. Nobody likes to be handed a draft and told that it needs to be turned around in twenty-four hours. And if there simply is not enough time (and the copy is not too long), walk the copy around to the content experts and ask them to review it while you are waiting.

Make copy-review delays a matter of time and therefore of money. When the vice president for relief programs leaves for a three-week field trip to Patagonia before completing her review of copy for the annual report, don't hesitate to tell her secretary how much money this delay will cost in overtime at the printer. Devious editors have been known to ask the secretary to get the vice president to sign off on a memo requesting a budget exception to account for overtime expenses at the printer. Because nonprofits cannot afford to squander precious funds, the delinquent vice president would be well advised to find time for text review during her trip and to fax or e-mail her comments back to the office.

Never hesitate to invoke the reader. When the chief economist insists on putting back into the draft terms like "macroeconomic destabilization factors," and you know this term will not sit well with the CEO, say so—diplomatically of course. "I understand that those words explain what happened in more precise language, but we really have to make this report accessible to a general reader. Is there a way we can reword this so that our readers will understand it?"

Decide what to do (and apologize only if it turns out to be wrong): Suppose Joe Powerset's correction to a passage of text says, "Sixty percent of the children helped by Operation Teddy Bear made a more rapid recovery from surgery than children in hospitals not covered by the program. Of the remaining 40 percent enrolled in Operation Teddy Bear, 5 percent did not survive because their illnesses were too far advanced at the time of admission. The recovery rate for the remaining 35 percent was about the same as for children in hospitals not covered by the program." Jim Short's correction to the same passage reads: "Sixty percent of the children helped by Operation Teddy Bear made a more rapid recovery from surgery than children in hospitals not covered by the program. The remaining 40 percent either experienced a rate of recovery about the same as children in hospitals not covered by the program or did not survive because their illnesses were too far advanced at the time of admission." Powerset's version is more precise; Short's version is a little gentler because it is more imprecise and does not quantify the distressing fact that 5 percent of the Operation Teddy Bear children did not survive. Neither Short nor Powerset is available to consult about which version of the passage should be used in the report. Base your decision on what you think the CEO and the report's readers would prefer. (If you are new and still a little unsure, you can flag it for the CEO's attention: "This passage was reworded per Jim Short's advice; however, Joe Powerset suggested the following language, which is more precise. I was unable to resolve the matter because they are both out of the office. Which version would you prefer?")

EXHIBIT 7.6

How to Get What You Need When You Need It, Cont'd.

When only signoffs—not content input—are needed, invoke the negative response trick. "This is the proposed final version of the draft annual report. All comments by key reviewers have been incorporated. Please read the draft and return it to me with your comments by _____ . If I do not hear from you by that date, I will assume that you approve and have no further comments." (Of course, you would not try this with the CEO, but all others are fair game. Indeed, not only is this a favor to busy people, because they don't have to do anything unless they want to, it is also a hint that if they are not sure they reviewed the draft all that closely the first time, they had better do it now.)

Invoke the highest power whenever necessary. When the lawyers insist that several parts of the draft must be rewritten (because the wording could be misinterpreted and expose the organization to litigation) but can't turn their attention to the language for several weeks, tell them that this delay will get you in trouble with the boss. "Since this is so important, and you carry more weight with President Flintstone than I do, I'm sure you won't mind asking him for an extension of the deadline."

Toot your own horn. Doctors and other professionals deck their walls with certificates attesting to their professional credentials, and so should editors. Collect compliments, rave reviews, and especially awards, and let management know about it. Imitate your colleagues in the corporate sector. According to the National Investor Relations Institute (quoted in Crosse Point Paper Corporation, 1994), 63 percent of corporations that were surveyed in 1993 entered their annual reports in competitions. Frame award certificates and hang them in your office. Being the award-winning editor gives you credibility and clout. Content experts are much less likely to worry about your word and style choices if they are confident that outsiders (perhaps as knowledgeable as they themselves are) think you know what you are doing and are doing it well. (A caveat here is to seek only awards that are meaningful to your organization. Design awards, for example, may not be as impressive as awards for overall communications excellence.)

comments so that readers of the annual report will be able to understand what is meant. If the editor has to fax or mail the drafts, however, especially overseas, it may be difficult to get the necessary responses by the deadline that has to be met if the project is to remain on schedule.

If the draft is circulated via e-mail, the editor should ask reviewers to flag changed language by using [[double brackets]] or <angle brackets> or some other visual device. Then the editor, instead of having to reread the entire draft, only needs to check changed text against a master copy of the edited draft, again exercising editorial judgment about how the changes will be worded.

If the organization has an intranet, the editor may want to try getting reviews accomplished via this new medium. An intranet is especially useful if the organization has a presence around the world, and if all its offices have Internet access. Both e-mail and an intranet offer the advantage of defeating time zones and catching traveling reviewers wherever they may be (provided they haven't fled to their cabin in the Maine woods, the one with no telephone or electricity). Again, as with a draft circulated via e-mail, the editor can smooth up comments that have reintroduced jargon or over-specialized language.

It may be tempting to think that while the various pieces of the annual report are out for content review, the editor will now have time to visit his or her own cabin in the Maine woods. Then again, this may be the perfect time for tackling all the writing tasks that are usually left to the editor.

The Editor's Writing Responsibilities

The editor is usually the one who writes those portions of the report that are not part of the writer's assignment. For example, the editor may write the boilerplate sections that describe the organization's mission or tell potential donors how they can support the cause. The editor is also the person most likely to write the photo captions—and caption writing is an art unto itself; here is where the challenge of cramming pertinent information into a very tiny space is greatest. Of course, some photos don't require captions at all. Some don't require full-sentence captions. Some, because photo captions are the most-read feature of any annual report, require ministories that elaborate or illustrate points made in the text. Table 7.1 lists the many types of photo captions and shows examples of them.

Captions for the World Wildlife Fund annual report, written in the informational style, carry a lot of baggage: the identification of the plant or animal species pictured (including its Latin name), a unique characteristic of the species, and perhaps some information about the threats to its existence and what the organization is doing to help protect it. Even the pictures of the chairman and the president give their names and titles, tell where the pictures were taken and why the chairman or president was there, and say a word about the importance of those places to World Wildlife Fund.

Very much as in the World Wildlife Fund annual report, the photo captions in the 1999 annual report of the International Finance Corporation (IFC) explain a lot about the organization's work. These captions use a mix of the identifying and informational styles. For example, the caption for a picture of a plaster-spattered worker holding a trowel says, "Palestinian workers on the construction site of the Bethlehem Jacir Palace Hotel, the largest building project to date in the West Bank and Gaza. This is among 15 projects IFC has supported in the territory since 1994" (International

TABLE 7.1

Types of Photo Captions

Caption Type	Example
Identifying. These are the classic, traditional captions that identify people or animals or objects in the picture. The most typical example is the kind of caption you find in museum catalogs or art exhibits. These captions do not use complete sentences. Although this type of caption is the easiest to write, in an annual report it is also boring and does not add much to editorial impact.	(picture of dinner plates in a museum exhibition catalog) Dutch majolica dishes. ca. 1590–1650. Tin-glazed earthenware on obverse; lead-glazed on reverse.
Informational. An expansion of the identifying caption, these captions offer interesting facts about the subject of the photo. The information can be drawn from the body of the text, but it's more interesting for the reader if you can expand on the subject matter in the photo caption. In an annual report, these can add to editorial impact and reader identification with the "product."	(picture of a bird in the Everglades) Food sources for the white ibis and other waders that live in the Everglades will be greatly improved through restoration of near-natural water flows to the system.
Pull (or callout) quote. This type of caption is used most often when there are mug shots of people mentioned in the text. Instead of simply using an identifying caption, the editor searches the body of the text for an illuminating or controversial quote from the person pictured. The purpose of the pull-quote caption is to entice the reader to read the article. This type of caption works in an annual report only if the quote is short.	(picture of VP for Ferret Adoption Programs) "Our goal is to give ferrets a good home, and that sometimes means training the adoptive parents."
Mood-evoking. These often pick up a cloud formation, shadows and lighting, or facial expressions in a photo and translate the mood into words. The editor does this to remind the reader of the quality of the photography or art used, to evoke an emotional response to the issue being discussed, and even to suggest in an editorializing way how the reader should view or judge a subject. These captions can work very well in annual reports if not overdone and if the text presents the facts clearly. The example at the right is not a pull quote because it pulls nothing from the text. Rather, it uses a few lines of poetry to evoke a mood and, the editor hopes, trigger a positive emotional response in readers.	(picture of breaching whale with shoreline in the background) There is a pleasure in the pathless woods, There is a rapture on the lonely shore, There is society, where none intrudes, By the deep sea, and music in its roar: I love not man the less, but Nature more. —Byron

Finance Corporation, 1999, p. 39). Captions can also be used to expand the annual report's coverage by briefly discussing topics not covered in the text. The same report took this approach in its review of operations, which covered Central Asia, the Middle East, and North Africa. A single sentence in the text referred to Morocco: "Foreign direct investments in the Middle East and North Africa nearly doubled (to $5.9 billion) in calendar year 1998, largely because of recent programs in Egypt, Morocco, and Tunisia" (p. 36). But the caption for a photo showing business executives standing outside a new building added new information: "Settavex has begun an expansion that will boost the competitive position of Morocco's textiles sector. With IFC financing, the management team featured here will hire 50 more people and diversify its product mix. Employee-friendly, Settavex is divided into self-sustaining profit centers. Each minicompany promotes team spirit and fosters a sense of ownership and responsibility in employees" (p. 41).

Cramming so much text into scarce space can be difficult, which may explain why photo captions in the annual reports of some nonprofit organizations truly "travel light." The 1998 annual report of the National Trust for Historic Preservation (see Exhibit 7.7) features an evocative color photograph that spans the front and back covers. Here is an old, probably abandoned, building—perhaps a schoolhouse?—on a vast plain under a low sky. Is this building historic? We will never know, for there is no caption, only a credit. The other photos are as small as their very short identifying captions, like "Great Falls' Tenth Street Bridge," or "Hood Hall at Livingstone College" (National Trust for Historic Preservation, 1998). In both cases, the stories near the pictures function as captions.

Ducks Unlimited's 1999 annual report may have had stunning photographs of ducks, but readers must have strained their eyes to find out what species they were. When they finally managed to locate the captions—in tiny, difficult-to-see type on the cover, inside back cover, and page 6—and found only "wood duck" or "mallards" or "egret," they surely wondered if the effort had been worthwhile. Were these waterfowl threatened? Was their habitat shrinking? What was Ducks Unlimited doing to protect them? Inquiring readers would have wanted to know why these pictures were in the report.

The editor also needs to manage where captions are placed—preferably as close to their photos as possible. Designers sometimes tend to think of photo captions as clutter and may try to put them somewhere far away from the images, where they won't interfere with the overall design. Arrows, or words like "bottom left" or "top right" are somewhat helpful in guiding readers to the photo identified by the caption, but placement near the photo is almost always better. For example, the 1999 annual report of Conservation International featured a photo of a deerlike creature at the bottom left-hand

Exhibit 7.7

Cover, National Trust for Historic Preservation 1998 Annual Report

Source: *National Trust for Historic Preservation 1998 Annual Report.* Photograph by Eric Meola, Image Bank. Reprinted by permission.

corner of a page somewhere in the middle of the report (there were no page numbers, for some reason). Intrigued by this photograph, I nearly concluded that it had no caption. There was a caption opposite the animal, on the facing page, but that caption belonged to the photo of a book in the right-hand column of the facing page. Most readers drawn to photographs of wildlife would be likely to give up in frustration, but I persisted until I finally located the caption—at the top right-hand corner of the page. The creature, by the way, was a juvenile red-flanked duiker, and I suspect that many readers of this annual report also wanted to know whether duikers were endangered and what Conservation International was doing to protect them.

In the case of the American Friends Service Committee, the Boy Scouts of America, Girls Incorporated, and even the Christian Children's Fund, pictures of the people being served by these nonprofits are to be expected. Perhaps readers don't need to know who these people are and why they are being pictured, but it leaves a somewhat incomplete feeling in the mind not to have this information. And sometimes one wonders whether those smiling, rosy-cheeked, healthy adults and children in scouting uniforms are real scouts or actually models. It is so much better not to have to wonder, so much easier to see, for example, a picture of a field with hedges in the 1997 annual report of the Consultative Group on International Agricultural Research and to learn from the caption that "contour hedge rows are used to control soil erosion in Philippine farmlands" (Consultative Group on International Agricultural Research, 1997, p. 28), or to see wooden boats laden with brightly colored foodstuffs and learn from the caption that the organization "is committed to ensuring future food security, exemplified by this floating Thai market" (p. 29).

Writing photo captions—very much like finishing a homemade dress by putting in a hem, making buttonholes, and sewing on the buttons—always comes at the end of a long and laborious process. The temptation is to let it go for lack of time or lack of space, but the annual report, like the dress, is not useful or usable until it's really finished. It is always a relief to reach the stage where text is final. Reviewers' comments have been taken into account, and the text has been copyedited one last time. The donor lists have been put into alphabetical order, and any spelling queries have been resolved.

Once hard copy and electronic files have been turned over to the designer, the editor can catch up on all the tasks that had to be postponed during the editing process. But turning the report over to the designer does not mean that the editor's work is done. The editor's role as manager of visual coherence and impact has only just begun.

Chapter 8

Integrating Text with Design

SOME EDITORS operate on the assumption that good graphic design is like the Supreme Court's definition of pornography: you know it when you see it. But others approach the design phase with fear and loathing: the fear that they will not know a good design when they see it and the loathing that usually stems from feelings of inadequacy. People trained to polish prose tend not to see themselves as skilled shapers of physical space; the editor's eye tends to concern itself with the impact of words or thoughts, not with shapes or colors, and editors are likely to conclude that if they can't draw or aren't artistic, then they can't possibly tell good design from bad. (Never mind that there is a difference between an illustrator and a graphic designer—not all designers draw, nor do all illustrators do graphic design—and never mind that a discerning eye can tell the difference between good art and bad art, just as a discerning ear can tell the difference between good music and bad music.)

At any rate, an annual report is not a work of art. It is a tool for communicating, marketing, and raising funds. Therefore, a well-designed annual report is one that communicates and motivates. And, because the annual report is but one piece of the organization's overall communications strategy, it should resemble—and thereby reinforce the strength and unity of—the organization's other communications products.

The Beauty of Consistency

Just as a corporation achieves a coherent visual identity through consistent application of its trademark, a nonprofit "brands" itself with its audiences through consistent treatment of its visual identity. For example, the organization's logo is always rendered in the same colors and appears in the same place and in relatively the same size wherever it is used: on the home page of the organization's Web site, on the letterhead of press releases, on stationery and business cards, and on every publication, including the annual report. Typography is restricted to one or two typefaces (which include all the styles within those typefaces), and publications are designed to conform to a standardized grid. Although these design standards may somewhat restrict the designer's artistic freedom, they do give the nonprofit a coherent visual identity. The nonprofit's publications look familiar, and familiarity breeds "brand loyalty."

Design standards, especially flexible standards that do not absolutely stifle creativity, are expensive to develop, however, largely because of the time the designer must spend consulting key people and refining concepts to suit the client's preferences and needs. Many newly founded, very small nonprofits find the cost of developing design standards to be beyond their modest means, but they should also recognize that not having design standards can also be expensive because the designer is being paid for a totally different look each time there is a publication to design. Fortunately, the world is full of design students eager to make their mark, and even some of the more experienced professional designers may be willing to donate their time to a worthy cause. If neither of these approaches works, however, a struggling nonprofit can benefit from even the most basic design standards. If the organization already has a logo, then minimal standards can be established by sticking to a couple of typefaces and establishing some rules about placement and use of color, as demonstrated by the simple graphic design standards shown in Exhibit 8.1.

It is useful here to point out the difference between consistency and uniformity. Whereas an emphasis on uniformity tends to put the designer in a straitjacket, producing results that often fail to communicate or motivate the audience, an emphasis on consistency establishes boundaries within which the designer can execute an appropriately motivational design.

This is where the editor plays such an important role. It is the editor's job, not the designer's, to understand the organization and its goals. The editor knows the audience, and the editor must make the annual report motivate that audience to respond favorably—and generously. That said, the annual report can communicate and motivate only if it is read.

The Power of First Impressions

Despite all the admonishments we heard from Miss Murgatroyde in the fourth grade, we can't help judging people by first impressions and books by their covers. The annual reports is no exception. When the cover portrays

EXHIBIT 8.1

Creating a Coherent Visual Identity—Newsletter

Dames, Inc.

Women's Work

Dames, Inc.

Detroit Chapter Wins Civic Award

On March 18, 2001, the Detroit chapter of Dames, Inc., won an award from the Mayor's Council on Downtown Development for the chapter's work to place low-income women in training that will help them develop skills to run their own businesses.

"We are so honored," said chapter president Margaret Battle. "But we are also blessed that so many women entering our training program are taking that next important step toward economic independence by opening their own businesses."

In addition to recognizing the chapter's decades-long efforts to reach out to women of Detroit's inner city, the Mayor's Council cited the chapter's most recent efforts to engage the Department of Social Services in cooperative efforts to help women enrolled in training also find affordable housing. *(Continued on page 3)*

Albany President Seeks Corporate Sponsors

Sandra Karlson, president of the Albany chapter, has decided it's time for local businesses to give back. She has approached Gray Office Products Company with an offer to join forces in helping Albany's low-income women stock their offices with supplies they can purchase on credit.

"We know that women in general, but especially women just getting started in business, have trouble getting credit," says Karlson. "But they are also major potential customers for companies like Gray."

J. D. Anderson, president of Gray Company, says he will actively consider Karlson's proposal. "This could be one of those rare win-win propositions that we cannot ignore," he says. Anderson and Karlson will be finalizing the details of the arrangement at a meeting in July.

The Albany chapter boasts three women-owned businesses within a three-block radius of Gray's store. *(Continued on page 6)*

Vol. 6, No. 3. June 2001   *making "women's work" worth it*

EXHIBIT 8.1

Creating a Coherent Visual Identity—Letterhead

Dames, Inc.

Making "women's work" worth it

Dames, Inc.
12 West 33rd Street
Detroit, MI 48095
(616) 496-9987

Fax: (616) 496-9988
E-mail:
dames@dames.org

President
Anna Humdinger

Vice President
Natasha Wagner

Treasurer
Anita Filberti

Board

Jane Allison
Beverly Blondelle
Vanessa Camp Bell
Katherine Koch
S. H. Mettes
Annabelle Robinson
Yvonne Black
Marilyn Wallsmith
D. L. West
Persephone Winfret

Visit our Web site at
www.dames.org

January 12, 2001

Jane Allison
Editor in Chief
Girls' Talk Magazine
33 Broadway
New York, NY 10016

Dear Jane:

Well, I survived the trip to Los Angeles and the visit from the in-laws this Christmas. As luck would have it, Dan got the flu, and the children caught it soon afterwards. For some miraculous reason, I escaped unscathed.

I gather your holidays were not as hectic as mine, and I envy you the peace and quiet of Italy this time of year.

We missed you at the December board meeting, but your assistant did tell me that you had been called away to deal with a major cover crisis for the February issue. I hope all worked out for the best because we need your presence at the next meeting.

We are planning to hold the May meeting in San Antonio at a River Walk hotel as yet to be arranged. You can expect to receive a packet of materials for that meeting sometime in April.

We picked San Antonio because our Dallas chapter president, Johnny Sue Baker, tells me that there is a pressing need for us to put San Antonio on the list of new sites that we will be considering for chapterhood.

As you may recall, we had to table our expansion discussion because we did not have a quorum at the December meeting. (Not your fault!) But please be prepared to dream big at the May meeting. This past year has brought Dames, Inc., so much in the way of growth that it appears we might be able to add more new chapters than originally planned.

Another reason I need you at the May meeting has to do with the election of a successor to Caroline McClain, president of the Chicago chapter. She is planning to retire next month. Because the Chicago chapter is at such a critical crossroads,

EXHIBIT 8.1

Creating a Coherent Visual Identity—Annual Report Cover

Annual Report
2001

You've come a long way, boss.

EXHIBIT 8.1

Creating a Coherent Visual Identity—Business Card

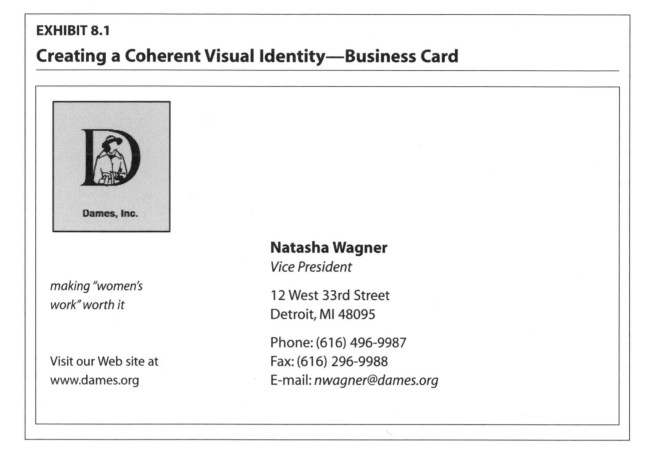

Dames, Inc.

making "women's
work" worth it

Visit our Web site at
www.dames.org

Natasha Wagner
Vice President

12 West 33rd Street
Detroit, MI 48095

Phone: (616) 496-9987
Fax: (616) 296-9988
E-mail: *nwagner@dames.org*

the organization and its mission clearly and is visually appealing, the annual report will be opened. To communicate clearly, the cover needs only a few basic elements: the organization's logo, the title of the report, a catch-phrase to capture the theme, and (if funds permit) some kind of illustration that reinforces the organization's mission and the report's theme. But what if the organization has no funds for photography or illustration, as well as a very tight printing budget? The designer for the fictional American Geography Education Foundation might present four possible cover designs for the association's 2001 annual report, as shown in Exhibit 8.2.

The text found inside the cover must be readable, with heads that clearly demarcate the report's main sections, and with major points emphasized by graphics, color, pull quotes, or other devices that catch the reader's eye. The report's pages should not be so text-heavy that readers decide that reading the report is not worth the investment of their precious time.

"Our advice to clients," says Jim Pizzo, account representative for the design firm Curran and Connors, "is keep it tight. Do not overwrite and edit, edit, edit. The report needs to be as visual and scannable as possible."

One design element that can give the report a more appealing, less dense appearance is white space. And don't forget the photo captions. If, as

EXHIBIT 8.2

Four Sample Cover Designs for an Annual Report

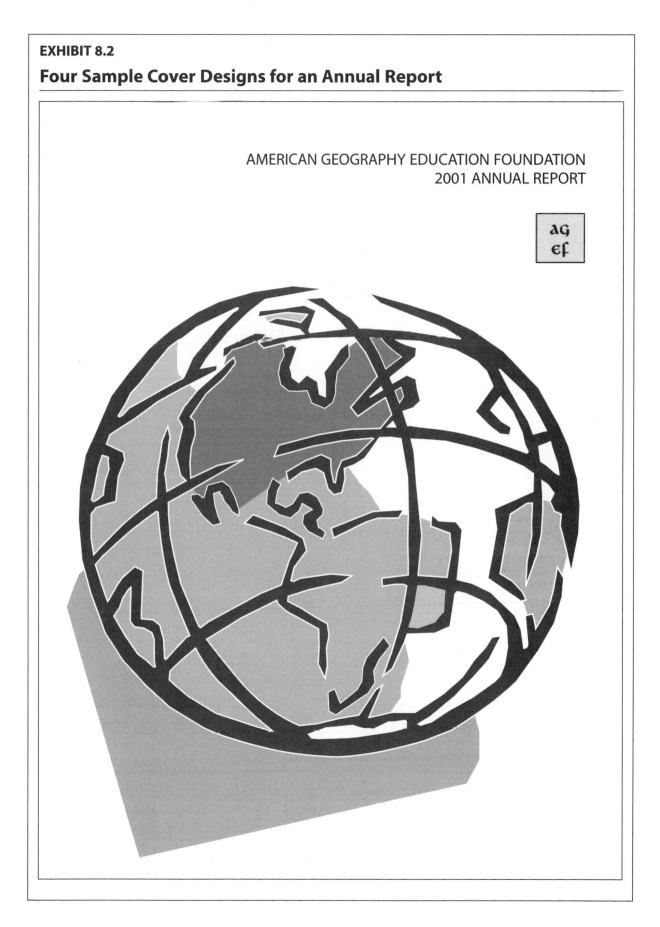

EXHIBIT 8.2

Four Sample Cover Designs for an Annual Report, Cont'd.

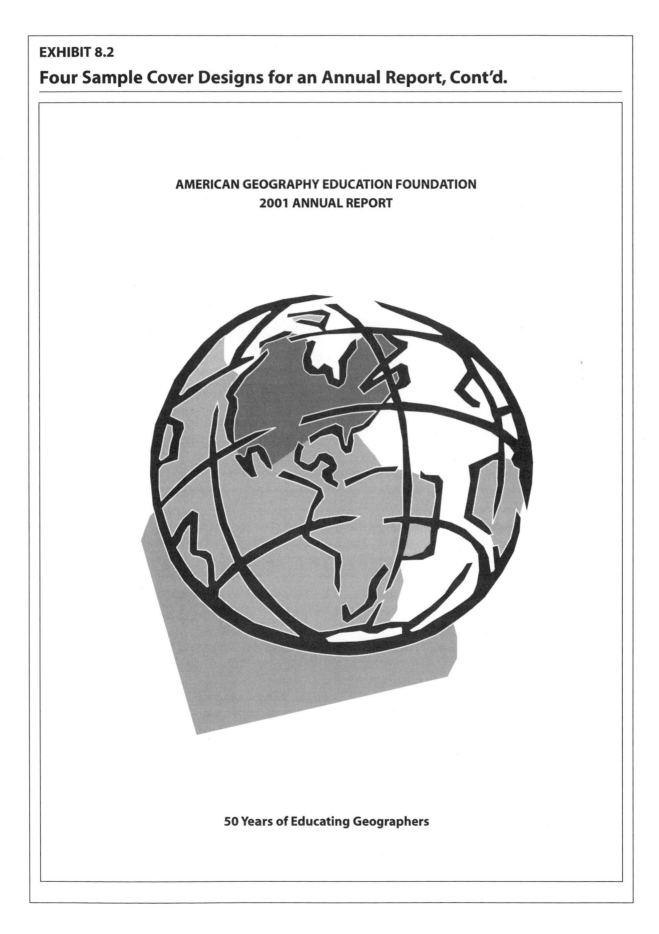

**AMERICAN GEOGRAPHY EDUCATION FOUNDATION
2001 ANNUAL REPORT**

50 Years of Educating Geographers

EXHIBIT 8.2

Four Sample Cover Designs for an Annual Report, Cont'd.

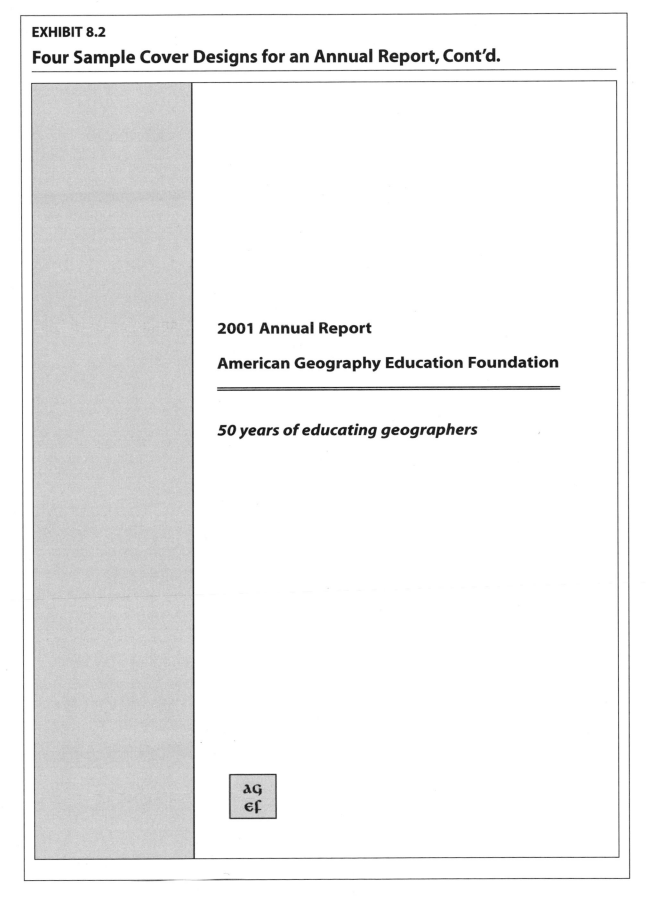

2001 Annual Report

American Geography Education Foundation

50 years of educating geographers

aG
ef

EXHIBIT 8.2

Four Sample Cover Designs for an Annual Report, Cont'd.

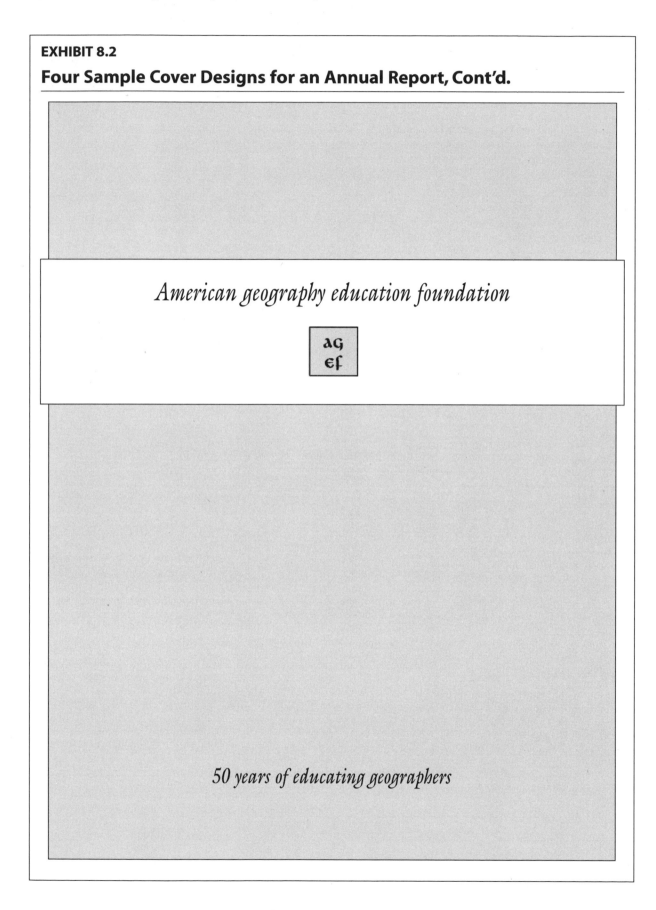

American geography education foundation

50 years of educating geographers

we've seen, photos are the first thing readers look at, then the captions will be the first thing they read. The captions should be informative. They should also emphasize the report's major themes and the organization's successes for those readers who are simply not going to read any farther. The designer for the fictitious Dames, Inc., working under the same budget limitations as those faced by the American Geography Education Foundation, might execute two designs for the inside text of the organization's 2001 annual report (see Exhibit 8.3).

The Client Is (Almost) Always Right

Although interpreting the nonprofit's mission and work to the annual report's audience is clearly the editor's responsibility, the editor must also pay heed to how the design enhances the verbal message. The annual report's design must be approached as a problem in communication that requires the most effective solution. This does not mean that all editors must be graphic designers. But they should cultivate enough design sense—or have enough confidence in the designer's design sense—to know what might look good but does not enhance the message. Experienced designers of annual reports know that the most effective annual reports are those in which the design follows the message. As Marc Meadows of Meadows Design Office points out, "Appearance is derived from content. Style should not suppress promoting the product."

The editor should know—or be able to find out by consulting development staff or by searching through correspondence and e-mails—what the organization's key supporters like and don't like about its publications. The wise editor keeps a "fan mail" file that contains both positive and negative comments about the organization's publications (including its Web site). When it comes to comments on a publication that is mailed to five thousand people, one letter is just as important as an e-mail, a telephone call, or a conversation between the vice president for development and a prospective donor. People who have bothered to share their opinions should be heeded.

The editor's colleagues and superiors in the organization should be heeded as well. Even if what they say seems highly subjective, they, too, know the organization and what it is trying to accomplish. This does not mean that the editor must act on every piece of advice (unless, of course, that advice originates with the CEO). It is necessary only to remember that the designer does not know what the editor knows about the organization and its supporters, just as the editor does not know what the designer knows about graphic design.

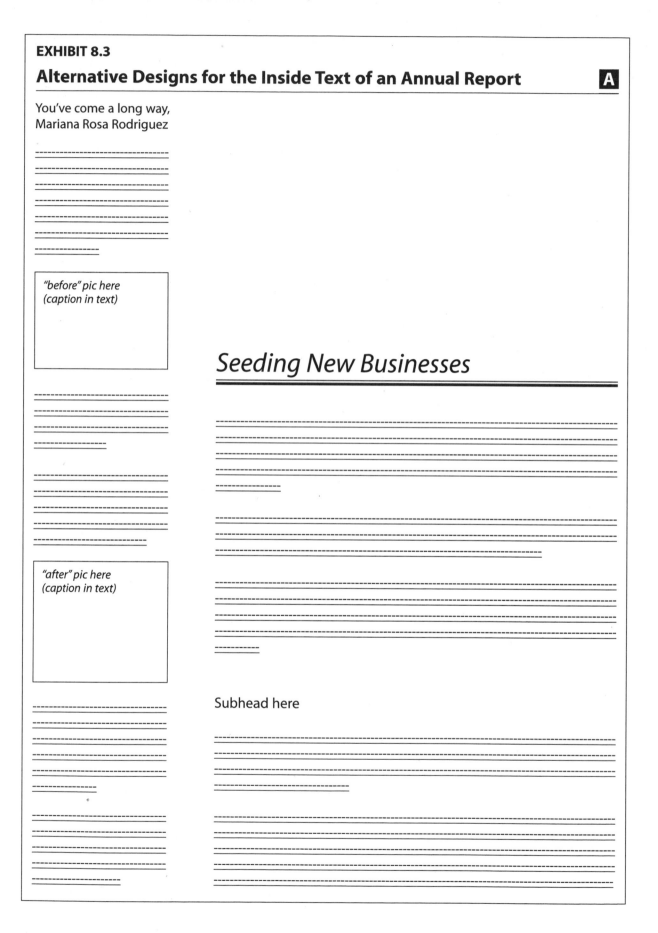

EXHIBIT 8.3

Alternative Designs for the Inside Text of an Annual Report

A

You've come a long way,
Mariana Rosa Rodriguez

*"before" pic here
(caption in text)*

*"after" pic here
(caption in text)*

Seeding New Businesses

Subhead here

EXHIBIT 8.3

Alternative Designs for the Inside Text of an Annual Report A

Participating Banks in Fiscal Year 2000

"Before Mariana opened her salon, I had to ride across town on three different busses. Now, it's a five-minute walk for me."

— Consuelo Martinez, 76

Pic of First National Bank loan officer John Waggoner goes here

Caption to photo goes here....................................
....

EXHIBIT 8.3

Alternative Designs for the Inside Text of an Annual Report   **B**

You've come a long way,
Mariana Rosa Rodriguez

Seeding New Businesses

Pic of Rodriguez here

W————————————————————

Subhead here

Pic of Rodriguez's hair salon here

Caption to photo opposite
goes here.............................

EXHIBIT 8.3

Alternative Designs for the Inside Text of an Annual Report B

Pic of First National Bank loan officer John Waggoner goes here

"Before Mariana opened her salon, I had to ride across town on three different buses. Now, it's a five-minute walk for me."

— Consuelo Martinez, 76

Caption to photo goes here..............................

Participating Banks in Fiscal Year 2001

The designer knowledgeable about annual reports will ask the right questions. Shirley Geer, senior information officer for the Consultative Group on International Agricultural Research, fills out a questionnaire that the designer provides at the beginning of the process. The designer, says Geer, "can be much more helpful to us if we answer these questions: Who is the audience? What is the most important message of the report? What do we want people to take away? How will the report be used? Is it part of a larger strategy? What is the goal? What are we trying to convey?"

"Designers must be responsive to you," says Jennie Ziegler, director of external relations and corporate secretary for the Ethics Resource Center. "You must, in effect, speak the same language, or you will not be able to pull the report together as a harmonious whole." Because choosing the best designer is more than a matter of money or expertise, Ziegler highly recommends outsourcing the design of a product this important.

Insider or Outsider?

At first glance, the staff designer may appear to be the most logical choice for designing the organization's annual report. He or she probably already knows what the take-away message is. Nevertheless, as in the decision about whether to use a staff or freelance writer, there are advantages and disadvantages to having the report designed in house versus engaging an outside designer. Staff designers do know the organization better, but they also may have other claims on their time. If the designer does have time to tackle the annual report, it certainly will be less expensive to have the report designed in house.

But using an outside designer also has its advantages. For one thing, in the words of designer Marc Meadows, "the outside designer brings a totally fresh perspective on the client and its work." Moreover, every institution practices some kind of internal politics and has a pecking order. The outside designer, according to Meadows, "tends to be free of the institutional politics that can really hamper progress," whereas the in-house designer is often a mid-level person whose creative ideas can be overruled by senior managers, content experts, and others who must review and approve the report but very often do not know good design when they see it. As the Urban Institute's Kathleen Courrier points out, "It is difficult to address the concerns of content reviewers who have strong opinions about the report's design but no background in design or publications." Furthermore, although it is simply impossible for any individual designer to satisfy all the different notions of good design held by all the managers involved in producing the annual report, most outside designers routinely work on widely different products and tend to be given more opportunities than staff designers are to expand their portfolios. Finally, nonprofit managers, like other managers, typically subscribe to the adage "When in doubt, bring in a consultant." Therefore, unless the organization's senior managers, especially the CEO, are totally thrilled with the quality and timeliness of in-house design, it is likely that the decision will be made to hire an outside designer for the annual report.

What do corporations do? According to a survey by the National Investor Relations Institute (1999), of the 97 percent of corporations giving clear responses, only 14 percent designed their own annual reports, whereas 64 percent engaged outside firms and the remaining 19 percent used a combination of in-house and outside designers.

How much do corporations pay for design? The National Investor Relations Institute (1999) reports that for a corporate annual report about fifty pages long, on the average, the fee paid for design in 1999 was $64,500, compared to $39,600 in 1996. For many nonprofits, fees in that range would exceed annual gross revenue. The cost of designing the annual report can be lowered significantly if the report is shortened, if use of color is restricted, and if a limit is placed on the number of photographs that are acquired from commercial sources. There is no harm, either, in asking the designer to donate a portion of his or her services to the nonprofit to further the organization's good works.

Choosing a Designer

Choosing the person who will design the annual report, like choosing the writer, is an important decision. It involves budget considerations, time frames, and the designer's ability to listen to the editor's and the organization's particular needs and apply them to the design. The editor's all-important ability to speak the same language as the designer is so crucial to success that it is worthwhile looking at the relationship from the designer's perspective.

What qualities do designers want in the editor of an annual report? According to Jane d'Alelio, president of Ice House Graphics, "The annual report editor should keep to the agreed-upon schedule, have sharp editing skills and flawless visual taste, be fun to work with, have good mediation skills, be understanding and patient, and take the designer to expensive restaurants for lunch at every phase of the project." Neither the editor nor the designer, of course, will have time to lunch at expensive restaurants at every phase, but taking the designer to lunch is not too high a price to pay for a successful outcome.

If an editor is producing the organization's first annual report, or if the editor is not satisfied with the designer who has been used in the past, the tips shown in Exhibit 8.4 may help in locating a truly professional designer who fits the budget and can speak the editor's language.

The process of soliciting proposals for design may become quite technical in the corporate world, where company profits are riding on the outcome, but the checklist developed by Ameritech (Sweet, 1999e), as adapted for nonprofits (see Exhibit 8.5), certainly merits consideration. Keeping these essentials in mind, the editor can overcome any crisis of confidence in the designer

---

EXHIBIT 8.4

How to Find the Right Designer

1. Ask a trusted colleague for names of designers who do good work and who work well with that colleague.

2. Collect well-designed annual reports, and contact the people who designed them.

3. Interview prospective designers and examine their portfolios. (Editors who believe they know good design when they see it can learn a lot by looking at samples of annual reports in a designer's portfolio. Editors who class themselves in the "fear and loathing" category may want to keep one or two samples to show people whose aesthetic judgment they respect.)

4. Ask for a list of references, preferably the names of other nonprofits for which the designer has done annual reports. Ask these references some frank questions:

   • Has Dana Designsmith done more than one annual report for you?

   • How did you find out about her and her work?

   • Did you find her easy to work with, or was getting what you wanted a frustrating battle of wills?

   • Did you think her fees were reasonable? If not, why?

   • Did she pay attention to typography—killing widows, dividing words correctly at the end of a line, not ending a page with a hyphenated word, making sure type sizes of heads and subheads were consistent, and so on?

   • Did she take good care of slides and transparencies, not scratching them, and keeping track of them?

   • Did she know how to check color proofs and have them corrected to your satisfaction?

   • Did she meet her deadlines?

5. Call the printer and ask if there were any problems with the designer's file preparation, whether there were problems at the blueline stage stemming from the designer's errors, and whether the designer conducted a competent press inspection.

by asking the prospective designer to submit samples of his or her work before a hiring decision has been made and by showing these samples to people whose judgments and artistic temperament the editor trusts. The editor can also ask the designer chosen for the annual report to present more than one design concept and can then go over these concepts with the same people.

Most graphic designers worth their salt will base a design on what they think best visually represents the client's product. These decisions will be grounded in objective reality rather than subjective personal likes and dislikes. For example, if the potential donor base is made up of people who consider themselves conservative or traditional, then the report should be designed to appeal to their tastes. The designer who slavishly follows the

---

EXHIBIT 8.5

Checklist for Prospective Design Firms

Please respond to these issues in your proposal:

- The design firm will demonstrate depth of experience in annual reports for a range of clients.

- The design firm will exhibit creativity, initiative, and exceptionally responsive client service.

- The design firm will dedicate its most creative staff, including the principal or partner, to the report. The design firm will have the internal resources to support a report of this scope, will identify who will have primary, end-to-end responsibility for the project, and disclose the number of other design projects that this person will be handling during the time frame for producing this report.

- The design firm will produce the report on Macintosh computers, using Quark XPress software.

- The design firm will maintain off-site backup of the annual report files on magnetic media.

- Quick cycle time and accuracy are important. The design firm will proofread text changes and verify them.

- The design firm will explain how it charges for design, art direction, and production. The design will explain overtime charges, if any, for working after 5 P.M. or on weekends. The design firm will provide price ranges for design, photography, and printing for similar-sized reports it has done in the past.

- During the project, the design firm will provide monthly reports that compare actual expenses with the budget. The design firm will provide a sample of the reporting format it uses.

- The client will not pay agency commissions or markups on outside services. The design firm will review invoices and will bill expenses and subcontracted services direct to the client.

- The design firm will submit three annual reports with design, photography, and printing costs listed for each. The design firm will provide at least three client references and two printer references.

Source: Adapted, with permission, from B. Sweet (ed.), *Ragan's Annual Report Review,* Aug. 1999, p. 2. For further information, call (800) 878-5331.

latest design trends, without regard to the purpose or audience of the annual report, may be headed for the designers' hall of fame, but probably at the expense of the nonprofit organization. A nonprofit should not allow its annual report to be placed at the leading edge of modern graphic design unless the nonprofit is a cutting-edge, avant-garde sort of organization.

The editor and the designer can work magic together. The editor interprets the organization's words to the public, and the designer interprets the organization's image.

"What we really need to hear and learn is senior management's vision for the company," says designer Wendy Pressley-Jacobs. "It's not just a report of what happened last year, but . . . how what happened last year affects the future and the vision of the company" (cited in Sweet, 1999b).

This opinion is shared by Jim Pizzo of Curran and Connors.

"The client for an annual report is often very senior," Pizzo says. "We are dealing with the investor relations officer, chief financial officer, or CEO. They know the organization better than we do, and they know what message needs to get across in the annual report."

The Designer and the CEO

Many designers prefer to work directly with the CEO. It makes sense because it ensures that the CEO's thoughts will not be garbled in transmission. But CEOs are busy people and often do not have time to work one-to-one with the designer. One solution is to make the designer an integral part of the planning. "We can bring efficiencies to the process in terms of time and materials," says designer Marc Meadows.

It is particularly helpful to involve the designer in the planning when the nonprofit has not done an annual report before and is not familiar with the publications process, but it is always helpful to the designer to hear exactly what the CEO wants from the CEO's own lips. Richard Lewis, chairman of Corporate Annual Reports, Inc., believes that it is simply not possible to create an annual report without knowing what the CEO wants, given the CEO's leadership role (cited in Herring, 1990).

The more people the CEO's messages are passed through, the more garbled these messages may and do become. Suppose, for example, that the CEO says, "I want this report to be evocative but corporate." These are abstract terms, and it is quite likely that everyone who hears this pronouncement will have a slightly different idea of what it means. Further discussion may enlighten everyone, or it may simply muddy the waters. One of the editor's responsibilities is to see that the CEO's message has been clarified before it reaches the designer.

It is most helpful if all the key decision makers are involved at the beginning, when the report is planned. "We need to know what message is important to the organization to communicate, and what audience the report is intended to reach," says Jim Pizzo. Nevertheless, it is difficult to schedule a planning session at a time convenient to the many busy managers who are expected to participate in the production of the annual report, and it is often impossible to include the designer in that session. This is why many nonprofits, especially those that have been producing annual reports for a number of years, make the editor responsible for ensuring that the CEO's views are communicated to the designer (the actual design work, of course, is left to the designer). The editor tells the designer what is required and then challenges the designer to come up with a concept that expresses those requirements visually.

Designers who know how to communicate through print may start off with a so-called artistic temperament, but they are well trained. In addition to good communications skills, the designer of a publication as complicated as an annual report should have a four-year fine arts or graphic design degree and, preferably, another four years of studio experience.

According to Marc Meadows, "Not only must designers have mastery of the technology, they must also know how to communicate through design." According to Meadows, technical mastery of desktop publishing programs is the hallmark of a good desktop artist, not a good graphic designer.

Jane d'Alelio of Ice House Graphics agrees. "Designers are trained in layout, typography, illustration, use of photos, and computer skills," she says. "Desktop operators have computer training but not necessarily visual communication skills. For example, a desktop operator may not understand the history and origins of type design. Not having this perspective and depth, the desktop operator can end up selecting ugly, inappropriate typefaces of questionable taste and using them poorly and illegibly on the page."

The technological revolution, with its consolidation of typesetting and design, has put an additional burden on the designer. In the days of waxed galleys and paste-ups, the transition from manuscript pages to typeset galleys and made-up pages and then to an image ready for printing looked something like what is shown in Figure 8.1. The typesetter was concerned solely with producing typeset copy in galleys and then in made-up pages. Because the typesetter often rekeyed the text on computerized typesetting equipment, the typesetter was responsible for proofreading the typeset text against the original manuscript and correcting any errors that had been made. The typesetter was also responsible for correct letter spacing, word spacing, leading, word division, and column alignment.

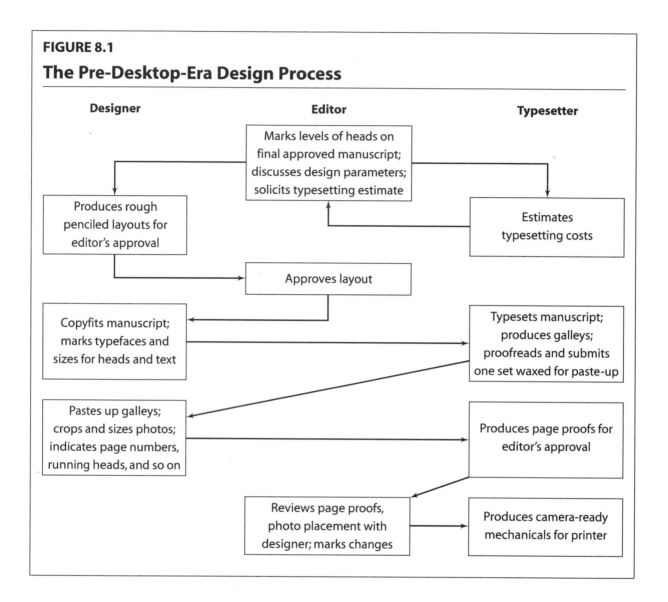

FIGURE 8.1

The Pre-Desktop-Era Design Process

With the advent of sophisticated desktop publishing, however, all these functions, with the exception of proofreading, have devolved on the graphic designer, in a process that, at least in smaller design firms, looks something like what is shown in Figure 8.2.

Getting to Work

Once a designer has been chosen, the actual design process gets under way with a meeting between the editor and the designer. At this meeting, they discuss the report's theme, the particular features to be included (sidebars, pull quotes, maps, and so on), the general printing specifications (estimated

FIGURE 8.2

The Design Process Today

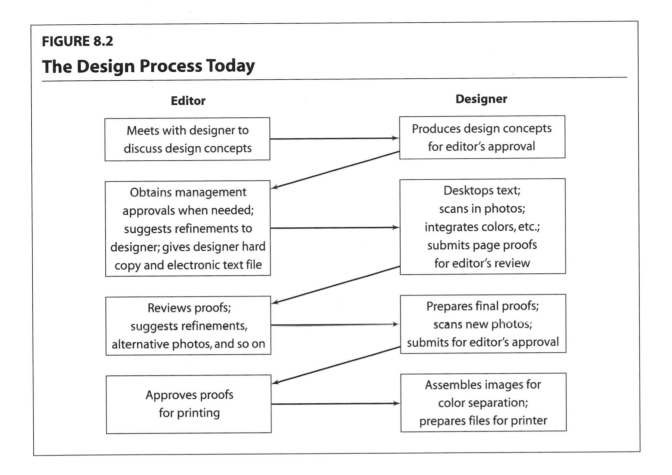

Editor	Designer
Meets with designer to discuss design concepts	Produces design concepts for editor's approval
Obtains management approvals when needed; suggests refinements to designer; gives designer hard copy and electronic text file	Desktops text; scans in photos; integrates colors, etc.; submits page proofs for editor's review
Reviews proofs; suggests refinements, alternative photos, and so on	Prepares final proofs; scans new photos; submits for editor's approval
Approves proofs for printing	Assembles images for color separation; prepares files for printer

print run, overall size of the report, number of pages, type of paper stock, ink colors, and the like), and the number and types of illustrations to be used.

Some editors try to have the text and all photographs and other illustrative matter ready at the same time so that the annual report can be handed to the designer as a package that is complete, more or less. Other editors find that handing over a complete package is "mission impossible." For one thing, the designer may be the one who suggests cover illustrations and color schemes; for another, it is difficult, and perhaps a waste of precious time, to research photographs while the text is still in a state of flux. For example, there may be a last-minute decision to cut the story about the Kosovar refugee who used the women's cooperative seed money to start a bookstore, and the photo of the refugee in front of her bookstore can no longer be used. Instead, the editor must scramble to find before-and-after photographs to illustrate the replacement story about emergency grants to repair a fire-damaged cooperative in Uganda. Nevertheless, this kind of last-minute scramble for the perfect illustration can consume a lot of time and cause headaches, which is why the editor is well advised to begin by giving the designer as much information as possible.

If this is the organization's first annual report, or if it is a completely revamped version of previous reports, then one key item to give the designer is a rough sketch, or "thumbnail" (see the glossary of graphic arts and mailing terms, p. 193), that shows the order in which the editor imagines the material will be presented. Using the synopsis shown in Exhibit 4.5, and assuming a report that will be twenty-four pages long, Figure 8.3 shows how one editor plotted a thumbnail for the designer.

Initial Concepts

When the designer and the editor have worked together for years, and when the general format of the report is well established, there may be no need for the editor to give the designer a thumbnail, and no need for the designer to give managers rough layouts and a full-color preview in the form of "comprehensive dummies," or "comps" (see the glossary of graphic arts and mailing terms, p. 193). Even in these cases, however, the previous year's postmortem (see Chapter Eleven) may have revealed a few design features that can be tweaked for better results this year; for example, perhaps the type was too small, or the layout too cluttered. The editor needs to pay particular attention to the readability of the type at this stage. The annual report must communicate clearly and quickly, and so the type fonts that are used should be simple, without too many font changes. According to Sweet (2000b), "The fewer fonts used in a document, the less chance the design has of distracting or confusing the reader. That is not to say that there might not be a time when liberal use of fonts is appropriate. It is just highly unlikely to occur within an annual report."

Perhaps this year there is a need to spend less money on the report, and so last year's full-color report must "morph" into a two- or one-color job. Unless there have been numerous complaints, however, about the report's being too slick and expensive-looking, care must be taken not to give the report an excessively low-budget appearance. It is important not to create the impression that the organization is incapable of high-quality performance. Or perhaps there have been text changes that call for new design elements—pull quotes, sidebars, testimonials from donors, even miniature maps or other types of symbols—that were not used in previous reports. The editor must make sure that these different elements are used sparingly so that there is no question on any page about where the reader's eye should be drawn first.

FIGURE 8.3

Friends of the Ferret 2001 Annual Report: Thumbnail

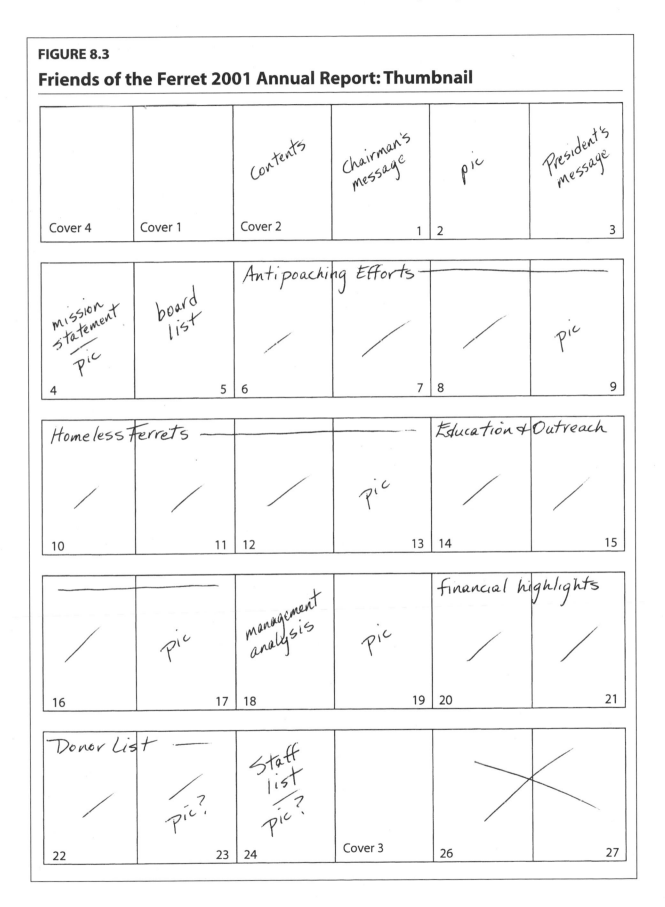

Even if there are no fundamental changes to the report, it will not have the same theme as it did last year. The editor may have some suggestions for visual treatment of the theme, but it is the designer who has the expertise to select the typefaces, layouts, and colors that best represent the new theme.

Fortunately, modern desktop publishing technology has made it possible for the designer to produce layouts that are very close to what the actual printed piece will look like. "Very close" is not quite there, however, and the editor needs to understand that color laser copies or color photocopies are not exact and that photo reproduction will not be as sharp, nor colors as true, as in actual printing. The initial layout sketches and comps are intended to show rough concepts and to give the organization's managers an opportunity to veto color, type, and presentation choices that they don't like. But buyer beware: it is standard in the industry for the designer's fee to cover only one set of initial concepts, and it can become quite expensive—sometimes doubling the cost, if changes are radical—to ask the designer to redesign and then redesign again. That is why it is so important for the editor and the designer to understand each other and work together to arrive at a concept that will involve, at most, only minor changes.

The truly professional designer will explain his or her choices in objective terms, and the editor should respect the designer's views. When in doubt, however, the editor should question a troubling design choice, whether it involves format, type style, type size, or layout (see Table 8.1). The editor's first question should be "Why does this bother me?" The editor's next question is for the designer: "Why did you make this particular choice?" The truly professional designer will also alter a design concept, within reason, to suit the client's wishes. That is why it remains the editor's responsibility to represent the organization's interests by managing the visual presentation of the annual report at the earliest possible conceptual stage.

Once the basic layout has been established, it is still possible to reposition copy, change type sizes and colors, and so on. These changes are usually made at the page proof stage.

Proofs

The designer produces desktop page proofs of the text and the other elements of the report, including maps, photos, tables, graphs, and drawings. If, as is usually the case, there are going to be type corrections to the first set of proofs, to fix inaccuracies and supply text that was not fully approved at the time the report was first handed to the designer, then the proofs should be produced as close to original size of the printed page as

TABLE 8.1

Bothered and Bewildered?

Problem	Ask Yourself	Ask the Designer
Unpleasant colors	Why do I dislike this color? Are readers likely to have the same reaction?	Could you tell me why you chose this particular color?
Type too small	If I'm having trouble reading it, will readers also have the same problem?	Could you tell me why the type is so small?
Type style too fancy or too difficult to read	Does this type style best represent my organization and its work? Would something simpler be easier to read?	Could you tell me why you chose this particular type style?
Type overprinting a photograph difficult to read	Are readers likely to skip this because they can't read it easily?	Could you tell me why the type overprints the photograph? Can you make it more readable?
Distracting shadow graphics behind the text	Do these visuals invite readers to read or discourage them from reading?	Are the shadow graphics necessary? Or would they never be missed?
No space for photo captions	Will readers want to know what the photo is about, or does it speak for itself without a caption?	How difficult would it be for us to put photo captions where needed?
Captions too far away from photos	Will readers find the caption where it is now located?	Could you place the captions closer to the photographs they identify?
Hard-to-read type reversing out of a light color or a screen	What makes this type hard to read? Will readers skip over it?	Does there need to be more contrast to make the type readable, or should the type not reverse?
Layout looks cluttered	Are there too many elements—photos, graphics, text blocks, heads—on the page? Is the page too busy?	How could we simplify this layout and make it more coherent to readers?
Too many typographical distractions—big type, small type, sink initials, shadow initials, bold, bold italics	Does this entice readers by focusing their eyes on critical elements, or does it distract their attention?	How could we simplify the typography and make the text more inviting?

possible, and in black and white. (Color desktop proofs are more expensive and time-consuming to produce, but they are advantageous at subsequent proof stages, after most type corrections have been made.)

When marking proofs, the editor can use two different colors to indicate author's alterations (those text changes that will be paid for by the nonprofit because they are not the designer's mistakes) and what are called "printer's errors" (changes made to correct the designer's or typographer's mistakes). Most designers of annual reports charge an hourly rate for corrections and do not separate author's alterations from printer's errors. If the overwhelming majority of the corrections will be made to rectify printer's errors, however, then the editor should call this to the designer's attention and ask for the designer to assume the cost.

With color proofs, the editor can check the use of color blocks and screens. The editor can also check heads for readability, contrast against a colored or screened background, and color consistency and make sure that the colors used for graphs and maps are appropriate. For example, the designer may have rendered a map with land masses in purple and oceans in green, whereas it would make more sense to render land masses in green and oceans in purple, or the financial pie charts may look like candy wafers because the colors chosen for them are too vivid. In this case, the solution may be to change the colors altogether or to add some black to tone them down.

The editor also reviews the page proofs to be sure that photos are cropped and scaled (sized) for maximum effectiveness. Where the designer has exercised aesthetic judgment in cropping and scaling a photograph, the editor must exercise editorial judgment. For example, the designer probably knows that it would be inappropriate to eliminate someone's arms or legs from a photo, but the editor knows that the only available photo of Ms. Fiscal, the vice president for finance, should definitely be cropped at the waist because it was taken at last year's staff picnic and shows Ms. Fiscal in short shorts. Is this dishonesty? No, it's diplomacy. A photo of Ms. Fiscal wearing shorts would tend to suggest that she and, by extension, the organization that employs her are not serious. Naturally, the editor faced with this problem will also make a note to see whether, budget permitting, a more businesslike photo of Ms. Fiscal can be commissioned for next year's report. The editor who has not worked before with a designer may find it helpful to consult the list of design "no-no's" shown in Exhibit 8.6.

After all of the issues that concern layout and design have been settled, the designer and the editor should work together to integrate the annual report's final visual element: the illustrations.

EXHIBIT 8.6

Design No-No's

- A type style that is inappropriate to the medium (and the message)
- Type that is too small to read (especially for age-challenged eyes)
- Type that is difficult to read because of overprinting a contrasting background like a photograph or a ghosted drawing
- Too-small type reversed out of a dark or light background
- A line of text longer than the length of one and one-half alphabets
- Red ink in the financial statements
- Poorly laid-out photos
- Poorly cropped or scaled photos
- Headline type that looks like this:
  A
  N
  N
  U
  A
  L
- Headline type that looks like this:
  A
    N
      N
        U
          A
            L

- Red that looks pink when screened
- Photos so small that the subjects can't be identified
- Elements that form an L shape when arranged on the page
- Yearbook-style arrangement of mug shot photos of board members or staff
- Too many different type styles and sizes
- Inconsistent use of the design grid from one page to another or one section to another
- Inconsistent size and style of heads and subheads
- Failure to use word division to even up line lengths in unjustified copy
- Too many hyphens in a row at the end of a column of text

Chapter 9

Illustrations and Graphics

IN AN IDEAL WORLD, the editor of an annual report would give all the illustrations (whether drawings, paintings, or photographs) to the designer at the same time as the manuscript. The designer could then work out which photos or illustrations should go on which pages, and how much space is available for them. As we've seen, however, finding appropriate illustrations can take a lot of time, and very often the editor does not know which illustrations will be used until the manuscript is in nearly final shape—that is, until it is far enough along in the review process for wholesale story substitutions to be unlikely.

In the real world, the collection of illustrations tends to begin late enough in the process to make the designer's and the editor's lives much more complicated. At this late stage, it is tempting to wonder whether it might be possible to print the annual report without any illustrations at all.

That temptation should be resisted. There is simply no better way to represent the organization's work and mission than through illustrations. As we saw in Chapter Three, people who read annual reports think that photos make the reports more interesting. This is not to say that photos are the only way to illustrate an annual report. In some cases, photos simply don't work, or the budget is too small to allow for photos. In others, the organization's work is too abstract or difficult to illustrate through photography. Moreover, even if an organization has abundant photos of refugee camps, impoverished inner-city ghettoes, or starving children and adults, such negative images can do more harm than good, by creating the impression that the organization is not achieving its desired results. Evidence abounds, of course, that the Four Horsemen of the Apocalypse still stalk the Earth. The poor may always be with us, and there will never be an end to the devastation caused by natural disasters. Nevertheless, nonprofits established to ameliorate suffering must do everything possible to show the positive side of their work in their annual reports.

The Ethics Resource Center uses graphics and pull quotes. The pull quotes in the organization's 1998 annual report accomplish in words what pictures cannot, as illustrated by this quote from Ira A. Lipman, president and chief executive officer of Guardsmark, Inc.:

> *Each year, Guardsmark's 14,000 employees participate in updating our Code of Ethics, first adopted in 1980. This bottom-up process, incorporating input from employees at all levels, makes our code a living document. We believe that the world and the country would be better places for mankind with ethics programs in all organizations and businesses. We look to the Ethics Resource Center Fellows Program to encourage that development [Ethics Resource Center, 1998, p. 4].*

Finding high-quality photos also poses problems for Nancy Kelly, communications and outreach officer for the Asia Foundation. "We can spend quite a lot on stock photos," she says, "but we would rather have photos from the field. Yet among our fourteen offices throughout Asia where we work, there is an uneven quality to staff photos." The Asia Foundation has even hired photographers and sent them to Asia, but it was costly.

"I think our photos could be better," says Bill Warren, senior writer for the National Trust for Historic Preservation. He used stock photos for the cover of his organization's 1998 annual report (see Exhibit 7.7 in Chapter Seven). The smaller photos came from the organization's photo archives, which, Warren notes, are in need of updating: "Our report could be greatly improved if we hired a photographer to shoot the historic properties and other program activities."

Photo Research

Many mid- to large-sized nonprofits maintain some sort of photo library or archive of photos of key staff, conferences, activities, and fieldwork. Although these may be excellent images from the editorial standpoint, they may not be of the best technical quality, in terms of focus, lighting, composition, or contrast, because they may have been taken by staff or nonprofessionals. But archival photos should never be overlooked: some amateur photographers are quite good, and the organization's archives may be the only repository of images that are directly related to specific aspects of its work.

Budget permitting, however, the editor may choose to go beyond the archives, in search of the ideal cover photo and other illustrative material that is not available internally. Within existing budget constraints, photos can be found to illustrate all but the most challenging subject matter. This photo research should begin the moment the report's theme has been established, and it should continue until all the necessary photos and illustrations have been acquired.

Where to look for photos? There are various sources, which are described, from least to most expensive, in the following sections.

Staff Members and Volunteers

The chance to have their photos appear in an annual report is an incentive to many amateur photographers. With automatic-focus cameras, staff members and volunteers can take decent photographs of the organization's staff at work or of people the organization is helping.

It helps to give some guidance in advance. Ask the photographer to write down the names of all the people in a photograph, to name the place where the photograph was taken, and to identify any objects or animals or plants in the photograph. This kind of detail may seem a bit burdensome, but a photograph can't really be used if that information is missing. In exchange for the time and effort they've put into collecting this information, the editor can offer to reimburse staff members or volunteers for the cost of the film and its processing.

Clip Art

In its native form, straight out of a catalog or off a disk, clip art may be tasteless. Nevertheless, it can be artfully reconfigured by a clever designer, or it can be used in such a way that it resembles commissioned artwork.

The Internet

Corbis, Picturequest, and other stock-photo Web sites sell royalty-free images that can be used in a number of ways, with some restrictions. For example, visitors to Picturequest.com can purchase a CD with a single image or with multiple images, for prices ranging from $68 to $499 each, and single images go for $20 to $220 each. PhotoDisc.com offers Web visitors ninety thousand downloadable, royalty-free images from well-known photographers.

Nevertheless, because many digital images are not available at a high enough resolution for clean, sharp print reproduction, it's crucial to check with the designer to find out the lowest possible resolution that can be used for high-quality print reproduction. Printers, especially sophisticated printers of annual reports, prefer transparencies or slides.

But the Internet is definitely a good place to conduct photo research. Simply conducting a keyword search can often lead the researcher to a Web site where adequate images can be obtained at low cost. Like the commercial stock-photo agencies, many professional photographers also have their own Web sites.

Public Archives

Public archives, too, have Web sites. The Library of Congress, the Folger Shakespeare Library, the Smithsonian museums, the National Gallery of Art, the National Portrait Gallery, the National Archives, and other public institutions often permit the photos in their archives to be used in publications. The quality of such photos varies, from professional to amateur, and there is usually a nominal fee involved for one-time use. There is an even stiffer fee if the image is lost.

Private Institutions

Embassies, tour and travel agencies, private museums, cultural organizations, and even other nonprofits may be willing to lend the images in their archives, or allow their use for a fee.

Stock-Photo Houses

The myriad commercial stock-photo houses publish catalogs, both in hard copy and on the Web, that show the kinds of images that can be purchased for one-time use. These images are usually of high quality and are taken by professional photographers. The fee will depend on the size and location of the photo in the annual report and on the number of copies that are printed.

Commissioned Illustration or Photography

The most expensive and time-consuming way to obtain illustrations is to hire a professional to create them. Corporations do this frequently, but nonprofits seldom have the funds. Nevertheless, commissioning artwork may be the only recourse if the subject matter is difficult or abstract.

In commissioning either illustrations or photography, it is essential to spell out the conditions of copyright (such as outright ownership versus ownership for certain purposes only) that will affect the cost of the commissioned work. If a nonprofit wants to own a photo or an illustration, which can then be used as the organization wishes, the cost will be much higher than if the organization purchases rights to use the photo or illustration only in certain publications, and only for certain specified purposes.

Working with a Photographer

Let's assume that the budget has no limits, and that a photographer will be employed to photograph the CEO of Friends of the Ferret at one of the homeless-ferret shelters. The editor (and the graphic designer, if one is available) must "art direct" the photo shoot to be sure that the photograph is editorially appropriate for use in the report. First, however, the editor must be sure that the photographer is as well prepared as possible. The editor who is hiring a photographer should be prepared to specify what is wanted by answering the questions in Exhibit 9.1.

Sometimes the photographer will have to shoot without much direction—for example, if the editor, by interviewing the person to be photographed, becomes part of the action. But usually it works better if the editor can guide the photographer to those subjects that should be photographed, especially in a group situation like a reception or conference. The editor should also be aware of the background: the CEO holding a homeless ferret against a background that shows nuclear cooling towers, for example, would not be appropriate, and the photographer should be directed to locate the subject against a less distracting background.

The editor in the role of art director should also be specific about the comfort level of the people being photographed. Ask these questions:

- Is the photographer expected to stay out of the action and take his or her shots at a distance, using a zoom lens? (Many photographers say that the closer the camera can get to the subject, the greater the chances of getting a high-quality image.)

EXHIBIT 9.1

What the Photographer Needs to Know

- Will the photo shoot take all day or only half a day? (Most photographers charge by the whole or half-day, plus film and processing.)
- Black and white or color film? If color, do you want prints, slides, or 4-by-5-inch transparencies?
- Will the photo shoot take place indoors or outdoors?
- What subjects will the photographer be photographing? People or buildings or landscapes or objects?
- Should the shots to be posed or candid?
- How much equipment can the photo subjects tolerate? (Some CEOs dislike a lot of equipment and lighting cluttering up the landscape or disturbing their offices, but if the shot is indoors, lights will most likely be needed.)
- Close-up or distance shots, or a mix of the two? (The photographer needs to know what lenses to bring.)

- May the photographer get in close and converse with the subjects so as to catch the life in their eyes or the action of their hands? (This approach often yields photos with sparkle and vitality.)

- Is it permissible to move furniture around to get the best setting? (If moving furniture irritates the person being photographed, that irritation is likely to show.)

If the shot is indoors and requires lights to be set up, the editor should stand in for the person being photographed while the setup is going on. Making the principal sit through often time-consuming preliminary adjustments is a waste of that person's time (Hurley, 1977, p. 167). Indeed, it is advisable to ask the photographer how much time it will take to set up the shot. Then the schedule can include time for the setup, to be followed by the actual photo shoot.

When objects or buildings are to be photographed, the desired outcome has to be clear. Should the photographer capture the whole building, just the architectural details, or a mix of both? With buildings or landscapes, should the photographer aim for vertical shots, horizontal shots, or a mix of both? When photographing an object, should the photographer frame it against a background, isolate it, or both? The editor should also be specific about what is not wanted. If posed shots—the speaker standing at a lectern with a microphone in front of his face, or a succession of "mug shots"—are not wanted, it's important to say so.

The editor, the photographer, or someone else on the scene should make sure that every object, person, and animal in the camera's frame has been carefully identified when the photo shoot is over, and that permission has been sought from the parents of any minors who have been photographed (this permission will be followed up with a written release that parents should sign). The editor should also be sure to give the photographer a deadline for delivering contact sheets, prints, slides, transparencies, or whatever other medium was requested at the outset. The photographer should be asked to mark or somehow identify the best-quality images; that way, the editor won't have to pore over a hundred or more images, looking for the best shot. The editor may not agree with the photographer about what the best image is, but it helps to start with the preferred shots first.

Commissioning photography and art may be the most expensive way to illustrate the nonprofit annual report, but acceptable results are more likely with this option than with any other—*if* the photographer clearly understands what is being sought. This is why it is wise to err on the side of too much art direction. Nothing would be more wasteful of the editor's time, and perhaps even board members' or the CEO's, than to have to reschedule a photo shoot because the photographer didn't "get it."

Because time is a precious commodity in the annual report's production cycle, it is wise to commission photography as early as possible in the process. Then, if the camera malfunctions or the lights fail, the photographer can be given a chance to reshoot—time permitting, of course.

But suppose the shoot comes off without a hitch and that the photographs that were commissioned are excellent. The images need to be tracked because they will pass through many hands before they are ready to be returned to the source that provided them (see Figure 9.1). If a system for tracking images through the process is already in place, then it's time to begin matching photos to the stories in the annual report. If no image-tracking system has been established, however, the organization may wind up having to pay hundreds or even thousands of dollars for lost or damaged images. Table 9.1 shows what a simple image-tracking system might look like.

In addition to keeping a record of image sources, the annual report's editor keeps a record of where each image appears in the annual report, and of the date when each image was sent from one key player to another. The

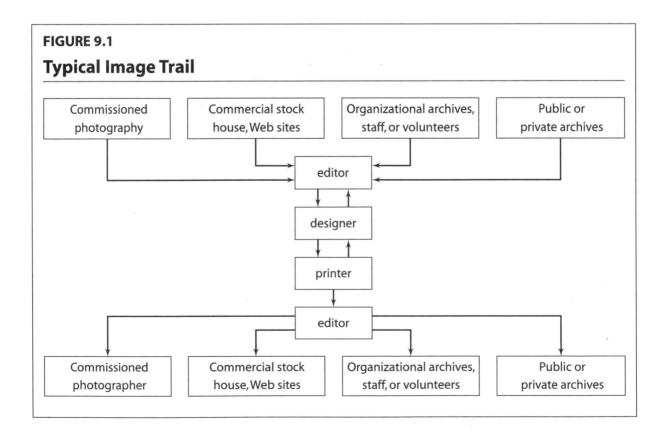

FIGURE 9.1

Typical Image Trail

TABLE 9.1

Dames, Inc., 2000 Annual Report Images

Image	Received from	To Designer	To Printer	To Dames	Returned to
Cover: Detroit shops in a row	Minden Stock 4/3	7/1 rejected			7/5 Minden
Cover: Chicago Pro Temps, Inc.	Pro Temps 7/30	7/31	9/5	10/30	11/3 Pro Temps
p. 2 CEO photo	Archives 5/2	7/1	9/5	10/30	10/31 Archives
Review Ops, p. 4: classroom scene/ Dallas	John Finch[a] 4/3	7/1	9/5	10/30	10/31 Archives
p. 6: Mrs. Page/ Omaha	John Finch[a] 4/3	7/1	9/5	10/30	10/31 Archives
p. 8: Joyce's Cut 'n' Curl/Chicago	Cut 'n' Curl	7/1	rejected 9/15 (scratch)		9/30 Cut 'n' Curl
p. 8: Joyce's Cut 'n' Curl/Chicago	Joyce Joyner	9/17	9/17	10/30	11/3 Joyner
p. 12: woman w/briefcase and child/Albany	Minden Stock 4/3	7/1	9/17	10/30	11/3 Minden

[a]Commissioned photography.

editor also keeps copies of the slide labels that identify subjects and photographers. In the case of prints, the editor records information about subjects and photographers so that this information is ready to hand when it is time to write captions and photo credits.

Making the Photo Communicate

When working with photos that already exist (that is, photos that were taken for some other purpose than to illustrate the annual report), the editor must exercise both judgment and imagination. Pictures have a more immediate impact than text, so every picture must count. Yet very often the pages of nonprofit annual reports are dotted with small pictures that seem to have been included simply to fill space not taken up by text. The editor who tends to place a higher value on words is well advised to remember that readers look for illustrations first. Therefore, the editor has to be brutal, cutting text, if necessary, to allow the illustrations to play their crucial role.

A few small pictures may have to be included because the CEO has insisted that there be a photo of a particular all-important meeting. Chances are that most of the available pictures of that meeting will show the backs of people's heads and a table cluttered with papers and half-empty coffee cups. Pictures like these do not communicate, even if their captions do list everyone in attendance. The challenge is to make pictures of this kind speak volumes, by suggesting that the photos be artfully cropped and scaled to show the intensity of concentration on one participant's face or to reveal a heated negotiation between two participants. Perhaps another such photo can show a flip chart or an overhead projection of a graphic or talking points that tell what the meeting is about.

Why isn't this a job for the designer? The answer is that the editor is the one who must respond to the CEO's directive to put boring but politically necessary pictures into the report. The designer who is given such pictures is likely to request either that they not be used or that better versions of them be found. For example, when designer Marc Meadows looks at an image, he wants to know "whether the resolution is adequate for the scale of the final image size, or whether deep shadow areas or other dark portions of the photo might suffer from dot gain on the paper stock that has been specified. I also look for sharp focus and color contrast." In other words, he is looking for the best images, in terms of their aesthetic and reproductive qualities. But the editor may not have a better-quality image of the particular event that must be illustrated in the annual report. The editor and the designer must work with the materials at hand, and working with the materials at hand means looking carefully at all possible options, to find the one possibility that will communicate something interesting. It does not mean simply settling for the standard all-inclusive shot of everyone who attended the meeting. Readers looking at small, static pictures will not find them compelling and are very likely to conclude that the pictures are small because the organization didn't find them compelling, either. Big is better because big is bolder.

But big merely for the sake of big can also be counterproductive. For example, suppose the designer's layout for the introduction to each major section of the report allows for a large photo that covers one full page and extends part of the way onto the facing page. In this case, the technical quality of the photograph has to be good enough for the photo to be scaled up to that size, but the picture itself also must *require* that amount of space to tell its story (see Exhibit 9.2). It must be a picture that cannot be cropped to focus the reader's eye on one small element. It must not be a picture in which one small focal element is lost in a vast landscape—unless that is precisely the point that the picture is supposed to make.

The trick is to develop a trained eye, which takes some practice. But at some point, and with a little help from the designer, the editor can judge which photos work better small and which work better big. To keep things interesting, the editor will use a mix of big and small, always keeping in mind that the smallest photo should be large enough to be understood at a glance (Hurley, 1977, p. 31). After selecting all the photos that may be useful, and that must be used for internal political reasons, the editor should ask the designer to pick those of high quality that are visually the most compelling and place them where they look best in the overall design scheme.

Enlisting the Designer

"It's really better to have the designer be a part of the photo selection process," says Marc Meadows. "Reproductive quality is a serious issue. Sometimes that ideal image simply can't be enlarged or reproduced without looking grainy."

This is particularly true of digital images, many of which are not at a high enough resolution to reproduce well in a high-quality four-color publication. According to Meadows, "To achieve high-quality printing of a four-color annual report, digital images must be at least 300 dpi [dots per inch], in the final size that will be reproduced, and in either TIFF or EPS file format."

In the ideal team arrangement, the designer worries about technical considerations and the editor exercises judgment about the image's editorial appropriateness, an issue that includes its location in the publication. If the designer has placed a photograph of monkeys or baboons on the page that lists a conservation organization's board of directors, the editor sees to it that the photo is replaced with one less likely to provoke snickers. Likewise, if the annual report is issued by a cultural or historical organization, a photo of Machiavelli or Mao opposite the page containing the CEO's executive message may be visually stunning but editorially inappropriate in that it may invite unkind comparisons.

If the nonprofit works with people in any way, it is best to try to include photos of those people in the annual report. There should be an effort to find positive images of these people in the places where they work and live, images suggesting that the people are benefiting from the organization's outreach. Every attempt should be made to include the full range of people served, in terms of age, sex, race, income, and education level (see Exhibit 9.3). If the nonprofit saves animals, there should be photos of a wide range of representative species in the report.

EXHIBIT 9.2

Two-Page Spread, World Wildlife Fund 1996 Annual Report

Source: *World Wildlife Fund 1996 Annual Report.* Photograph © Kevin Schafer. Reprinted by permission.

World Wildlife Fund gratefully acknowledges the support provided by the donors listed on the pages that follow for our conservation efforts in fiscal year 1996. By choosing to contribute significant resources to WWF, these individuals, foundations, and corporations are leading the fight to save life on Earth. As Partners in Conservation, they are key to WWF's ability to conduct and expand conservation activities in Africa, Asia, and the Americas. Partners provide funds for far-reaching programs, such as WWF's worldwide forest conservation campaign, "Forests for Life," which seeks to protect these vital harbors of biological diversity for generations to come. Partners also give emergency assistance to protect highly endangered species like tigers, rhinos, and pandas. Perhaps most important, Partners are a dependable source of ongoing support that ensures our capacity to protect wildlife and wildlands whenever and wherever they are threatened.

Emperor penguins *(Aptenodytes forsteri)* breed in colonies of hundreds or thousands. Well-adapted to Antarctica's frigid temperatures, their feathers remain undisturbed even in winds approaching 40 miles per hour. (Kevin Schafer)

EXHIBIT 9.3

Page, Girl Scouts of the USA 1999 Annual Report

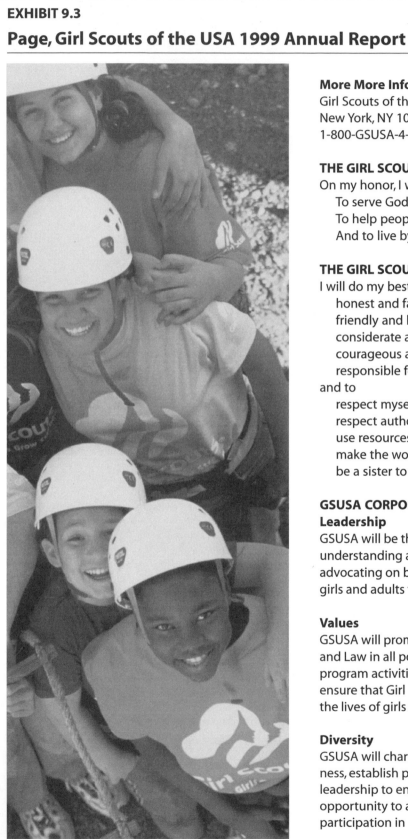

More More Information:
Girl Scouts of the USA, 420 Fifth Avenue
New York, NY 10018-2798
1-800-GSUSA-4-U / www.girlscouts.org

THE GIRL SCOUT PROMISE
On my honor, I will try:
    To serve God and my country,
    To help people at all times,
    And to live by the Girl Scout Law.

THE GIRL SCOUT LAW
I will do my best to be
    honest and fair,
    friendly and helpful,
    considerate and caring,
    courageous and strong, and
    responsible for what I say and do,
and to
    respect myself and others,
    respect authority,
    use resources wisely,
    make the world a better place, and
    be a sister to every Girl Scout.

GSUSA CORPORATE GOALS FOR 1997–2002
Leadership
GSUSA will be the recognized authority in
understanding and addressing the needs of girls,
advocating on behalf of girls, and preparing
girls and adults for leaderhip roles.

Values
GSUSA will promote the Girl Scout Promise
and Law in all policies, practices, partnerships,
program activities, and communications to
ensure that Girl Scouting positively impacts
the lives of girls and society as a whole.

Diversity
GSUSA will chart innovative paths for inclusive-
ness, establish partnerships, and attract diverse
leadership to ensure that every girl has the
opportunity to achieve her full potential through
participation in Girl Scouting.

Source: *Girls Scouts of the USA 1999 Annual Report.* Reprinted by permission.

At World Wildlife Fund, we were careful to include photos of the charismatic megafauna (giant pandas, tigers, elephants, gorillas) as well as of wild species that people may not imagine when they think of wildlife (spiders, orchids, frogs, warblers, even snakes and lizards; see Exhibit 9.4). In the corporate world, especially when it comes to the cover, putting the product in the report is an absolute must. In the nonprofit world, putting the product in the report means ferrets, for Friends of the Ferret; scouts, for the Boy Scouts of America; and historic buildings, for the National Trust for Historic Preservation.

Any showroom designer can explain that how a product is displayed counts as much as the product itself. The Boy Scouts of America and Girls, Inc., select or commission photos of healthy young people who are smiling and who make direct eye contact with the reader. Imagine how diluted the impact would be if the photos showed scouts or young girls looking off to the side or not smiling. When it comes to historic buildings, readers need to see the whole building, or at least the portion of it that evokes its history. There must be no question in readers' minds that the building is old and, even better, so distinctive or beautiful that it must be preserved.

A duck may not need to be looking directly at the reader, because ducks are often more colorful when viewed in profile. For many animals, however, a photo has much greater impact if the animal appears to be looking at the reader. The reader should be able to see the "catch light" of the photographer's flash reflected in the animal's eye; otherwise, the animal may end up looking like a stuffed toy. If the organization's mission is to protect wildlife, then animals must appear to be in the wild, with no zoo fencing or electrical power lines or well-kept pathways or concrete walls to reveal to the careful eye that the animals were photographed in captivity (even though that is most often the case, especially with rare and endangered species). And, just as a picture of a suffering child would not be placed on the cover of an annual report for an organization that helps children, the editor would not select a photo of a suffering animal for the cover of a report for an organization that protects animals. In fact, it is advisable not to include any photos of animals snarling at the camera, dining on prey, or busily engaged in procreation.

Pictures of miserable refugees or orphans of war, or shots of people slaughtering whales, or photos of animals caught in traps do speak more than a thousand words about the organization's mission to alleviate suffering—but they should not appear in the annual report. The annual report, after all, is essentially a success story, and readers should not be encouraged to think even for a moment that the organization is losing the battle, regardless of the astronomical odds. Readers should have an instant impression that the organization is achieving results and spending donors' money prudently.

EXHIBIT 9.4

Page with "Product" Photo, World Wildlife Fund 1997 Annual Report

Madagascar's panther chameleon *(Chamaeleo pardalis)* lives in the humid jungles of Madagascar's moist forests, a Global 200 ecoregion. More species of chameleon are found in Madagascar than anywhere else on Earth. (Kevin Schafer)

Source: *World Wildlife Fund 1997 Annual Report*. Photograph © KevinSchafer. Reprinted by permission.

Of course, readers will also have an opportunity to examine the financial statements carefully, and that is why graphics are often used to draw readers' attention to key financial data.

Making Graphics Work

Most investors are quite adept at reading the financial statements in an annual report, but poring over figures is only part of understanding the fiscal side of things. Very often there is a story behind the numbers, a story best told through some kind of graphic that synthesizes the information and presents it in such a way that the reader gets the point instantly.

According to designer Marc Meadows, "Graphics can help the organization present key information in an attention-grabbing way that is simply not possible with a table." Suppose, for example, that Friends of the Ferret wants to show readers a phenomenal growth in membership in the four years since the organization was founded: there were 1,800 members in 1997, 2,300 in 1998, 3,200 in 1999, and 4,800 in 2000. The typical annual report compares the current year's earnings to those of the previous year, and so a comparison of the membership revenues for 1999 and 2000 could be presented as in Table 9.2.

Readers can see from the table that revenues from individual members increased by $13,909, but growth in the actual number of members is shown much more clearly and dramatically in Figure 9.2. The data merely support the CEO's claim that membership has increased, but they do so much more clearly than a table does. Readers can now see at a glance that membership was slightly over 3,000 in 1999 and is hovering near 5,000 in 2000. Of course, the executive message will mention the "phenomenal 50 percent increase in membership since 1999." Even more dramatic, however, would be a graph title that states the main point: "Membership Has Grown 50 Percent in One Year." Indeed, chart expert Gene Zelazny (1996) believes that the desired message should determine any chart that is used, and that this message should be made the chart's title.

TABLE 9.2

Friends of the Ferret Statement of Activities

Revenue	2000	1999
Foundations	$ 68,904	$ 56,738
Individual members	76,498	62,589
In-kind donations	9,748	8,629
Total revenue	$ 155,150	$ 127,956

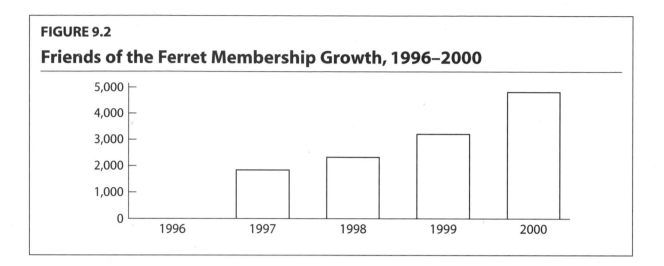

FIGURE 9.2

Friends of the Ferret Membership Growth, 1996–2000

In its 1998 annual report, the International Fund for Animal Welfare placed two bar charts—one showing growth in income and the other showing growth in supporters from 1994 to 1998—side by side on the same page. Not only could readers see at a glance how closely growth in membership was linked to growth in revenue, they could also see that this growth had been steady over the four-year period (see Exhibit 9.5).

The primary function of graphics is to reveal data. A well-conceived graphic also invites readers to consider the facts rather than their presentation. It does not distort the data or present them in a confusing manner; it is integrated with statistical or verbal descriptions, and it encourages readers to draw inferences and make comparisons (Tufte, 1983).

The challenge for the editor is to work with the designer to ensure that graphics are not cluttered up with decorative elements that may look interesting but actually detract from a graphic's central message. When a staff desktop operator with little design experience does the design preparation of graphics, the editor may need to don the art director's hat again. Today's software-based "chart wizards" and other aids may be relatively simple to use, but the results may be difficult to understand. For example, if a graphic has many different elements but there is only one color to work with, the desktop operator may be tempted to use hash marks, crosshatching, and fine lines to differentiate one part of the graphic from another. But graphics like these may produce optical effects that are literally hard on the eyes, as shown in Figure 9.3.

When only one color is available, the graphic should be kept as simple as possible (see Figure 9.4). Note also how the graph achieves greater impact with a change in title.

EXHIBIT 9.5

Graphics Showing Income and Membership Growth, International Fund for Animal Welfare 1998 Annual Report

For the Year Ended June 30, 1998   US Dollars (in thousands)

BALANCE SHEET

ASSETS

Cash and equivalents	$ 23,700
Prepaid expenses and other current assets	2,209
Fixed assets, net	2,516
Total assets	$ 28,425

LIABILITIES

Accounts payable and other current liabilities	4,159
Other liabilities	865
Total liabilities	5,024
Net assets	23,401
Total liabilities and net assets	$ 28,425

INCOME STATEMENT

PUBLIC SUPPORT AND REVENUE

Supporter contributions	$ 56,039
Bequests	3,807
Other income	2,407
Total public support and revenue	62,253

EXPENSES

Program and operating expenses	62,997
Total expenses	62,997
Surplus/(deficit)	$ (744)

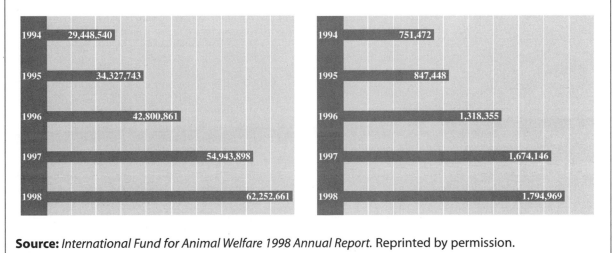

Financial History of IFAW, Total Income in US$

1994	29,448,540
1995	34,327,743
1996	42,800,861
1997	54,943,898
1998	62,252,661

IFAW Supporter Growth

1994	751,472
1995	847,448
1996	1,318,355
1997	1,674,146
1998	1,794,969

Source: *International Fund for Animal Welfare 1998 Annual Report.* Reprinted by permission.

FIGURE 9.3

Friends of the Ferret Chapter Members in Chicago, Dallas, and Denver, 1997–2000

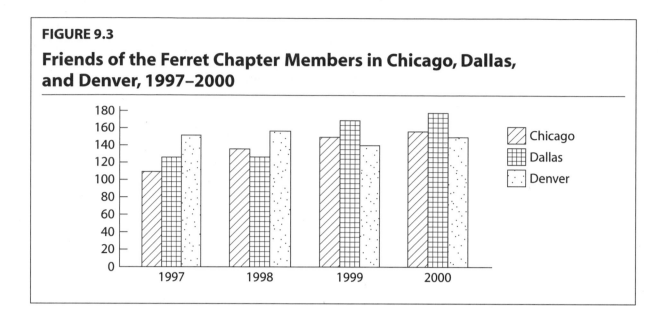

FIGURE 9.4

Friends of the Ferret Membership Has Grown Fastest in Dallas

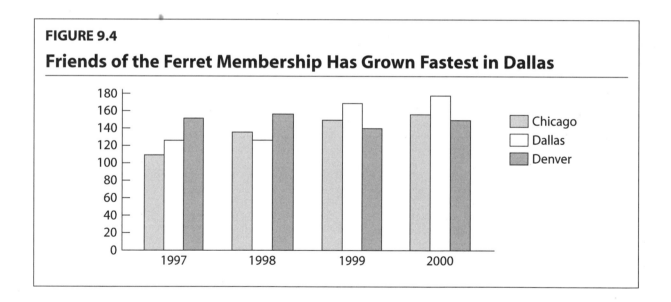

Types of Graphics

There are four basic types of graphics—fever charts (often called line charts), bar charts, pie charts, and tables. Each type has its own strengths and weaknesses, and each will be discussed and illustrated here in its simplest form. The editor who wishes to render graphics in a more sophisticated way than illustrated here should tap the designer's expertise.

Fever Charts

Fever or line charts show the movement of a set of data over a period of time. Usually the time is plotted on the horizontal axis, with measures of quantity plotted on the vertical axis (Holmes, 1984). The growth in membership for Friends of the Ferret could have been displayed in a fever chart (see Figure 9.5), but the message would not have been as dramatic: a fever chart has its greatest impact when it depicts a recovery of some kind, and Friends of the Ferret experienced no decline in membership from which it then recovered. A bar chart is a more powerful way to communicate growth in membership. Moreover, if there is too much information or too little variation in quantities, a fever chart may work less well than a bar chart (Holmes, 1984).

Bar Charts

The bar chart is used mostly to compare different quantities over the same period (Holmes, 1984). For example, a bar chart might be the graphic of choice if Dames, Inc., the fictitious charity that helps low-income women start their own businesses, wanted to show the readers of its annual report the number of women-owned business startups that received the charity's help in the five cities where Dames, Inc., focused its attention in 1999 and 2000 (see Figure 9.6).

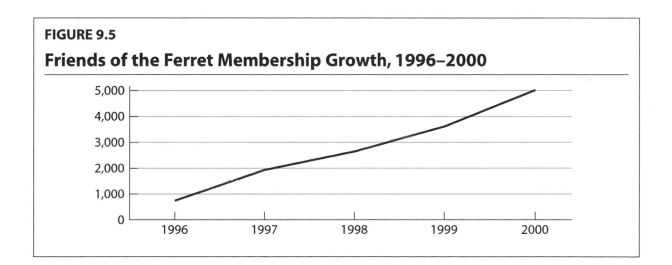

FIGURE 9.5

Friends of the Ferret Membership Growth, 1996–2000

FIGURE 9.6

Detroit Outpaced Other Dames, Inc., Chapters in Business Startups in 1999 and 2000

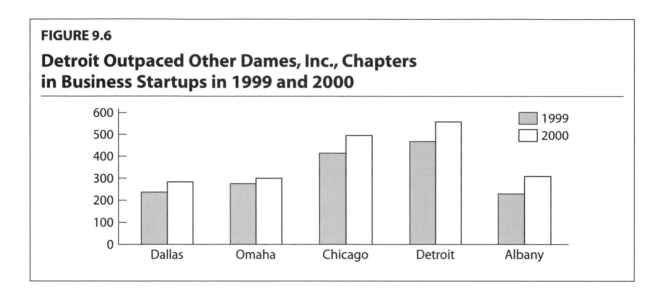

When should a bar chart be used instead of a fever chart? Holmes (1984, p. 47) offers this advice: "It is appropriate to use [the bar] chart when the priority is to comprehend individual numbers within a series. If an overview of Dow Jones statistics for a few months is required, use a fever line. If a detailed look at the last two weeks' daily closings is what's needed, use a bar chart."

Pie Charts

The pie chart is most often used to show the components of a whole (Holmes, 1984). Most pie charts in annual reports show sources of revenue or expenses by category, as in Figure 9.7.

Many nonprofit annual reports limit their graphics to two pie charts, one illustrating sources of revenue and the other showing how expenses are categorized. A pie chart that appears in the section on financial highlights should be easy to comprehend at a glance, and it should be as subdued and straightforward as the text it interprets. Bright splashes of color in an otherwise staid graphic layout may create the impression that the organization itself lacks seriousness—or, worse, that the designer got carried away with the color palette, much as a child with a new box of crayons might do.

Another trap of pie-chart design involves trying to put words inside a space too small to hold them, or placing words at an angle that forces the reader to turn the report upside down and sideways to read them. One solution was tried in the World Bank Institute's 1999 annual report, with

FIGURE 9.7

Program Expenses and Operating Revenues, World Wildlife Fund 1999 Annual Report

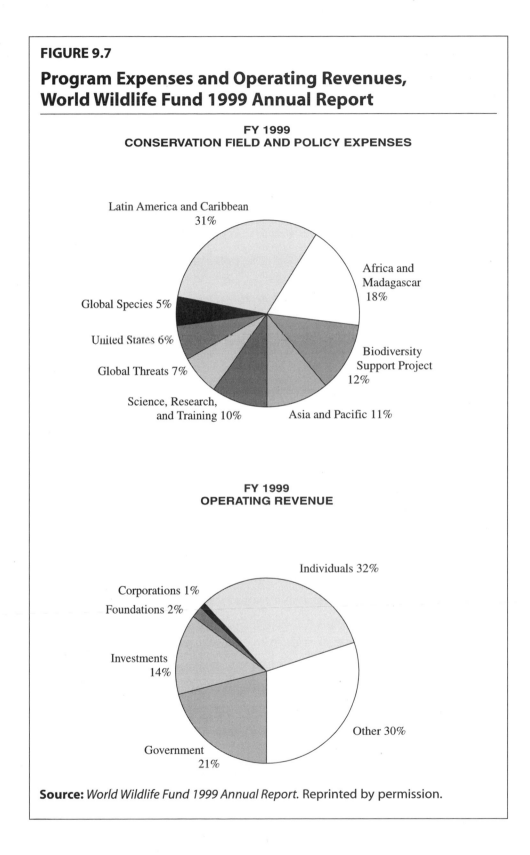

**FY 1999
CONSERVATION FIELD AND POLICY EXPENSES**

Latin America and Caribbean 31%

Africa and Madagascar 18%

Global Species 5%

United States 6%

Biodiversity Support Project 12%

Global Threats 7%

Science, Research, and Training 10%

Asia and Pacific 11%

**FY 1999
OPERATING REVENUE**

Individuals 32%

Corporations 1%

Foundations 2%

Investments 14%

Other 30%

Government 21%

Source: *World Wildlife Fund 1999 Annual Report.* Reprinted by permission.

mixed results. Abbreviations used in the graphic were keyed to related information in the financial table, but because the abbreviations themselves meant nothing at a glance, readers had to search for their meaning in the table above the graphic (World Bank Institute, 1999, p. 31).

Holmes (1984) cautions that a pie chart may become unreadable if it has more than eight divisions, if a piece of the pie is smaller than 2 percent of the whole, or if the labeling text is so long that it must be placed outside the pie, with a line leading to the piece to which it refers. If the copy and the data cannot be simplified, a table will probably work better than a pie chart.

Tables

The table is the editor's best choice when it is important to report exact numbers, and when the spread is too great to be easily charted. Most statements of activities in annual reports are presented in table form, but tables can be dull and should be restricted to situations in which no other form of graphic presentation will suffice (Holmes, 1984).

When graphics are used throughout the annual report, not just in the section dealing with financial highlights, they must be thoroughly integrated with the design; otherwise, they will appear to be afterthoughts (which they do sometimes tend to be). As an example of integrated graphics and design, consider the Urban Institute's 1999 annual report. Right on the front cover, where a gridlike image overlays a photograph of children (see Exhibit 3.2 in Chapter Three), the report sets the context for the graphics to come. The grid theme is then carried forward throughout the text, as background, and the review of operations uses this theme in many graphics. The mission of the Urban Institute is to study domestic policy issues, and the graphics greatly enhance the stories about the results of some of the institute's studies. For example, in the section about the institute's New Federalism project, a bar graph (see Figure 9.8) shows the "percentage of U.S. households receiving welfare below 200% of poverty with children" (Urban Institute, 1999, p. 7). Boldface text to the left of the graph emphasizes the major point: "Poor noncitizen households with children use welfare far less than citizen households do." In the section on the institute's State Policy Center (see Figure 9.9), the bar graph showing murder arrests per 100,000 population demonstrates that "young adults are more likely than juveniles to commit murder" (p. 45). Nevertheless, some of the graphics seem to be merely decorative or are difficult to read. For example, a "graph" used in the section on the institute's Income and Benefits Policy Center is simply a picture, with a faint grid overlay, of what appears to be a line of job applicants (p. 29). Worse, the table in the section on the institute's Metropolitan Housing and Communities Policy Center (p. 37) is titled "Comparison of Denial Rates by Race and Ethnicity by Applicant Income," but the light-dark gradient of the table partially obliterates the first word of the title, and, at the right, a photograph of houses completely swallows the figures for low-, moderate-, and middle-income blacks, Hispanics, and whites, in a part of the table titled "MSA Denial Rates" (see Table 9.3). The latter two examples demonstrate the wisdom of an old design adage, represented by the acronym KISS: Keep It Simple, Stupid.

FIGURE 9.8

U.S. Households Receiving Welfare

Poor Noncitizen Households with Children Use Welfare Far Less Than Citizen Households Do

Even before welfare reform, poor noncitizen households with children received welfare at significantly lower rates than did their citizen counterparts. Most children in these households are U.S.-born citizens. Following welfare reform's enactment, use fell to half the rate of citizens' use—a drop that could reflect confusion over eligibility and noncitizens' fears that applying for programs jeopardizes their future.

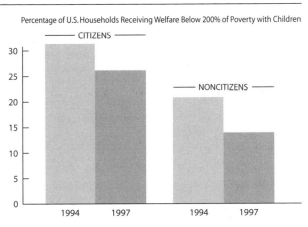

Source: *Urban Institute 1999 Annual Report.* Originally from "Trends in Noncitizens' and Citizens' Use of Public Benefits Following Welfare Reform: 1994–1997" (March 1999) by Michael Fix and Jeffrey S. Passel, Urban Institute. Reprinted by permission.

FIGURE 9.9

Murder Arrests per 100,000 Population

Young Adults Are More Likely Than Juveniles To Commit Murder

Should anti-crime policy focus on juveniles? "Yes" shouldn't be an automatic answer, given the facts.

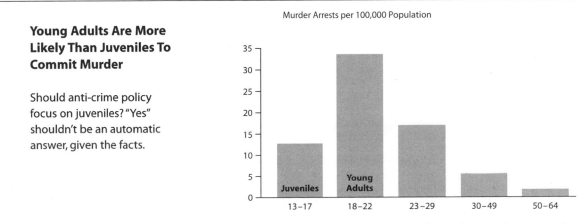

Source: *Urban Institute 1999 Annual Report.* Originally from Urban Institute Analysis of Federal Bureau of Investigation data, 1999. Reprinted by permission.

TABLE 9.3

Lender Denial Rates by Race and Ethnicity

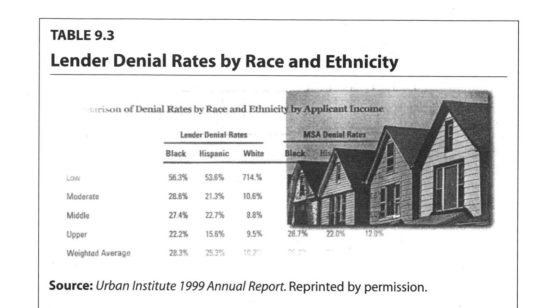

...rison of Denial Rates by Race and Ethnicity by Applicant Income

	Lender Denial Rates			MSA Denial Rates		
	Black	Hispanic	White	Black	His...	
Low	56.3%	53.6%	714.%			
Moderate	28.6%	21.3%	10.6%			
Middle	27.4%	22.7%	8.8%			
Upper	22.2%	15.6%	9.5%	28.7%	22.0%	12.0%
Weighted Average	28.3%	25.3%	10.7%			

Source: *Urban Institute 1999 Annual Report.* Reprinted by permission.

Bar charts and pie charts are simple and can even be produced on a personal computer with Microsoft PowerPoint or Microsoft Excel. It should be noted, however, that a graphic produced in this manner serves best as a "mockup" of the final print-resolution graph that is prepared by the designer. Other types of graphics—maps, or any graphics that must display a three-dimensional view—may be more complicated and therefore must be rendered with great care by the designer. This doesn't mean that the editor has to treat such graphics with awe or accept a graphic that doesn't make sense. Indeed, the editor's role is to serve as the first reader of a graphic, and if the editor doesn't get it, surely the readers won't either. If the designer has created something beautiful but incomprehensible, the editor owes it to the readers to see that the graphic is comprehensible, even if beauty must fall by the wayside.

Once the graphics have been created and the photographs have been scanned into the document, the editor has a first opportunity to review the annual report as a whole. This is also when it is least expensive to make changes of any kind—photo substitutions or relocations, type changes, and color changes—before the entire report is output for printing. Beyond this stage, as the report moves through the various stages of printing, the cost of making alterations increases.

Chapter 10

Printing and Distribution

IN A DESIGN course I once took, the class project was for each student to design and produce—in those days, using dry-transfer lettering and glue—a magazine that made use of typography, color, layout, photography, and printing. We could use "Greek" text (gibberish) or simply draw lines to indicate where the text would be on the two-page spreads, but we were required to render the headlines and illustrate each topic, on a theme unrelated to graphic design. Because I was working in the population field at the time, I chose people. In fact, the title of my magazine was *Demo-Graphics.* For my typography spread, I used dry-transfer lettering to form human faces and titled the section "True to Type." For the layout spread, I found a picture of a gymnast coming out of a midair tumble and doing the splits upside down; I titled that section "Balancing Act." Printing was easy: I found a picture of a woman giving birth, and I titled the section "Reproduction."

Printing, much like childbirth, gives physical form—in this case, to the ideas, hopes, dreams, and plans of the publication's creator. And just as highly trained professionals are there to assist the miracle of childbirth, highly skilled printers are there to transform the editor's thoughts and the designer's imagination into a collection of symbols and images rendered in ink on paper.

As we have seen, many nonprofits must publish their annual reports by an established deadline. Murphy's Law dictates that by the time the annual report is ready to be printed, there will be no time left for printing. Publication deadlines can slip by a few days, but the printer is usually the one who has to put in the overtime to get the report published in time. This chapter outlines what is involved in printing the annual report—from receipt of electronic files to delivery of bound reports—and offers tips on how to pick reliable printers, work effectively with them, and recognize high-quality printing.

Some editors know the printing process inside out; others are more comfortable hiring designers who have that kind of knowledge. (For editors who would like to know more about printing, books that discuss the printing process in detail can be found in the References and the Recommended Reading section at the back of this book.) Suffice it to say, printing is more a craft than a manufacturing process; each step of the process demands knowledge, skilled craftsmanship, and attention to detail.

Editors unfamiliar with printing processes will also discover that printers speak a strange language. It sounds like English but isn't readily understood without mastery of a specialized vocabulary. For example, what does the printer mean when he says, "The designer's photo files really choked my rip"? He means that the volume of data in the designer's files was so huge that the rasterized-image processor, or "rip," took a very long time to digest the information and make an image of the film. What does the designer, just back from a press inspection, mean when she says, "It turns out I didn't need to worry about picking, but there were some problems with dot gain and a couple of hickeys"? She means that she didn't need to worry about white spots showing up in inked areas, but there were some problems with halftone dots that printed larger on the paper, and there were two doughnut-shaped spots on a heavily inked page. (Editors unfamiliar with this language, or with other jargon used elsewhere in this chapter, can find help in the Glossary of Graphic Arts and Mailing Terms at the back of this book.) The editors' knowledge of printing may vary almost as widely as the printers' capabilities.

Most of us know high-quality printing and binding when we see it. Colors are vivid and accurate. Text looks sharp and clear. The binding holds together, even after the book is opened and pushed flat. Ink does not come off on hands as the reader thumbs through the pages. There are no untrimmed pages, no spots, and no faded images, let alone pages printed out of sequence or upside down. And yet printers can and do make all of these careless errors. If errors like these show up in the annual report, however, it is the editor, not the printer, who may soon be reading the want ads.

Of course, a poor printing job can be rejected and sent back to be redone at the printer's expense, but this means that the long-awaited report will be late—perhaps too late for that important board meeting or conference. The prudent editor averts disaster by choosing the right printer. In organizations where cost control is paramount, the editor bids out the printing of the annual report only to printers who are capable of doing it justice—at a reasonable price, of course.

Choosing a Printer

The process of selecting the annual report's printer is much like the process of choosing a graphic designer, but there are some important differences. Editors who are producing a first annual report, or who are not satisfied with the printers they have been using, may find the tips in Exhibit 10.1 helpful.

If it is the organization's policy to solicit bids, the next step, following decisions about which printers are capable of doing a good job, is to prepare a print specification sheet ("spec sheet" for short) and ask the printers who have passed muster to submit price quotations based on the specs. Sometimes the designer, as the one most familiar with the printing process required to achieve the intended result, performs this function. If the report is a simple two-color job, however, the editor can just as easily prepare the print specs, provided that the editor knows enough about printing to ensure that the specs are complete. A good printer's rep will also help an inexperienced

---

EXHIBIT 10.1

How to Find the Right Printer

1. Ask a trusted colleague for names of printers who do good work and who work well with that colleague.

2. Collect high-quality annual reports and contact the companies that printed those reports.

3. Interview prospective printers and examine their samples. Notify them in advance that you want to see samples of annual reports. If there are no samples, cross the printer off your list. Some printers offer a discount if you make your report the first one they print, but the risks are high.

4. Ask for a list of references—preferably, the names of other nonprofits for which the printer has done annual reports. Ask these references some frank questions:

   • Has Perfection Press done more than one annual report for you?

   • How did you find out about the company and its work?

   • Did you find the printer's representative easy to work with and knowledgeable about printing, or was the rep more of a salesperson?

   • Did the printer's rep manage your job throughout the whole process? [Printer's reps worth their salt take personal responsibility for the quality of the work for which they will be earning a commission.]

   • Did you think the price was reasonable? If not, why?

   • Did the printer's representative call you if there were problems with files, color matches, and so on?

   • Did the printer take good care of slides and transparencies, not scratching them or losing them?

   • Did the printer meet your deadlines even when you were late submitting files?

5. Call designers who have used this printer on annual reports and ask if there were any problems, such as faulty film output, dirt, uneven inking, or sloppy binding.

editor put together a list of print specifications. Often this happens informally when the printer's rep gets the specs, finds gaps in them, and calls the editor for the missing information. Sometimes the printer's rep—again, if this is an *experienced* rep—will suggest less expensive paper stock, or a more cost-effective arrangement of full-color photographs, or a better binding method. If the printing specs change as a result of this dialogue, the editor who is seeking competitive bids must be sure that the print specs are uniform for all printers who are asked to bid on the annual report. Exhibit 10.2 illustrates what is needed for a simple two-color annual report. An example of a price quote for a more complex annual report is shown in Exhibit 10.3.

EXHIBIT 10.2

Sample Print Specifications

Title:	Friends of the Ferret 2001 Annual Report
Text:	
No. pages:	48 pp. plus cover
Trim size:	8.5 by 11 (bleeds all sides)
Paper stock:	70-pound uncoated offset book
Ink:	black and PMS 377U green
No. of halftones:	50 (printer to scan)
No. of screens:	10 (on disk)
No. of reverses:	throughout (on disk)
Cover:	
Paper stock:	10 pt. Mark V CIS white
Ink:	black and PMS 377U green (2/0)
No. of halftones:	1 (printer to scan)
No. of screens:	0
No. of bleeds:	all sides
Binding:	saddlestitch on the 11" side
Art provided:	Zip disk and color-separated proof sheets
Proofs:	Text and cover bluelines
Press inspection:	yes
Print run:	10,000 + additional 1,000s
Ship to:	500 advance copies to Friends of the Ferret; balance to mail house[a]
Delivery date:	November 15, 2001
Art ready:	October 11, 2001

[a]*The spec sheet should say whether the mail house is a local address for the printer or an out-of-town location that will involve shipping charges.*

EXHIBIT 10.3

Sample Price Quote for a Complex Report

R E Q U E S T   F O R   P R I N T I N G   E S T I M A T E

MEADOWS DESIGN OFFICE
4201 CONNECTICUT AVENUE
NORTHWEST · SUITE 407
WASHINGTON, D.C. 20008
TELEPHONE 202·966·6007
FACSIMILE 202·966·6733
E-MAIL MEDOWS@AOL.COM

Date 4 May 1998

Our Job Number 3019-97

Project IFAW annual report

Client Meadows Design Office

Contact Marc Meadows

Specifications Project supplied on Mac diskette in Quark Xpress 3.3.2r5

Dimensions   **Width** 8.75 inches   × **Height** 11.75 inches

Length

52 total pages + cover: **40 text pages + 12 color plates bound in as single sheets + cover**

Color plates fall on the following pages: 1-2, 3-4,7-8, 17-18, 25-26, 35-36
[six sheets of leaves = 12 report pages]

Paper Stock

Text Gilbert Voice 100 lb text, white   **Color Plates** Scheufelen, Pheono Star Plus 100 lb text, gloss white

Cover Scheufelen, Pheonon Star Plus 100 lb cover, gloss white

Dustjacket   **Flaps**

Other

Stock Options none

Ink

Text 4CP + 1 PMS throughout (5/5)   **Color Plates** 4CP throughout (4/4)   **Finish**

Cover 4CP throughout (4/4)   **Finish** UVCoat cover 1 & 4

Photos

■ **50 Separations:** 2 Double spread bleeds, 11 Full page bleeds, 37 third-page to minimum   **Line Screen** 200

☐ **Duotones**   **Line Screen**

☐ **Line Art**   ■ **Tint Screens** on financial page only for graphs

■ **Bleeds**   ■ **Traps**   ☐ **Reverses**   ■ **Tight Registration**

☐ **Silhouettes**   ■ **Heavy Coverage** Color plates and covers

Service Bureau   ■ **Output** by printer, **2540 dpi** from Quark v3.32r5 files.

Binding

■ **[Notch] Perfect**   ☐ **Paperbound**   ☐ **Smyth Sewn**   ☐ **Spiral**   ☐ **Saddle Stitched**

☐ **Clothbound**   ☐ **Endleaves**   ☐ **H&F Bands**

Boards

Cloth

Stamping

Packing Conveniently in cartons   ☐ **Shrinkwrap**

☐ **Units per Box**   ☐ **Skids**   ☐ **Other**

Proofs   ■ **Random color/Chromalins**   ■ **Blueline and color composites of complete piece**   ■ **Press Inspection**

Shipping To be arranged with printer separately. Approx. 2,300 to worldwide destinations and balance to two US destinations.

NOTES We anticipate mechanicals ready next week, need 15–20 working day turn around by printer.

Quantity

10,000 copes   addn'l 1,000s

Source: Meadows Design Office, 1998.

Evaluating Bids

Every printer has a different system for producing price quotes. For that reason, it is important to read the price quote carefully, to be sure that it is accurate and complete. In the case of a four-color printing job, for example, one printer may include the cost of color separations in the overall price, whereas another will quote a separate cost for each separation. If a printer's price quote is not complete, the editor should ask for a corrected submission.

When all the bids have come in, it is time to see which printer gets the job. Because only highly qualified printers have been asked to bid on the job, the decision can be based on the lowest bid. Nevertheless, the editor may feel more comfortable working with the printer's rep for a company that offered a slightly higher bid. Annual reports are highly subject to Murphy's Law, so it's a good idea for the editor to trust his or her instincts: a few more pennies now can mean fewer hassles later on.

According to Dana Lane of the International Finance Corporation, "Once the printer is selected, it's important to sit down with the designer and look at potential problems." She adds, "You can save money by doing accent colors with color builds instead of an additional PMS color, but color builds that look terrific on a Mac screen may not translate to ink and paper in the same way."

The designer and the printer can also work together on paper options, to determine which stock is best for holding traps and bleeds. Once these decisions have been made, the designer sends the files to the printer for prepress preparation.

Reviewing Proofs

The editor's next job is to review proofs. In the predesktop era, the blueline proof, with its light blue ink on yellow photosensitive paper, offered the first opportunity to see all the elements—including photos, reverses, and screens—as they would appear in the printed piece. The blueline is quite similar to today's desktop proofs except that its pages are output as signatures rather than two-page spreads.

Because the blueline offers such a complete view of what the finished product will be, editors and others who review it are often tempted to make substantial changes. Things suddenly jump off the page after having escaped the editor's notice at the proofreading stage: somehow Ms. Fiscal's knees are showing beneath her short shorts, despite instructions to crop her photo at the waist; text describing the southernmost tip of South America mentions the Cape of Good Hope instead of Cape Horn. Why errors like these emerge at the blueline stage remains a mystery—and a costly one at that, for if the blueline is made from plate-ready negatives, then any changes will mean that the printer has to generate new film from revised electronic files. Of course, editors should correct major mistakes that were missed in proofreading. If content has changed because of late-breaking events—for example, if the vice president for policy is now the executive vice president for legislative affairs—then the correction must be made regardless of the expense.

Blueline alterations can be expensive, says Annie Williams of Virginia Lithograph, especially if changes are made in areas where there are color builds in a four-color job: "A change on one page of the blueline may mean that changes will have to be made in *all* of the film that contains the same color builds, so that the color is consistent throughout. This is because the chemicals in the film-making machinery change and wear down in time, so the chemical composition of the film on Monday will not be the same as the chemical composition of the film on Friday—even though it may still be within [industry] tolerances." Williams has this advice for editors who know there are likely to be text changes to the financials at the last minute: "Do them [the financials] in black on a white background, or on a background build having no black in it, so that the type can be changed without having to go back to composite film for changes that affect pages with color builds on them." Although many printers are careful to bill blueline alterations at a fair price, Williams cautions that a printer who is less than scrupulous, or who has "low-balled" a price quote to get the job, may discover that billing for blueline alterations offers a chance to recover some costs and make the job more profitable. "Even if you trust your printer," she says, "you should address the issue of blueline-alteration costs immediately—not when the invoice finally arrives."

Time and money are both excellent reasons why editors should resist the urge to rewrite whole portions of text or make wholesale substitutions of photos at this stage. Instead, the blueline should be regarded primarily as a prepress proof that enables the editor to check for halftone placement, cropping, and scaling, for color breaks, page sequences, alignment of rules and other gutter-jumping elements, for dirt, and even for trim size. Designers very often output desktop proofs at a reduced size so that a two-page spread can be placed on one sheet of paper; therefore, an editor who, having worked with these smaller proofs, requests an increase in the type size for the photo captions may be astonished at how large the type is when all the elements show up in the blueline at what will be their actual size. Editors who are reviewing blueline proofs for the first time can benefit from the tips in Exhibit 10.4.

EXHIBIT 10.4

How to Read a Proof

When examining a proof, keep these items in mind:

Slow pace. Take your time. Don't let a deadline make you careless.

Individual features. Make a list, then check each feature throughout the entire proof. For example, go through once just to confirm page sequence. Next, check borders and rules for alignment and crossovers. Continue to examine headlines and display type for typos and placement. Finish by studying areas of critical register and color.

Photos. Check every photograph to verify that the correct image is in the correct space, is scaled and cropped properly, and faces in the proper direction. Look for sharp focus, especially in portions of the image farthest from the center.

Flaws. Boldly circle every blemish, flaw, spot, broken letter, and anything else that seems wrong.

Previous corrections. Double-check any corrections made on previous proofs.

Instructions. Write directly on the proof in a dark pencil. Be very clear and explicit in your instructions.

Finishing. Anticipate bindery problems. Measure trim size. Check that folds are in the correct direction and relate to copy as planned.

Correct colors. Confirm that you know what copy prints in what color. Double-check to make certain.

Overview. Stand back to view the proof as a whole. All the elements should work well together, and the message should be presented in a clear and attractive manner.

Questions. Ask about anything that seems wrong. Asking questions that seem stupid is a lot better than printing mistakes.

Costs. Discuss the cost of changes and agree about who pays for what.

Source: Mark Beach and Eric Kenly, *Getting It Printed: How to Work with Printers and Graphic Imaging Services to Assure Quality, Stay on Schedule, and Control Costs* (Cincinnati, Ohio: North Light Books, 1999), p. 73. Copyright 1999 by North Light Books. Reprinted by permission.

If blueline corrections are numerous, or if the text changes in any way, it is advisable to ask for a second, corrected blueline proof, just to make sure that all the changes have been made and that they have not affected the copy flow. The final "OK to print" signals the printer to begin makeready on the presses. When the graphics and color screens are not particularly complicated, an annual report done in one or two colors usually will not require a press inspection unless the editor is not fully confident that the PMS colors will reproduce as desired, or unless the editor has doubts about the printer's capabilities. Press inspections cost money, but they are necessary for a report that uses four or more colors. For that type of report, the press inspection is usually preceded by a review of color proofs.

Color proofs and match prints are close to true color, but they are not exact. Nevertheless, color corrections can be made at this prepress stage for a lot less money than when the report is on press. When it comes to checking color proofs, even the editor who understands color separations and printing relies heavily on the designer's knowledge and expertise. For one thing, the designer probably has a keener eye for color and can more readily spot when flesh tones are too yellow or too red, or when a specified color tint is not the intended hue. The designer also knows how these faults can be corrected—by reducing yellow or adding more cyan, for example.

"I check the accuracy of the proof to the original transparency for color and contrast," says designer Marc Meadows. "Some clients demand an exact match of color; others are happy to have what we call 'pleasing color'—the image looks fine even if not an exact match to the original."

This is not to say that the editor has no role to play; four eyes are always better than two. The editor may notice, for example, that a halftone has been incorrectly flopped, or that a color photograph is out of registration. Or the editor may notice one of many flaws that have hitherto passed unnoticed in examination of slides or transparencies, but that now loom large in the color proofs: in his photo, esteemed scholar Dr. Doctrinalli has a spot on his tie that looks like a food spill, for example, or a scratch on the slide makes it appear that a thin straight line extends from the top of the sky straight through the chairman's dark blue suit, or little spots appear all over that adorable giant panda (the spots may be the residue of the bamboo he is eating, but they will look like inking errors in the final printed piece). Working together, the editor and the designer can determine whether these flaws can be fixed by some creative color correction and, if so, whether there are ethical reasons why they ought not to be fixed. (Why clean up the panda if he is naturally dirty?) Finally, it is the editor's judgment that must be brought to bear on the decision about whether the expense of color correction makes photo substitution a more cost-effective approach at this stage. Nevertheless, there are some decisions that the editor should be sure not to make solely on the basis of cost.

Printers can literally save a job once it is on press. They can color-correct photos of board members to lighten red noses or hide dandruff. They can eliminate shadow areas behind heads and remove five o'clock shadows. (When the top brass looks good, so does the editor.) Printers can even remove a flock of tiny white birds from a photograph of sea and blue sky because in the printed piece the birds will look like hickeys. Nevertheless, the cost of corrections while a job is on press far exceeds the cost of minor corrections made earlier in the proofing stage, and time is lost while press corrections are made.

If the editor is working with printers who have not been used before, or if the printers are using a process that they haven't used before (for example, direct-to-plate printing), the editor will probably want to do a press inspection. This is not a signal of mistrust, and if the printer suggests that it is, the editor should find another printer. Even if the editor has great confidence in the printer, and even if the printer is not trying a different process, the editor is well advised to request a press inspection for reports that use four or more colors.

Usually the editor who employs an outside designer for an annual report has the designer conduct the press inspection because the designer is likely to be more familiar with printing and will know what to look for.

"Even when there is really good prepress," says Marc Meadows, "a press inspection offers your only chance to see exactly what the ink looks like on paper. Depending on the press, the paper, the inks, and even the weather, ink saturation can be different from one day to the next."

And press inspections can be grueling: Meadows, who has designed annual reports for twenty years and has done World Wildlife Fund's annual report for more than ten years, usually spends seventy-two hours on the press inspection. During that time, he is constantly on call to review sheets as they come off the press.

"Sleep deprivation becomes a factor after three days," he says. "But stopping the presses so that I can catch a few winks is not an option."

Meadows prefers to conduct the inspection without the editor present. The job at this point should be completely satisfactory from the editorial standpoint, he says. The editor should be on call, however, to answer any questions that may arise during the inspection.

Annie Williams of Virginia Lithograph agrees. Here are some of her tips for a first press inspection:

- Make sure that the colors are right. Look at the color bars and screen blocks under the loupe to make sure they are not plugging. If the color looks too washed out or plugged, ask for a densitometer reading.

- Check the registration by eye and then under the loupe. If the loupe shows, say, half a dot off registration, perhaps trying to correct it is not technically possible. Something clearly off registration, however, should be corrected. Look not only at the registration marks but also at the images.

- If the job prints front and back, make sure the color integrity is held on both the wire and smooth side of the press sheet.

- Bindery jobs are also critical when it comes to gutter jumps and cross-overs, although any problems should have been spotted at blueline stage and corrected before the job went to press.

Williams warns that changes on press can be even more expensive than at the blueline stage. One of her clients, for example, misspelled the boss's name and didn't notice it until the job was on press. "She ran up $5,000 in extra costs because that one change meant having to go back to film and back to plate," says Williams. "And then there was all that paper on which the misspelled name appeared that had to be thrown out."

Once the press inspection is over and there are press sheets to show everybody, it's time to sit back and wait for the printers and binders to do the rest of their magic. At last, the day everyone has been awaiting through all these miserable months has finally arrived. The report is sitting on the editor's desk. It's beautiful. But it's not yet time to break out the champagne—not until the pesky details of distribution are dealt with.

Distribution

Most typically in a large nonprofit organization, the annual report's editor does not handle distribution. In a smaller organization or nonprofit, however, where the editor is the development person responsible for seeing that the complete package is put together and mailed at the right moment, there are a few arrangements that have to be made. First, if the annual report is accompanied by a letter from the CEO, someone must write that letter and get it signed and duplicated. Very often, the CEO's letter will feature a gift table, like the one in Table 3.1 in Chapter Three, which tells donors how much work the organization will be able to accomplish with the help of a certain amount of money from them. The information for this gift table most often is supplied by development staffers, who are the ones working most closely with actual and potential donors, and who are most familiar with the kinds of work that donors are most interested in supporting.

If responsibility for distribution devolves on the editor, and if the annual report is a separate publication rather than a partial or full issue of a regularly published magazine or newsletter, it is helpful to use a "to do" list like the one shown in Exhibit 10.5.

After the editor has discharged his or her final responsibilities for the annual report, it's time to disappear to that cabin with no electricity or

EXHIBIT 10.5

"To Do" List for Distribution

- Work with the development database manager to ensure that the names and addresses of intended recipients are accurate, complete, and compiled in a file format that the mail house can handle. (Seed the list with your own name and address so that you will know when the report is actually received in your ZIP code area.)

- Make sure that there is an adequate supply of carrier envelopes and postage-paid return envelopes (or get some printed) to be inserted in the package so that donors can mail their contributions.

- Assemble all package ingredients—report, cover letter, gift table, carrier envelope, and reply envelope—and weigh a sample package to assess postage costs.

- Solicit bids from mail houses and select the winner.

- Issue the purchase order or contract for the mail house.

- Deposit to the postal account sufficient funds to cover postage.

- Arrange for delivery of all package ingredients to the mail house and for return or discard of any "overs."

telephone in the Maine woods. It is far too soon for the editor to expect any feedback from colleagues or superiors about the report's impact, but what they say when the editor returns from this well-deserved break sets the stage for the final step in the annual report's production process: the postmortem.

Chapter 11

Evaluating Success and Spotting Trouble

HAVING GONE through purgatory to produce a high-quality annual report by the specified deadline, the editor often faces a period of long, ominous silence, with no feedback from the CEO, colleagues, or readers. Do senior managers simply not like the report, or are they busy with other matters? Most editors can be reassured that silence is golden at this point. If there were problems, the editor would be the first to hear about them—and probably from the CEO.

So it's safe to go ahead and celebrate. But while the editor is still suffering from the aftereffects of that well-deserved magnum of champagne, it's useful to take a hard look at the report (along with a couple of aspirin) to see what needs to be done to make things work more smoothly and effectively next time.

Now that it's all together in one piece, does the report accomplish its purposes? As Herschel Lee Johnson of the NAACP Legal Defense and Educational Fund puts it, "We always want to improve the writing, to try to find ways to make it more concise and compelling. At the same time, we want to greatly improve the look of the publication. These two elements, of course, go hand in hand in providing the reader with a valuable and entertaining experience."

To what extent does the annual report contribute positively to the organization's overall image? Does it appear to be a separate, stand-alone publication, or does it reinforce the organization's image and message in readers' eyes because it resembles other communications from the organization? Is the annual report's overall message a drumbeat that emphasizes, through repetition, what has been said in other communications? Are the visual elements well integrated with the text? Are there any printing or binding problems? In retrospect, what could have been done differently? Should more money be budgeted for next year's report? Should more time be allowed? Should the format be changed? These are all good questions, the answers to which can be found in a number of ways. One way is to look for signs that the report is accomplishing its intended objectives.

Signs of Success

For the nonprofit that uses the annual report as a fund-raising tool, the true test of the report's effectiveness is the amount of money it raises. Not many nonprofits track the funds raised by their annual reports, but those that include a response device can attribute some funds to the impact of their reports. For example, the World Wildlife Fund's 1998 annual report raised more than $220,000 in funds that could be directly traced to a response device that was included with the report. The National Wildlife Federation sends its annual report to its top donor audience with a business reply envelope. "We occasionally receive five-figure gifts from those donors," says the federation's Natalie Waugh, especially if the report "comes at a time [when] people are in a giving frame of mind."

Many nonprofits do not use their annual reports to raise money, however. For them, there are several other success measurements, which have been covered in previous chapters of this book. I have pulled these criteria together in Exhibit 11.1.

Signs of Trouble

Evaluating the report for signs of success is a lot more fun, of course, than looking for signs that the report is not achieving its intended purposes. Sharp declines in membership, especially accompanied by letters complaining about the annual report, seldom occur; only truly dissatisfied customers complain. But that is why the editor should make careful note of every critical remark made about the report and then exercise some judgment to determine which criticisms merit consideration and which do not. If too many people complain about the size of the type, the editor would most likely make sure the next report is easier to read. If only one person criticizes the use of purple as a second color, the editor could respond politely but take no further action until there are other similar complaints. If some people complain that the report is probably a waste of donors' funds, the editor should be prepared to explain what it cost and how much money it has brought in to the organization.

EXHIBIT 11.1

Ten Criteria for a Successful Annual Report

1. Does the report contribute positively to the organization's overall image?

2. Is the cover enticing?

3. Is the text succinct, colorful, accurate, and easy for readers to understand?

4. Is the theme expressed visually as well as verbally?

5. Has the report attracted new members and additional support?

6. Does the report meet watchdog agency standards?[a]

7. Does the executive message tell where the organization is headed?

8. Has the report won awards for communications excellence?[b]

9. Did the report come out on time and within budget?

10. Does the CEO like it?[c]

[a]*Council of Better Business Bureaus Wise Giving Alliance standards can be found at http://www.give.org/standards/cbbbstds.asp.*

[b]*Awards are an excellent sign that the report meets independent standards of quality. Being able to claim that the organization publishes an award-winning annual report also enhances the organization's image.*

[c]*In addition to the CEO, do board members and other important recipients of the report like it?*

Nonprofits have to be particularly concerned about complaints that funds used to publish the annual report could be better spent on the organization's work. "When you have foundation heads saying they won't make a grant to any organization whose annual report costs more than the average size of the foundation's grants, you've got a real problem," says World Wildlife Fund's Bill Eichbaum. In such cases, it is wise to have on hand a form letter that addresses complaints of that nature.

World Wildlife Fund sometimes receives letters criticizing the expense of its annual report, which is produced in full color on glossy paper. The organization justifies the expense on two basic grounds: unlike many other environmental groups, it does not publish a full-color magazine, and its annual report helps raise funds for conservation.

The editor may be tempted to change the report simply to take a fresh approach, especially when the editor has been putting out the annual report for several years. The editor may be bored with the same old format and style every year, but if readers love it and have come to expect more or less the same thing, it may be wise to hang on to what's working for them until there are sufficient clues that change will be welcomed rather than condemned.

This is why the involvement of development staff members is crucial. As front-line contacts with actual and potential donors, they know what works and what doesn't work. Showing development staffers initial concepts and full-scale page proofs may seem to take up precious time, but in the long run it will save heartache—and possibly money—if the editor makes sure that there are no red flags for donors.

Funds permitting, it may be helpful to have the report evaluated by an outside expert. "From time to time," says Jim Wilson of the Boy Scouts of America, "we have our reports reviewed and critiqued by Annual Reports Incorporated." According to Wilson, after the Boy Scouts had experienced five or six years of "significant grief" in getting the annual report produced, Annual Reports, Inc., helped the organization "focus on the audience" of key corporate managers and "recognize that we didn't need a theme and that we had the greatest photos possible in an annual report—kids in action within the Scouting program." Annual Reports, Inc., offers consultations at $2,500 plus travel expenses. Further information about the company's services can be obtained from Christopher J. Doyle, president, Annual Reports, Inc., 1250 Park Avenue, Franklin, IN 46131; (800) 729-5071; http://www.annualreportsinc.com.

From Postmortem to Progress Next Year

Although an independent outside evaluation can be helpful and is probably advisable if the report is truly not accomplishing its objectives, an alternative approach in less dire circumstances is to hold a formal postmortem with the CEO and other managers to assess what worked, from their perspective, and suggest what could be improved.

"It's useful to have a postmortem for any major project," says Kathryn Fuller, president of World Wildlife Fund. "You need to review what works and what didn't and whether the process can be improved."

Using the ten criteria for a successful annual report as a point of departure, the evaluators can also discuss issues such as these:

- Whether more money would solve problems or make the report better next year (and whether spending more money is advisable)

- Whether photographs or illustrations need to be commissioned to add visual impact

- Whether it is time to change designers to get a fresh approach

- Whether it is time to change printers to get better quality or greater responsiveness (if the printer did not meet the final production deadline)

Because these decisions can increase the overall cost of the report, the editor can get stuck in a catch-22 situation, with few options for improvement.

Would cutting the report's length help? One survey found that more than half of those surveyed did not want to see the traditional comprehensive annual report replaced by a smaller version (Potlatch Corporation, 1995). No wonder many editors are turning to Internet technology.

Online Annual Reports

Most businesses and many nonprofits have already invested in Web sites. The advantage of putting an annual report on the World Wide Web is clear: less money is spent on paper and printing, and distribution is cheaper and faster. Before switching to this new medium, however, it may be helpful to take a look at what corporations are already doing.

In September 1999, corporate annual report guru Sid Cato called the idea of annual reports on the Internet "an urban legend." He claimed that he had been unable to locate annual reports on most of the Web sites that he visited on two different occasions. By March 2000, he had changed his tune: he had not seen the print version of IBM's 1999 annual report, but he thought it would be exceptional even if it was only half as good as the version on the Web.

Readers who want to view IBM's annual report online are invited to visit the IBM Web site at www.ibm.com. The report is not easy to find, however. Visitors have to intuit that the annual report is on a link called "About IBM." The text and pictures together are wider than many monitors; therefore, to see everything, visitors must scroll both horizontally and vertically. Certainly, IBM must remain on the leading edge of new technology, but some less technologically savvy visitors to the site in 1999 were surely dismayed to discover that they would have to download Macromedia Flash 4 if they wished to read the Web version of IBM's report. By 2001, IBM had made things easier by offering flash and nonflash versions. Visitors must move beyond the cover page to find the 2000 annual report's various sections. Once there, however, viewers can find the contents listed across the top of the page.

In 1999, IBM's "Review of Operations" section featured twenty-eight separate photos, each linked to a short description of the company's services or products—although it was not clear from the photo what the product or service was. By 2001, IBM had made things easier: each of the 2000 report's chapters listed in the table of contents for the review of operations also had a short blurb describing which aspects of the business were discussed in that chapter. IBM had also taken advantage of the annual report's archiving function by offering Web visitors the chance to read reports extending as far back as 1994.

Although 50 percent of the respondents to the Potlatch Corporation's survey (1995) showed interest in receiving annual reports electronically, many online corporate reports are hard to find and difficult to navigate. Ford Motor Company's 1998 annual report, for example, was four clicks away from the home page. According to Sweet (1999c), "Browsers must select 'corporate' from the home page. Then, on successive pages, the links are 'shareholders,' 'company reports,' and finally, 'annual reports.'"

A visit to Ford's Web site, www.ford.com, in 2001 showed that the 2000 annual report was easier to find. Under a major section titled "Our Company," visitors can click a bar titled "Investor Information," which leads to a paragraph that invites browsers to click on "2000 Annual Report." A small screen pops up that must be maximized for ease of viewing. In that screen, the report's major sections are listed down the left side. The typeface in this Web version is highly readable, and a "printable version" can be downloaded with Adobe Acrobat. Ford's Web site did not provide an archive of previous annual reports.

Like for-profit corporations, nonprofits that have annual reports on their Web sites also seem to have difficulty guiding readers to their reports. An exception is World Wildlife Fund, whose annual report, at www.worldwildlife.org, is only one click away from the home page and offers the complete text of the report online; visitors are also given a telephone number to call if they want a printed report. To find the Red Cross's annual report, visitors to www.redcross.org can click on "Publications" at the top of the home page. The 2000 annual report is only one more click away: a color picture of the print version's cover is accompanied by a table of contents offering PDF files of the report's various sections. There is no information about how to obtain a print version of the report, but viewers can also see PDF files of the 1999 and 1998 annual reports.

The home page of the Web site for the Girl Scouts of the USA (www.gsusa.org) offers a link to the 2000 annual report. There visitors can obtain the complete report in PDF format or view two sections, the joint message from the national president and the national executive director and a section called "Girl Scout Leadership Skills." The Girl Scouts' 1999 annual report is also available in PDF format.

Online annual reports are gaining in popularity, but many people still prefer hard copy. In fact, 90 percent of Fortune 500 respondents to a survey said that there will always be a printed annual report, and 85 percent indicated that they would like to have both printed and online reports (Potlatch Corporation, 2000). To keep them happy, the Web site version of any annual report should provide an e-mail hyperlink or an address for requesting a print copy.

When someone finally creates the perfect online annual report, will readers prefer it to a printed copy? And in the case of a publicly held corporation, how will the organization know that readers actually have read the report?

"A lot of people want stuff online today," says Lou Thompson, president and CEO of the National Investor Relations Institute, "but you've got to assure that if you're offering the annual report online in lieu of sending them a printed annual report, then you have to have some way of verifying that they received it" (cited in Sweet, 1999d).

The Securities and Exchange Commission requires companies to offer shareholders exactly the same information online as is offered in print, and shareholders must sign a form before a company can stop sending them the printed annual report. And, of course, shareholders can change their minds at any time and request a printed report. The cost implications are evident in such cases: online reports duplicate rather than replace the printed report. Indeed, online publishing simply shifts the cost of printing to the consumer. The report must be redesigned as an HTML document, and companies must offer readers a PDF file or other format in which they can download the material and print their own copies. There are other disadvantages as well (see Exhibit 11.2).

As is obvious to most of us by now, the Internet is here to stay and is going to change a lot about our lives. There are already a number of technology-oriented potential donors who are more comfortable with the Web than with print, and yet experts believe that we are at least a generation away from universal access to the Web in the United States. In 1997, according to Sweet (1999a), Intel Corporation surveyed its shareholders to see if they wanted to have their reports delivered on the Internet, and slightly fewer than 5 percent chose that option. A similar survey by the National Investor Relations Institute (1999) showed that 86 percent of corporations had no plans to make their annual reports available exclusively on the Web. Moreover, only 21 percent of corporations whose initial public offerings had taken place between 1995 and 1998 thought that the printed annual report was headed for oblivion (Potlatch Corporation, 2000).

More important, will online versions actually save money? According to Sweet (1999d), the CEO of MCI WorldCom Inc. claims that the company saved "more than $800,000 in printing, production, and mailing costs by

---

EXHIBIT 11.2

Browser Beware: Seven Reasons to Think Twice About Publishing the Annual Report on the World Wide Web

Putting an annual report online may be innovative and exciting, but it can also be costly and fraught with hidden dangers. Here are seven things to watch out for.

1. Text is more difficult to read online. Scrolling down and across a screen is not as easy as reading a page.

2. Photos—the annual report's most-read feature—are problematic. Many stock houses and professional photographers do not offer Web rights, or if they do, these rights can be prohibitively expensive. Photos and other graphic images also take time to load and thus slow readers' access to text.

3. Web page design can be expensive. Unless the report is straight text, with no graphics or visuals, money spent designing the Web version can eat up savings that could be made on printing and distribution. (If you are doing both a print and a Web version, you may actually be spending more.)

4. The report can't be carried from one place to another or stored for future reference unless is it downloaded and printed out. Therefore, it becomes less useful as an archival record.

5. Until the technology is standardized, different download speeds and slower, older browsers make it difficult to design online documents that please everyone.

6. People, especially donors, still want something they can hold in their hands and show to other people. The day has not yet arrived when a development officer can say to a prospect, "I know you'll love our annual report. Just visit our Web site at www.ferretfriends.org."

7. With the exception of those who seek only the financial information, most online visitors will have a difficult time developing a complete picture of the organization, its mission, and its performance when the medium has been designed to provide targeted information through a menu of click options.

---

scrapping its slick annual report in favor of a low-key book on plain white paper with no color pictures" and publishing it online.

The need to control costs has enticed many nonprofits to put their annual reports on the Web. Nevertheless, as long as their members and major donors expect print versions of annual reports, costs can actually be greater for both a Web-based and a print version, especially if the report includes stock or commercial photographs. Many commercial stock houses do not grant Web rights, and those that do charge fees based on the estimated size of the audience. On the Web, the audience may be huge, and so the photo rights may be hugely expensive.

A nonprofit that does not yet have a Web site can get its annual report of up to eighty pages published on the World Wide Web by the Annual Report Gallery for a flat fee of $2,500. Further information about this service can be obtained at www.reportgallery.com.

For the reasons listed in Exhibit 11.2, it is likely that prudent nonprofits will continue to issue print versions of their annual reports. The National

Wildlife Federation's Natalie Waugh views the Web report as an ancillary tool. "We will probably put our report on the Web," she says, "but never solely on the Web, because not all donors are Web-conversant. They want a hard copy in their hands." This sentiment is echoed by all the editors who were interviewed for this book. Although the nonprofits they represent have Web versions of their annual reports or are considering putting versions on the Web, none is planning to offer only a Web version.

CEOs also have strong opinions about Web-only versions. "I would not consider publishing [our] annual report solely on the Web," says Kathryn Fuller of World Wildlife Fund. "The photos are much too important. A computer screen is not going to show the photos as well as the printed copy does. Besides, people keep our report."

One fine day, when there is universal Internet access, when the technology has been streamlined, and when the majority prefers a paperless world, Web-only versions of annual reports may be justified. In the meantime, before abandoning paper and snail mail altogether, the prudent editor canvasses the audience to see how many have Internet access and, for those who do, how many would prefer to get the annual report on the Web. One way to get this information is to include a reader survey with the current hard-copy version of the report.

Surveying Readers

At first glance, reader surveys are a good idea. They can yield all kinds of information, such as assessments of whether the report is too slick, too dull, or just right. The problem is that very few people are inclined to fill out reader surveys and return them, partly because it takes time and partly because, more often than not, people perceive such surveys as thinly disguised marketing tools. Even though feedback can be minimal, however, it never hurts to ask, especially when part of the cost of asking is included in the cost of mailing the report in the first place. Exhibit 11.3 shows a hypothetical reader survey for Friends of the Ferret.

Annual Reports of the Future

Finding out what readers want for next year is one thing; gazing into a crystal ball to see what annual reports of the future will look like is quite another. Today's annual reports from the corporate world do offer some clues about what the future holds, even for nonprofits (Sweet, 2000a; see Exhibit 11.4).

EXHIBIT 11.3

Sample Reader Survey for Friends of the Ferret

Dear Reader:

We hope you like the Friends of the Ferret 2000 Annual Report. Because we value your opinions, we hope you will take a few minutes to fill out this survey and return it to us in the enclosed postage-paid envelope.

Which feature did you read first?

☐ president's letter
☐ donor list
☐ photo captions
☐ financial highlights
☐ other (describe) _____

Was the text easy to read?   ☐ yes   ☐ no

If you answered no, would it help to increase the size of type?   ☐ yes   ☐ no

If you answered no, please tell us what would make the report easier for you to read: _____

_____

_____

Were the text and financial highlights informative?   ☐ yes   ☐ no

If you answered no, please tell us what would make them more informative:

_____

_____

Do you have access to the Internet?   ☐ yes   ☐ no

If so, would you prefer to receive an online version of the report instead of a print version?   ☐ yes   ☐ no

Additional comments: _____

_____

_____

_____

_____

_____

_____

_____

EXHIBIT 11.4

Characteristics of Future Annual Reports

- *Connection.* Because individual investors are buying stock at record rates and competition is fierce in all industries, it has become crucial that companies connect with their audiences.

- *More Web presence.* The Internet offers investors and companies an unprecedented chance to communicate directly. Tomorrow's annual reports are likely to be more creative and interactive in their online presence.

- *Plain English.* As more investors develop an appetite for easy-to-acquire corporate information, they will come to expect financials they can understand. The plain-English movement has picked up speed in recent years and will become more popular in the future.

- *Environmental sensitivity.* Soy inks, recycled paper, and other Earth-friendly materials will be found in tomorrow's annual reports.

- *Increased graphic presence.* Annual reports have been using graphics for years, but next-generation books will be even more centered on photos, illustrations, charts, graphics, and color.

- *Virtual reporting.* Product shots will fade in importance and be replaced by photos that show products in use and, even better, pictures that reflect both why the products are needed and the effects of their use.

Source: Adapted from Bob Sweet (ed.), *Ragan's Annual Report Review,* July 2000, p. 4. Reprinted by permission.

As can be readily observed, the likely features of tomorrow's annual reports will not be so dramatically different from today's as to challenge editors unreasonably. It should be possible for the editor to adopt some of these features for next year's report while also integrating crucial information gleaned from the postmortem, from surveys, and from critiques by outside experts. For the nonprofit with a long production lead time, the cycle for the next report can begin practically as soon as the current report is delivered. For the organization with a shorter lead time, there may be a few months' respite, during which the editor can catch up on all the work that had to be set aside during the frantic months when the annual report was "job one."

For a period that is all too brief, there will be an opportunity to forget the frustrations and anxieties associated with this complicated publication. There will also be time to think about ways to be more successful as an editor the next time around (see Exhibit 11.5). If this book has done its job well, the next report just may be a little less frustrating to produce, not only for the editor but also for the other key players, from the CEO to the mail house.

EXHIBIT 11.5

Tips for Being a Successful Annual Report Editor

- *Be a realistic perfectionist.* Aim constantly for perfection, even though it is seldom achieved. If you end up wasting money or time in the quest for perfection, you will have failed. The perfect annual report is coherent, accurate, and on message; it is also cost-effective and timely.

- *Pay attention to every little detail.* No one else will. It's the little things—the typos, factual errors, and inconsistencies—that can make readers question overall quality.

- *Be diplomatic but firm with key players.* It is true that you can catch more flies with honey than with vinegar, but if vinegar is the only way you can capture someone's attention, go ahead and mix a little bitter with the sweet.

- *Think ahead.* Be prepared to deal with setbacks and roadblocks before you encounter them.

- *Be fair and honest in your dealings* with colleagues and outside writers, designers, printers, and mail houses. Do business only with those who are fair and honest in their dealings with you.

- *Strive constantly for freshness.* If you put out the same annual report year after year because that is what donors like and expect to see, look for a fresh angle, a different layout, or a new feature to make the report interesting and challenging to *you.* After all, if you find yourself yawning your way through the same old stories and presentation, you can't expect readers to find the report exciting.

- *Respect the knowledge, talents, and experience of key players* and use every bit of it to achieve the best possible product. (And, yes, take them to lunch at an expensive restaurant—they're worth it.)

- *Copy successful annual reports of other organizations.* Most annual reports are not copyrighted, and imitation is the sincerest form of flattery.

- *Make the CEO happy,* even if doing so costs time or money or violates your aesthetic sensibilities. If the CEO likes the annual report, it is by definition successful.

Glossary

Graphic Arts and Mailing Terms

BASIC CONCEPTS and vocabulary in the fields of typography and printing are defined here. More complete glossaries and definitions can be found in *Getting It Printed* (Beach and Kenly, 1999), *Production for the Graphic Designer* (Craig, 1974), *Editing by Design* (White, 1974), and the latest edition of the International Paper Company's graphic arts production handbook, *Pocket Pal* (2000).

alley the space between columns of type on a page

amberlith orange-colored masking material used in preparing a film negative for platemaking

aqueous coating a water-based coating that is applied like ink to a printed page to protect it from smudging

bitmap a condition that occurs in desktop publishing when the pixels that make up the halftone dots form an observable pattern on a halftone image

bleed printing that extends beyond the trim marks of a page or sheet so that no uninked area of the page shows after the page is trimmed

blueline (often called *Dylux,* after the photographic paper used to make the proof) a prepress photographic proof, with halftones in place, where all ink shows as a blue image

butt to join one color with another, or a halftone with a surrounding rule, so that there is no overlap or space showing

color bar a strip of colors printed near the edge of the press sheet to show ink density

color blocks areas of the printed page that have solid or screened ink coverage *color break* the place where one ink color stops and another begins

color builds overlaps of two or more process ink colors to create a different color

color-correct to retouch or enhance color-separated negatives

color separation the product that results from separating continuous-tone color images into one set of halftone negatives for each of the process ink colors that are used in four-color process printing

composite film film consisting of each of the colors required for the final printed piece, including black

comprehensive dummy (also called *comp*) a model produced by the graphic designer to show what the layout, typography, and color of a piece will be when it is printed

compressed files electronic files from which all unnecessary data have been removed, for ease in transmission

continuous-tone a term that describes a photographic image containing all gradations of black and white, or containing the full spectrum of color

cromalin or *crome* a prepress color proof

crop marks lines marked at edge of a photograph or illustration to indicate those portions of the image that are to be cropped out (that is, eliminated)

crossover See *gutter jump*

cyan one of the four process ink colors (sometimes erroneously called "process blue," a color distinct from cyan)

CYMK abbreviation representing the four process ink colors—cyan, yellow, magenta, and black—that produce the full spectrum of color in a printed piece

digital camera a camera that captures images by means of an arrangement of photo cells rather than by film

digital plate a plate made from a computer file rather than from film

direct mail a mail package—usually containing one or more letters, informational pieces, and a response device—designed to motivate the recipient to buy a product, donate money, or take other action

dot gain a condition in which the dots in a halftone show up larger than they should when printed on paper, with a consequent darkening of tones or colors *double-bump* to print a single image twice so that it has two layers of ink

dpi abbreviation of "dots per inch," a measure used to represent the degree of resolution in images that have been scanned or output on laser printers or imagesetters (the greater the dpi, the closer the scanned or output image will be to the original continuous-tone image)

draw down (sometimes called *rollout*) a sample of a specified ink and paper, used to evaluate color

dropout halftone a halftone in which the highlight areas contain no dots

dummy (also called *mockup*) (1) a preliminary layout showing all visual elements; (2) a simulation of a printed piece, using the paper specified for the job

duotone a photograph reproduced from two halftone negatives and printed in two ink colors

Dylux See *blueline*

EPS abbreviation of "encapsulated PostScript," a graphics file format that can be used with many different computers and printers and imported into most desktop publishing software

flood to cover a sheet with ink or varnish

flop to reproduce a photograph or illustration so that the image faces in the opposite direction from the original

form one side of a press sheet

format the size, shape, and overall style of a printed piece

four-color process the printing technique that uses the four process ink colors—cyan, yellow, magenta, and black—to simulate full-color photographs or illustrations

FPO abbreviation of "for position only," an indication on desktopped proofs that low-resolution images showing placement and scaling are to be replaced by higher-resolution images before printing

FTP abbreviation of "file transfer protocol," a system for transferring files between computers on the Internet

gang to print two or more different pieces, or multiple copies of the same piece, on one sheet of paper

gather to assemble signatures into the proper sequence for binding

ghosting a condition in which the faint "ghost" of a printed image appears on a printed item in a place where it should not be

gloss a characteristic of any paper, ink, or varnish that reflects large amounts of light

glossy a photographic print made on glossy paper

grade a category of paper (the seven major grades of paper are bond, uncoated book, coated book, text, cover, board, and specialty)

graphic designer a professional who conceptualizes a design, plans how to produce it, and may coordinate the production of the printed piece

graphics art and other visual elements used in a printed piece to enhance its message

gutter between columns of type, the space where pages meet at the binding

gutter jump (sometimes called *crossover* or *bridge*) a condition in which the art on a printed page runs across the gutter to the opposite page

hairline a very thin line or space, about the width of a hair (1/100 inch)

halftone the product of converting a continuous-tone image into dots, for printing

halftone dots the dots whose varying sizes create the illusion of shading or of a continuous-tone image

hickey a doughnut-shaped spot or imperfection in a printed piece, most visible in areas of heavy ink coverage

house sheet general-use paper stock that is ordered in large quantities and stocked by the printer

image area (1) on a negative or plate, the portion that corresponds to the area where ink will appear on paper; (2) on a sheet of paper, the portion where ink appears

imposition the process of arranging pages on a form so that they will be in the correct order when the press sheets are folded

indicia postal-permit information printed on objects to be mailed, accepted in lieu of stamps by the United States Postal Service

knockout See *reverse*

layout sketch or desktop rendition of a design for a proposed printed piece, showing the position, size, color, and arrangement of text and graphic elements

leading (1) the amount of space, measured in points, between lines of type; (2) in type set by hand, a thin strip of metal inserted between lines of type to separate them ("10/12," or "10 on 12," means lines of 10-point type with 2 points of leading between them)

light table a translucent glass surface, beneath which are lights that illuminate slides and transparencies

line copy (also called *line art*) type, rules, clip art, or other images that can be printed without conversion to halftone

logo an assembly of type and art into a distinctive symbol that represents an organization, company, or product

loupe (also called *graphic arts magnifier* or *linen tester*) a magnifying lens used to inspect copy, negatives, and printing

M Roman numeral signifying 1,000 (a price quote for "additional M's" would be for additional units of one thousand copies)

magenta one of the four process ink colors

mail house (also called *lettershop* or *mailer*) a business that specializes in generating address labels, applying them to identical printed pieces, and mailing large quantities of the labeled pieces

makeready all the activities necessary to set up a press before printing can begin

matchprint an integral color proof

mockup See *dummy*

modem short for *modulator/demodulator,* a device that converts digital signals to analog tones, and vice versa, so that systems based on electronic memories can communicate via telephone lines

moiré in halftones and screen tints, an undesirable pattern that occurs when the screens are not properly aligned before printing

negative (1) a condition in which an image on film or paper contains white or clear areas that were black in the original subject, and black or opaque areas that were white or clear in the original subject; (2) the piece of film on which such an image appears

offset printing a method of lithographic printing that transfers ink from a plate to a soft rubber blanket and then from the blanket to the press sheet

opacity a property of a sheet of paper that determines whether images printed on one side are likely to show through to the other (see also *show through*)

outline halftone a halftone in which the background has been removed to isolate or silhouette an image

overprint to print over a previously printed image

overrun printing in excess of the quantity specified (standards in the printing industry usually allow a 10 percent overrun or underrun, and within this range the customer is not billed for overruns, nor is the printer required to go back on press if there is an underrun)

overs the printed pieces in an overrun

page count the total number of pages in a piece, including blank pages and unnumbered pages (a book's last numbered page may be 174, but the page count may be greater)

page proof a proof of the type and graphics as they will appear when the page is printed

pallet (also called a *skid*) a wooden platform used as a base for loading and moving paper and printed products

paper dummy a trimmed, folded, and, if necessary, bound unprinted sample of a proposed printed piece, using the paper specified for the job (often requested when the customer wants to know how much a printed piece will weigh, or if the customer wants to see how thick or thin the final piece will be)

PDF abbreviation of "portable document format," a file type created by Adobe Systems, Inc., that allows fully formatted, high-resolution PostScript documents to be transmitted over the Internet and viewed by any computer with Adobe Acrobat Reader software

perfect-bind to bind sheets by trimming them at the spine and gluing them to a paper cover

pica a unit of type measurement, equal to 1/6 inch

picking (n) an undesirable condition in which bits of fiber or coating come loose from the paper during printing, with resulting white spots in inked areas

pixel (short for *picture element*) a part of a dot made by a scanner or other digital device

pleasing color a color that does not exactly match original samples, scenes, or objects but is judged nevertheless to be satisfactory

plugged up said of a halftone in which ink has filled in the space around the dots, with a resulting loss of shadow detail

plus cover a cover using paper stock different from that used for the text

PMS abbreviation for the Pantone Matching System of ink colors

point a unit of type measurement, equal to 1/12 inch

prepress camera work, stripping, platemaking, and other operations that occur before a piece is put on the press for printing

press inspection an inspection of actual press sheets by the client to ensure that the printed piece is satisfactory

press proof a proof that is made using the actual plates, paper, and ink that were specified (press proofs are expensive)

press sheet one sheet as it comes off the printing press

print run the quantity of finished pieces that will be printed

process blue an ink color, sometimes confused with cyan, but not the same shade, and not used in four-color process printing

process colors the four primary colors—cyan, yellow, magenta, and black—used to print the full range of colors

rasterized image processor (RIP) a computer that converts desktop publishing files to bitmapped images for output to film

reverse type or other image that is reproduced by printing the background surrounding the image, rather than the image itself, so that the underlying color of paper or ink solid shows the shape of the letters or image; sometimes called *knockout* (for an example, see Exhibit 9.2 in Chapter Nine)

rollout See *draw down*

saddle stitch a form of binding that staples sheets together at the fold of the spine

scanner an electronic device that transforms physical artwork—slides, photographs, copy—into digital form for printing

score to compress paper along a line so that it will fold more easily and cleanly without cracking

screen a piece of film with dots of uniform density used to make plates that will print screen tints

screen tint an area of an image that is printed with dots so that the ink coverage is less than 100 percent and the area will simulate a lighter color

self-cover a publication in which the text and cover are printed on the same weight and grade of paper

self-mailer a printed piece that is designed to be mailed without an envelope *setoff* a condition in which the wet ink on top of one printed sheet rubs off onto the bottom of the next sheet as it comes off the press

sheetfed press a press that prints sheets of paper rather than rolls (sheetfed presses are used for flat products like bookmarks or postcards and for small to medium-size print runs)

show through printing on one side of paper that can be seen on the other side

side stitch a form of binding that staples sheets together along one edge

signature a sheet of printed pages that, when folded, becomes part of a publication

solid any area of the press sheet that receives 100 percent ink coverage

specifications complete and exact descriptions of trim size, paper, ink, binding, quantity, and other features of an item to be printed; often called *specs*

spine the binding edge of a signature or publication

spiral bind a form of binding in which a spiral of wire or plastic is inserted through holes punched along the binding edge of the paper

spot varnish varnish that is applied only to parts of a sheet

stripping assembling negatives in flats in preparation for making printing plates

tack a property in inks that makes them sticky

thumbnail sketch a rough sketch of a design or a rough sketch of a book or other publication showing generally what will appear on each page

TIFF abbreviation of "tagged image file format," a graphics file format for storing scanned images, including black and white, gray-scale, 8-bit color, and 24-bit color images

transparency a positive photographic image, usually in color, on film that allows light to pass through

trap a slight overlap of one ink on another or one image on another to create the impression that the two colors or images abut

trim marks lines on artwork, negatives, plates, or press sheets that show where the paper is to be trimmed after printing

trim size the size of the printed piece after the final trim is made *turnaround time* the amount of time it takes to complete a job or one stage of a job

typeface all type of a single design, which is identified by its name (for example, Helvetica or Garamond or Optima); sometimes erroneously called a *font*

type font all the characters and spacing of one size of a typeface (for example, 9-point Baskerville, or 11-point Times Roman)

type style the different forms of a typeface (for example, roman, italic, bold italic, bold, condensed, or expanded)

uncoated paper paper that is not coated and does not reflect a lot of light

underrun a condition in which fewer copies are printed than the quantity specified

up printing a piece "two up" or "three up" means printing the identical image two or three times on one press sheet, in one impression

varnish a clear liquid applied on press to protect the sheet from fingerprinting and to highlight artwork

web press a press that prints paper from a roll (web presses are used for large print runs that involve folded pieces or saddle-stitched or perfect-bound books because of the inline bindery machinery at the end of the press)

white space a term for areas of a page that contain no image or text

window an area on a layout showing where photos or illustrations are to be placed

Xerography photocopying on a Xerox machine

References

American Friends Service Committee. *Annual Report.* Philadelphia: American Friends Service Committee, 1998.

American Friends Service Committee. *Annual Report.* Philadelphia: American Friends Service Committee, 1999.

American Heart Association. *Annual Report.* Dallas, Tex.: American Heart Association, 2000.

Arnold, E. C. *Editing the Organizational Publication.* Chicago: Lawrence Ragan Communications, 1982.

Beach, M., and Kenly, E. *Getting It Printed: How to Work with Printers and Graphic Imaging Services to Assure Quality, Stay on Schedule, and Control Costs.* Cincinnati, Ohio: North Light Books, 1999.

Boy Scouts of America. *Annual Report.* Irving, Tex.: Boy Scouts of America, 1997.

Boy Scouts of America. *Annual Report.* Irving, Tex.: Boy Scouts of America, 1998.

Christian Children's Fund. *Annual Report.* Richmond, Va.: Christian Children's Fund, 1998.

Christian Children's Fund. *Annual Report.* Richmond, Va.: Christian Children's Fund, 1999.

Conservation International. *Focused Energy; Powerful Results.* Annual report. Washington, D.C.: Conservation International, 1999.

Consultative Group on International Agricultural Research. *Annual Report.* Washington, D.C.: Consultative Group on International Agricultural Research, 1997.

Consultative Group on International Agricultural Research. *Annual Report.* Washington, D.C.: Consultative Group on International Agricultural Research, 1998.

Council of Better Business Bureaus. "CBBB [Council of Better Business Bureaus] Standards for Charitable Solicitations." [http://www.give.org/standards/cbbbstds.asp]. 1999.

Craig, J. *Production for the Graphic Designer.* New York: Watson-Guptill, 1974.

Crosse Point Paper Corporation. *Annual Report: Strategies for Effective Communication.* St. Paul, Minn.: Crosse Point Paper Corporation, 1994.

Cunningham, M. *The Fannie Farmer Cookbook.* (13th ed.) New York: Bantam Books, 1994.

Ducks Unlimited. *Annual Report.* Memphis, Tenn.: Ducks Unlimited, 1999.

Environmental Law Institute. *Environmental Law Forum,* 1999, *16*(entire issue 3).

Ethics Resource Center. *Annual Report.* Washington, D.C.: Ethics Resource Center, 1998.

Girl Scouts of the USA. *What Does Strong Mean?* Annual report. New York: Girl Scouts of the USA, 1999.

Herring, J. *Annual Report Design: A Guide to the Annual Report Process for Graphic Designers and Corporate Communicators.* New York: Watson-Guptill, 1990.

Holmes, N. *Designer's Guide to Creating Charts and Diagrams.* New York: Watson-Guptill, 1984.

Hurley, G. D., and McDougall, A. *Visual Impact in Print: How to Make Pictures Communicate.* Chicago: Visual Impact, 1977.

International Federation of Red Cross and Red Crescent Societies. *Annual Report.* Geneva: International Federation of Red Cross and Red Crescent Societies, 1996.

International Finance Corporation. *Annual Report.* Washington, D.C.: International Finance Corporation, 1999.

International Fund for Animal Welfare. *Annual Report.* Yarmouth Port, Mass.: International Fund for Animal Welfare, 1998.

International Paper Co. *Pocket Pal: A Graphic Arts Production Handbook.* (18th ed.) New York: International Paper Co., 2000.

Loth, R. B. *How to Profit from Reading Annual Reports.* Chicago: Dearborn Financial Publishing, 1993.

National Council on Alcoholism and Drug Dependence. *Annual Report.* New York: National Council on Alcoholism and Drug Dependence, 1990.

National Council on Alcoholism and Drug Dependence. *Annual Report.* New York: National Council on Alcoholism and Drug Dependence, 1992.

National Council on Alcoholism and Drug Dependence. *Annual Report.* New York: National Council on Alcoholism and Drug Dependence, 1998.

National Investor Relations Institute. *Annual Reports: An Assessment of Trends and Practices in the Annual Report Process.* Vienna, Va.: National Investor Relations Institute, 1999.

National Trust for Historic Preservation. *Annual Report.* Washington, D.C.: National Trust for Historic Preservation, 1998.

National Trust for Historic Preservation. *Annual Report.* Washington, D.C.: National Trust for Historic Preservation, 1999.

National Wildlife Federation. *Making a Place for Wildlife in the New Millennium.* Annual report. Vienna, Va.: National Wildlife Federation, 1999.

New Israel Fund. *Annual Report.* Washington, D.C.: New Israel Fund, 1997.

Pinchot Institute for Conservation. *Annual Report.* Washington, D.C.: Pinchot Institute for Conservation, 1998.

Population Action International. *Annual Report.* Washington, D.C.: Population Action International, 1998.

Potlatch Corporation. *Your Annual Report Will Be Finished at . . .* Cloquet, Minn.: Potlatch Corporation, 1994.

Potlatch Corporation. *A Study of Corporate Annual Reports.* Cloquet, Minn.: Potlatch Corporation, 1995.

Potlatch Corporation. *Annual Reports in the New Economy.* Cloquet, Minn.: Potlatch Corporation, 2000.

Redding, W. C. *How to Conduct a Readership Survey: A Guide for Organizational Editors and Communications Managers.* Chicago: Lawrence Ragan Communications, 1982.

Samuelson, R. J. "I Love Coke's Report." *Washington Post,* Apr. 16, 1997, p. A17.

Sheets, T. E. (ed.). *Encyclopedia of Associations,* Vol. 1: *National Organizations of the U.S.* Farmington Hills, Mich.: Gale Group, 1999.

Sweet, B. "Despite Push to Online Annual Report, Few Investors Actually Ditch Print Versions." *Ragan's Annual Report Review,* Oct. 1999a, p. 8.

Sweet, B. "Don't Let Overexuberant Design Obscure the AR Message." *Ragan's Annual Report Review,* Nov. 1999b, p. 10.

Sweet, B. "Ford's Online AR Is Less Than the Sum of Its Parts." *Ragan's Annual Report Review,* Nov. 1999c, p. 9.

Sweet, B. "Online ARs Gain Support." *Ragan's Annual Report Review,* Sept. 1999d, p. 4.

Sweet, B. "RARR Checklist: 11 Criteria to Consider During Your Search for an AR Design Firm." *Ragan's Annual Report Review,* Aug. 1999e, p. 2.

Sweet, B. "Test Your AR Theme: Do Readers Remember It a Day Later?" *Ragan's Annual Report Review,* Nov. 1999f, p. 1.

Sweet, B. "ARs of the Future." *Ragan's Annual Report Review,* July 2000a, p. 4.

Sweet, B. "Making Your AR Flow Effectively with Smart Font Choices." *Ragan's Annual Report Review,* Aug. 2000b, p. 2.

Sweet, B. (ed.). *Ragan's Annual Report Review.* Chicago: Lawrence Ragan Communications, 2000c.

Tocqueville, Alexis de. *Democracy in America.* New York: Vintage Books, 1945. (Originally published 1835.)

Trust for Public Land. *Land and People,* 1999, *11*(entire issue 2).

Tufte, E. R. *The Visual Display of Quantitative Information.* Cheshire, Conn.: Graphics Press, 1983.

United Nations Children's Fund. *UNICEF Annual Report.* New York: United Nations Children's Fund, 1993.

Urban Institute. *Annual Report.* Washington, D.C.: Urban Institute, 1998.

Urban Institute. *Annual Report.* Washington, D.C.: Urban Institute, 1999.

Volunteers of America. *Engaging People.* Annual report. Alexandria, Va.: Volunteers of America, 1999.

White, Jan V. *Editing by Design: Word-and-Picture Communication for Editors and Designers.* New York: Bowker, 1974.

World Bank Institute. *Annual Report.* Washington, D.C.: World Bank, 1999.

World Wildlife Fund. *Annual Report.* Washington, D.C.: World Wildlife Fund, 1996.

World Wildlife Fund. *Annual Report.* Washington, D.C.: World Wildlife Fund, 1997.

World Wildlife Fund. *Annual Report.* Washington, D.C.: World Wildlife Fund, 1999.

Zelazny, G. *Say It with Charts: The Executive's Guide to Visual Communication.* (3rd ed.) New York: McGraw-Hill, 1996.

Recommended Reading

THE FOLLOWING list of books, periodicals, and Web resources is far from complete and is intended merely to offer resources that may be useful to editors of annual reports and to other publications professionals.

Books and Periodicals

American Showcase. *Creative Options for Business and Annual Reports.* New York: Watson-Guptill, 1995.

Bann, D., and Gargan, J. *How to Check and Correct Color Proofs: Everything You Need to Know to Guarantee a Great Printed Piece.* Cincinnati, Ohio: North Light Books, 1990.

Cato, S. *Newsletter on Annual Reports.* Kalamazoo, Mich.: Sid Cato Communications.

Craig, J. *Designing with Type: A Basic Course in Typography.* New York: Watson-Guptill, 1971.

Douglis, P. N. *Pictures for Organizations: How and Why They Work as Communication.* Chicago: Lawrence Ragan Communications, 1993.

Friedlob, G. T., and Welton, R. E. *Keys to Reading an Annual Report* (2nd ed.). Hauppauge, N.Y.: Baron's, 1995.

International Paper Co. *Pocket Pal: A Graphic Arts Production Handbook.* (18th ed.) New York: International Paper Co., 2000.

Ittelson, T. R. *Financial Statements: A Step-by-Step Guide to Understanding and Creating Financial Reports.* Franklin Lakes, N.J.: Career Press, 1998.

Pasewark, W. *Understanding Corporate Annual Reports: A Practice Set for Financial Accounting.* Blacklick, Ohio: McGraw-Hill College, 1997.

Press, E., and Redburn, T. (eds.). *Analyzing Financial Statements: 25 Keys to Understanding the Numbers.* New York: Lebhar-Friedman Books, 1999.

White, Jan V. *Editing by Design: Word-and-Picture Communication for Editors and Designers.* New York: Bowker, 1974.

Zinsser, W. *On Writing Well: The Classic Guide to Writing Nonfiction.* New York: HarperCollins, 1998.

Web Sites

Annual Report Gallery, http://www.reportgallery.com

Annual Reports, Inc., http://www.annualreportsinc.com

Index